Recession at Work

How has the recession affected the conduct of human resource management? How have HR departments and managers fared? Have leading firms taken measures to sustain and revive their businesses through innovative HR measures? How have union representation and influence been affected? Is the recession reshaping work and employment practices?

These are among the questions answered in *Recession at Work*, the first systematic study in Europe to deal with the effects of the economic crisis on people at work. Drawing on survey data for Ireland provided by nearly 500 managers responsible for human resources, on focus groups of HR managers and trade union officials and on detailed case studies of six major firms, the book provides an unrivalled picture of the effects of the current recession on how people are managed and how they are represented by trade unions. Examining the effects of the Irish recession on work and employment in the context of international experience and commentary, this book provides detailed information and analysis on the ways in which firms have sought to handle the challenges that have arisen since the severe reverse in Ireland's economic fortunes in 2008.

William K. Roche is Professor of Industrial Relations and Human Resources at the School of Business, University College Dublin and Honorary Professor at the School of Management, Queen's University Belfast. His most recent books are *Managing Workplace Conflict in Ireland* (with Deborah Hahn and Paul Teague; Government Publications 2009) and *Partnership at Work: The Quest for Radical Organizational Change* (with John Geary; Routledge 2006).

Paul Teague is Professor of Management at the Management School, Queen's University Belfast. He is author of *Employment Standard-Setting and Dispute Resolution in the Republic of Ireland* (with Damian Thomas) and *Managing Workplace Conflict in Ireland* (with Deborah Hahn and Bill Roche; Government Publications 2009).

Anne Coughlan is a part-time lecturer in the Smurfit School of Business, University College Dublin. She worked for the Irish Business and Employers' Confederation (IBEC) for more than twenty years, as both Senior Research Executive and as Head of the Research and Survey Unit.

Majella Fahy is a lecturer in Industrial Relations and Human Resource Management at the School of Business, University College Dublin (UCD). She is a graduate of the University of Dublin, Trinity College, and holds a PhD from University College Dublin. Prior to joining the Industrial Relations and Human Resources Group at UCD she was a Newman Scholar at the Centre for Quality and Service Excellence and undertook research on commitment-oriented HR strategies.

Routledge Advances in Management and Business Studies

For a full list of titles in this series, please visit www.routledge.com

Recession at Work

HRM in the Irish Crisis

**William K. Roche, Paul Teague,
Anne Coughlan and Majella Fahy**

NEW YORK AND LONDON

First published 2013
by Routledge
711 Third Avenue, New York, NY 10017

Simultaneously published in the UK
by Routledge
2 Park Square, Milton Park, Abingdon, Oxon OX14 4RN

First issued in paperback 2018

*Routledge is an imprint of the Taylor & Francis Group,
an informa business*

Library of Congress Cataloging-in-Publication Data

Recession at work : HRM in the Irish crisis / edited by William K. Roche,
 Paul Teague, Anne Coughlan, and Majella Fahy.
  pages cm. — (Routledge advances in management and business
 studies ; 55)
 Includes bibliographical references and index.
1. Personnel management—Ireland—History—21st century.
2. Recessions— Ireland—History—21st century. 3. Ireland—Economic
conditions—21st century. I. Roche, William K., 1957–
 HF5549.2.I73R73 2013
 658.3009417—dc23
 2012045360

ISBN 13: 978-1-138-34002-2 (pbk)
ISBN 13: 978-0-415-83246-5 (hbk)

Typeset in Sabon
By Apex CoVantage, LLC

Contents

Tables

Figures

Acknowledgments

The authors would like to acknowledge the funding provided by the Labour Relations Commission (LRC) for the research on which this study is based. Kieran Mulvey, Chief Executive of the LRC, initiated and commissioned the study, and was unstinting in his support and encouragement throughout the research project. Freda Nolan, Director of Advisory Services at the LRC, was invaluable to our work through her involvement in the conduct of the focus groups, and her professionalism, support and guidance throughout the project. We owe her a great debt, and we wish to acknowledge her contribution to the research. Members of the LRC Advisory Service, in particular Seamus Doherty and Leo Costello, played a valuable role in encouraging firms to participate in the employers' survey. Wendy Sullivan at the Chartered Institute of Personnel and Development (CIPD) also provided assistance with the survey. The Project Steering Group guided and assisted our work in various ways and we would like to thank, in particular, its external members: Michael McDonnell and Frank Kelly of the CIPD, Mary Connaughton of the Irish Business and Employers' Confederation and Esther Lynch of the Irish Congress of Trade Unions. Kieran Mulvey, Freda Nolan and Seamus Doherty also served as members of the Steering Group. Colman Higgins and Roisin Farrelly of *Industrial Relations News* provided helpful advice with respect to possible case studies for inclusion in the research. None of the aforementioned bears any responsibility for the analysis or conclusions reported in the study.

At UCD, Lisa Madsen provided excellent support to the management of the project and handled the production of the book manuscript with great skill, professionalism and good humor. Professor Dorothy Watson, at the ESRI managed the construction of the sampling frame and the weighting of the sample data with great skill. Caoimhe McGuckin transcribed the focus group interviews with great speed and accuracy, and Patricia O'Sullivan ably managed survey data entry and liaison with survey respondents. We would like to thank the HR managers and trade union officials who participated in the focus groups and the managers responsible for HR who completed survey questionnaires. We are also indebted to the companies who agreed to allow us to conduct case studies, as well as to the managers and union officials who were interviewed as part of the case study research but who are not named individually to preserve confidentiality. At Routledge, we are indebted to Laura Stearns, Terry Clague, Lauren Verity and Denise File for their support and encouragement, and we would also like to acknowledge the constructive and helpful comments of the anonymous reviewers who read and commented on our manuscript.

1 Introduction

Ireland is in the grip of the most serious economic recession in its modern history, which is having profound effects on the labor market and on the management of human resources. Trade unions charged with defending their members' pay and employment security face challenges without precedent in living memory. Other European countries affected by the financial, fiscal and economic crisis face pressures similar to Ireland's, but the Irish recession is among the most acute of all developed economies. The effects of the Irish recession on the manner in which people are managed at work and on how they are represented by trade unions is the subject of this study.

The context for this investigation is set out in Chapter 2. The impact of the international financial and economic crisis on the Irish labor market is assessed. Then, the Irish economic crisis is placed in a comparative European context to get a sense of the extent to which the response in Ireland has been similar to those pursued by other European Union (EU) member states. After this assessment a detailed review is conducted of the international literature and debates concerning the impact of recessions, past and current, on the conduct of human resources in organizations. This is followed by a detailed examination of the type of policies and practices available to organizations when making adjustments to difficult business conditions.

Chapter 3 sets out the findings of a survey of managers responsible for human resources. The survey examines the impact of the recession on changes in revenue and employment in firms to establish the commercial context for HR measures adopted. The chapter then goes on to examine the types and incidence of measures taken by firms, ranging from pay and headcount adjustments, to changes in working time arrangements and measures undertaken to preserve motivation and commitment. In addition to examining the range of individual measures adopted by firms, the manner in which firms combined these measures is also analyzed, as are the postures adopted by unionized firms in their dealings with unions during the recession. This is followed by an investigation into the role of the HR function in the recession. This investigation explores whether the work of HR functions and those who work within them has changed as a result of the recession, the function's influence on strategy formulation and implementation and the business role of HR. Finally, the chapter investigates the HR practices that survey respondents considered to be most effective in helping them manage the recession.

The findings of a series of focus groups with HR managers and trade union officials are outlined in Chapters 4, 5 and 6, and these cast a deeper light on the nature of the challenges arising and the responses adopted in the recession. Chapter 4 examines the effects of the recession as experienced by thirty HR managers representing a wide range of businesses. It reviews in detail the effects of acute cost, headcount and productivity pressures and the range of retrenchment measures that they were required to put in place. The chapter that follows examines HR managers' understanding of what constitutes 'good human resource practice' in recessionary conditions.

Chapter 6 presents the views and experiences of 17 union officials participating in union focus groups. The officials represented employees working in the private, commercial semistate sectors and, in some instances, the public sector. The chapter first looks at union officials' views on the effects of the recession on both their relationship with employers and with their own members. A significant element of their response was the negative change they perceived in the relationship between employers and unions. Following on from this is a discussion on their experience of collective bargaining in the recession. The union officials then give their viewpoint as to the features of good HR practice and the drivers of that good practice.

Chapters 7 and 8 present a series of six case studies that examine the responses of companies and unions to the pressures unleashed by the recession. The series of cases examined are regarded as instances of good practice in responding to different sets of recessionary pressures, and contain some significant innovative features. They were chosen because their responses to the recession are widely admired by their professional peers, because they had sought to accommodate employees' interests in responding to the recession and because the parties to employment relations succeeded in all cases in securing or strengthening the businesses affected by reaching different forms of accommodation that commonly involving significant changes to the operation of businesses, to terms and conditions of employment and to work practices.

Chapter 7 outlines the rationale for case study selection in detail before proceeding to the examination of the first three cases. The three cases involved the introduction of measures aimed at minimizing job losses. The first case study in Irish Life and Permanent (IL&P) charts the ebb and flow of efforts in IL&P to adjust to the onset of the financial crisis in Ireland, culminating in measures that included incentivized career breaks, a voluntary redundancy program, agreed pay rises and the freezing of service-related increments. In responding to the crisis the firm sought to institute new arrangements for the conduct of industrial relations with the trade unions representing its employees, operate through a unitary HR function (then in the process of being created), and win agreement on a series of cost-saving measures.

The second case study examines how Sherry Fitzgerald (operating in a sector almost devastated in the recession) developed its response to the recession when faced with the imperative to significantly cut costs, while at the same time deciding that its chief HR priority would involve employment protection and job security. Following the strategy adopted, Sherry Fitzgerald has managed to retain its position and brand identity in the industry in a period of severe and unprecedented contraction and has preserved and reinforced its culture.

Again, operating in a sector on which the recession has had a severe impact, the final case study in this section deals with the agreement reached between the Dublin Airport Authority (DAA) and the unions representing staff, on the Cost Recovery Programme and the innovative Employee Recovery Investment Contribution (ERIC) proposal. These agreements compose an innovative initiative in which management and unions, working mainly through traditional IR postures and processes, succeeded in reaching an accord that secured the viability of the company and that also provided for the restoration of pay levels once the DAA returned to profitability.

Superquinn, Medtronic and Ericsson were the subjects of the case studies in the next chapter and had to deal with different problems brought on by the recession. Superquinn struggled for its very survival, whereas Medtronic was actively engaged in defending its mandate within the multinational of which it was a subsidiary. Ericsson has sought to preserve competency development as a core HR practice while adapting to the recession by implementing redundancies at its Irish operations. The case studies chart the paths taken by the three firms to maintain and deepen cooperation and trust between management, employees and unions and to retain core HR practices while adjusting to the recession. The two key components of Superquinn's strategy were a negotiated survival plan agreement, which provided for the introduction of cost-cutting initiatives, such as redundancies and a pay freeze, and a new partnership-style procedural agreement. These agreements were essential to the survival of Superquinn in acute trading conditions.

The second case study follows the experience of Medtronic Galway (the only unionized subsidiary in this US multinational) through the recession, from the time its head office decided it needed to take action to improve profitability and cost competitiveness to the agreement reached with the trade union. It shows how the organization, despite having to renege on an agreement with unions that had been difficult to negotiate, still managed to face adverse business relations without jeopardizing trust relations. In reaching agreement, management and unions adopted a central principle of interest-based bargaining, which is to recognize and take on board the constraints of the other negotiating side. The final case study in the chapter examines Ericsson's retention of competency development as a core HR practice, while the company's Irish operations simultaneously maintained competitiveness. Significant job losses resulted but the company was still seen as possessing highly skilled and motivated people.

The final chapter addresses a number of major findings from the study in the context of the international literature. Discussion covers HR retrenchment programs, the role of the HR function, the effects of the recession on union representation and the effects of the recession on work and employment arrangements. The chapter ends with a discussion of the international import of Ireland's experience during the recession.

2 Recession, the Labor Market and the Conduct of Human Resource Management

2.1 INTRODUCTION

Ireland's employment growth in the 1990s was nothing less than spectacular. In less than a decade, a million new jobs were created, doubling the size of the labor market. If that much-abused term Celtic Tiger has any applicability, it is in relation to this hugely impressive job generation performance (Honahan 2006). Even in the first part of the noughties, employment creation was higher than most other EU member states, although the fact that 80% of the jobs created were in the construction industry should have caused some alarm bells to ring. But this exceptional employment performance came to a shuttering halt in the wake of the world financial crisis that started in 2007. It became apparent very quickly that Ireland was in the eye of this financial storm as its banks had become overexposed to bad debt due to profligate leading to property developers (Whelan 2010). Turbulence in the financial markets soon spread to other parts of the economy as consumer demand dried up and business confidence evaporated. The government has found itself in the position of needing to squeeze the public sector in an endeavor to stabilize the financial sector and public finances. Within a year, unemployment had increased to about 12.5% and job generation had ground to a virtual halt (Bergin et al 2010). The exuberance of the *vingt glorieuses* has been pushed aside as the gloom and doom of previous decades reappeared.

For companies in Ireland the financial crisis was a huge asymmetric shock. In the 10-year period up to about 2005, companies continuously struggled to fill vacancies. Recruiting and retaining staff preoccupied human resource departments almost everywhere. In an effort to help satisfy this big demand for labor, government, in an ironical historical twist, actively promoted employment migration. For example, in 1999, 6,000 work permits were issued to foreign nationals, a figure which jumped subsequently to 48,000 in 2003. Between 2000 and 2005 in excess of 100,000 non-European Economic Area (EEA) nationals alongside 50,000 EU citizens had taken up employment in the country. After the financial crash, the business environment changed completely. Large numbers of companies stopped hiring people while others, facing harsher economic times, began the process of shedding labor. Many human resource managers now face the challenging task of devising policies that would allow firms adjust to adverse market conditions in the short term without disrupting the potential to innovate and grow in the long term.

The main focus of this study is to assess the extent to which human resource managers have successfully faced this challenge by working closely with employees and unions, where they are found, and by pursuing policies that allow short-term cost pressures to be addressed without threatening the organizational conditions required for long-term business success. The purpose of this chapter is to set the context for this investigation. First of all, the impact of the international financial crisis on the Irish labor market is assessed. Then, the Irish economic crisis is placed in a comparative European context to get a sense of the extent to which the public policy response in Ireland has been similar to those pursued by other EU member states. After this assessment a detailed literature review is conducted on the impact of recessions, past and present, on the conduct and performance of human resources in organizations. The following section examines in detail the type of policies and practices that are available to HR when making adjustments to difficult business times. The penultimate section provides a snapshot, based on the data available, of the type of policies that firms have been implementing in Ireland since the onset of the financial crisis in 2007. The Conclusion section brings together the arguments of the chapter.

2.2   THE WORLD FINANCIAL CRISIS AND THE IRISH LABOR MARKET

The recent world financial crisis has had a hugely negative impact on economies, although some have been affected more adversely than have others. Ireland was among those worst hit by the crisis mainly as a result of the way the economy operated between 2000 and 2007. During this time bank credit expanded rapidly. The availability of easy money encouraged a boom in construction activity and property prices, which in turn fuelled domestic spending more widely (Honahan 2006). This cycle of unsustainable growth not only came to a halt, but also went into reverse when financial markets crashed. Almost overnight bank credit ceased up, construction activity came to a virtual stop and domestic demand plummeted. The resulting contraction in the economy has been severe and unprecedented. Banks have been brought to the edge of collapse due to a mountain of bad debts. The government has been forced into a big fiscal consolidation program in an effort to repair the deterioration in public finances, culminating in the EU/ International Monetary Fund (IMF) loans and the four-year austerity program of November 2010. All in all, the economy has been shrinking and prices falling and unemployment rising, the classic symptoms of a country in recessionary times. Moreover, all indicators suggest that it will be some time before the return to normal functioning of the economic system.

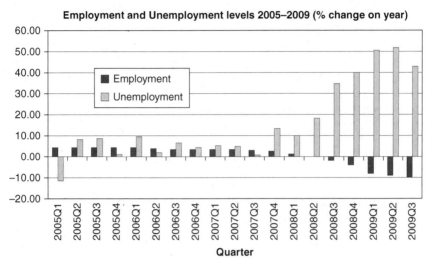

Figure 2.1   Employment and unemployment in Ireland
Source: CSO Labour Market Statistics 2010

Labor market activity has experienced the full ravages of the downturn. Employment and unemployment trends are immediate and reliable indicators of labor market performance. Figure 2.1 shows that the recession has had a huge negative impact on the Irish labor market. On one hand, net employment growth has been negative, with more jobs being lost than being created: in 2007 there were 2.1 million people in jobs, but by 2009 this had fallen to 1.9 million. On the other hand, there have been big annual percentage increases in unemployment: in 2007 the unemployment rate stood at 4.4%, but by 2009 it had increased to 12.5%. Toward the end of 2010 the level of unemployment stands at 13.6%. Thus, the virtuous era of employment growth has come to an end. For the most part, companies seem to have responded to bad economic times by reducing factor quantities (employment), but they have also moved to adjust factor prices (wages). It is difficult to get comprehensive, up-to-date figures with regard to earnings, but Figure 2.2 provides the information that is available from official statistics. Later in the chapter, other indicators of trends in pay and pay bargaining are reviewed. Three noteworthy points emerge from the figure. First, employees, across the board, enjoyed yearly healthy increases in wages during the early 2000s. Second, wages have declined quite sharply in the construction sector since 2007, which is hardly surprising given the steep slump in business activity in this part of the economy. Third, although the picture varies from sector to sector, an economy-wide fall in wages in response to the recessions appears not to have occurred from 2007 through 2009—some sectors even recorded small increases during this period. To some extent, this trend should not be surprising as real wages are relatively rigid downward. But this picture can change if the effect of deep recession will be to force prices down in all

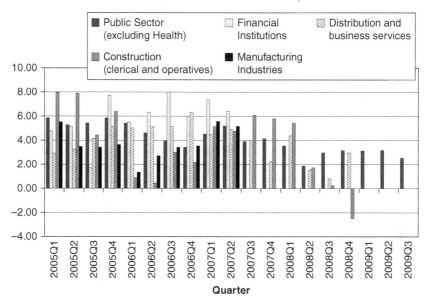

Figure 2.2 Average earnings growth by sector
Source: CSO Earnings Statistics 2010

sorts of markets, including labor markets. Thus, it is instructive to note that the Central statistics Office (CSO) in late 2010 reported a modest decline (of 0.2%) in hourly earnings in the private sector over the 12 months to the third quarter of 2010.

Unemployment has affected some groups and sectors more than it has others. Men are losing their jobs at a much faster rate than are women: from 2008 onward the fall in overall male employment has been running at three times the rate of the fall in female employment. Moreover, in 2009 whereas the unemployment rate for females was approximately 8.5%, male unemployment was pushing 16.0%. Young people have been hit hardest by the economic downturn. In 2007, the unemployment rate for 15- to 19-year-olds was just over 16.0%, but in two years it had leaped to nearly 35%. The picture for the 20- to 24-year-olds is only slightly better: in 2007, unemployment for this group was just over 8%, but by 2009 it had jumped by a factor of three to around 24%. These grim figures threaten the return of the bad old days when young people thought that Ireland offered them no hope or opportunities and as a result emigrated in search of a better life elsewhere.

Unsurprisingly, the construction sector has seen heavier job losses than other parts of the economy. Since 2007 some 72,000 jobs have been lost in the sector, a decline of nearly 30%. Other sectors have been affected too. Employment has declined by 12.3% in agriculture, which is surprising given the strong employment growth experienced by the sector earlier in the decade. Just over 6.0% of jobs were lost in the industrial sector, which although regrettable is not as bad as other sectors. Overall, the

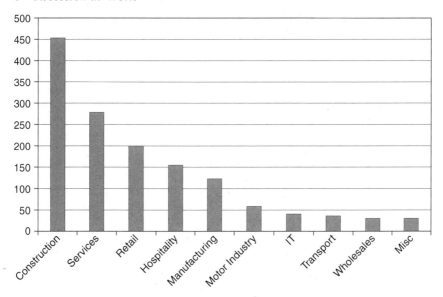

Figure 2.3   Insolvencies by sector
Source: CSO Insolvency Statistics 2010

manufacturing sector remains relatively healthy as indicated by the con-tinuing strong export performance of the Irish economy. The employment performance of the service sector has been mixed. Some parts of the public sector, most notably education and health, actually experienced job growth of about 3.6% between 2007 and 2009. But the need for sharp fiscal con-traction will reverse this picture: job losses in the public sector are likely to be significant in forthcoming years. Employment shedding has visited parts of the private-service sector, with jobs declining by around 6.8%, which amounts to 69,000 employees.

Company insolvencies were much higher in 2009 than in the two preced-ing years of the crisis, which tends to suggest that many companies were making desperate, but ultimately unsuccessful, efforts to stay in business. Figure 2.3 sets out in more detail the incidence of insolvencies in 2009. The figure shows that construction companies have been the main casualties of the economic downturn in Ireland, which again is not very surprising. How-ever, the table also shows that a significant number of service companies have also gone to the wall, which shows that the decline of business activity has become pervasive. A further interesting point emerging from the table is that more company insolvencies have occurred in the hospitality sector than in manufacturing, which is harsh proof that private consumption has significantly declined in Ireland. Data available for 2010 (see Figure 2.4) show the level of insolvencies for 2010 running close to the level for 2009 with two months remaining. Construction, services, retailing and hospitality continue to register the highest levels.

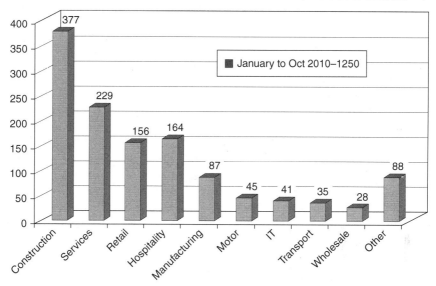

Figure 2.4   Insolvencies during 2010
Source: CSO Insolvency Statistics 2010

The distress being experienced by the business sector is also finding expression in the increased incidence of redundancies. There has been a steady increase in the number of redundancies since the onset of the economic crisis. Between 2008 and 2009, the rate of year-on-year redundancies has been increasing significantly across economic sectors. During 2009 the service sector experienced a 200% increase in redundancies; the corresponding figures for construction and manufacturing were 152% and 110%, respectively. In the second quarter of 2009, the number of redundancies was the largest on record, with about 22,000 people losing their jobs. These figures make it evident that many companies have found it difficult to face the challenges of the recession without shedding some of their workforce. This observation is reinforced when it is noted that the number of vacancies being registered with Foras Áiseanna Saothair (FAS), the government employment agency, has nose-dived over the past few years. Redundancy statistics available for the first 10 months of 2010 show a fall in the month-on-month levels recorded for 2009.

2.3   THE FINANCIAL CRISIS AND NATIONAL SOCIAL PARTNERSHIP

Jobs losses and rising unemployment have not been the only causalities of the financial crisis. Another was the system of national social partnership that had operated for more than 20 years as an institutional scaffolding for the labor market (Roche 2009). It is necessary to provide some historical context to appreciate the full import of the demise of social partnership. Historically, the key organizing principle of the Irish system of industrial relations was voluntarism (Gunnigle, 2002). A voluntary system of industrial relations is premised on freedom of contract and freedom of association, and, in terms of the British/Irish tradition, is based on free collective bargaining on one hand and relative legal abstention in industrial relations on the other. This principle of voluntarist industrial relations came under significant and sustained pressure in the 1970s and 1980s (Hardiman 1987). The incidence of industrial action, both official and unofficial, reached unprecedented levels, which appeared to question whether employers and trade unions left to their own devices could actually peacefully conclude collective agreements.

During these two decades, persistent efforts were made to move away from industrial relations disorder toward more stable, cooperative relations between employers and unions (Wall 2004). These efforts were mostly short-lived, but they paved the way for the establishment of a national system of social partnership that reigned in the country for more than 20 years. Between 1987 and 2009, the national social partnership performed a number of important economic and political functions. First of all, it governed the wage bargaining process through the conclusion of centralized pay agreements that normally lasted either for two or three years. For most of the period, these centralized pay deals led to pay moderation that contributed massively to the overall competitiveness of the extremely open Irish economy. Second, the national social partnership brought a large measure of stability to Irish employment relations, reversing the previous trend of highly confrontational employer–trade union relationships. It would be foolhardy to claim that social partnership eliminated the strong 'them and us' mentality that had prevailed between employers and unions. Nevertheless, it did have the effect of pushing adversarialism to the margins of the employment relations system. The prize provided to employers and trade unions for presiding over employment relations stability was significant influence over public policy: during the partnership years the government was most reluctant to introduce any measure that was opposed by either employers or unions (Roche 2007a).

Importantly, the national social partnership was a heavily centralized arrangement. Apart from the odd initiative here and there, for example, efforts to promote enterprise partnerships in the mid-late nineties, there was little attempt to influence in any serious way employment relations inside firms. In this respect, Irish social partnership stood apart from traditional corporatist industrial relations structures as practiced in continental Europe. A defining feature of these structures was how national- and company-level arrangements (works councils, for example) interlocked to influence, if not guide, interactions between trade unions and employers at all levels of the industrial relations system. In Ireland, the social partnership overarched the industrial relations system without impeding, to any significant degree, the activities of industrial relations actors—trade unions, employers and so on—at the enterprise level.

There are many differing interpretations of the nature and the consequences of the 23-year-regime of social partnership (Roche 2007b). But the longevity of the regime was impressive given that Ireland is widely seen as not possessing the type of institutions that support such arrangements. However, since about 2005 the operation of social partnership has come under pressure. The regime was finding it difficult to control nomimal wage increases just at a time when employment and productivity growth were flagging. Wage competitiveness relative to Ireland's main trading partners went into decline from the early 2000s. The impaired operation of the regime was reflected in the difficulties in securing a new pay agreement in 2008. Finally, a deal was done, but it was not long before the regime was once again in trouble. The source of the problem lay in efforts at securing a social partnership-led national response to the financial crisis. Trade unions were eager for the creation of a 'social solidarity pact,' which would involve unions agreeing to a combination of wages and public expenditure cuts alongside tax increases in return for a concerted government program on employment creation.

Discussions on this program ended in failure, and the government decided to follow its own recovery plan, involving large-scale cutbacks in public-sector pay and expenditure. This failure to agree was a hammer blow to the social partnership process. Trade unions announced their total opposition to the government plan and launched a campaign of action to impede its implementation. For its part, Irish Business and Employers Confederation (IBEC), the employers' organization, announced in November 2009 that it was withdrawing from social partnership. The significance of these developments for company-level responses to the economic crisis is that the overarching institutional framework that promoted consensus and accommodation is effectively absent. As a result, organizations are seeking to secure employee buy-in to restructuring plans in an industrial relations environment where the institutions encouraging trust and consensus have been weakened considerably and possibly fatally. The legacy of the social partnership was nonetheless reflected in the agreement between the government and public-service unions on pay and restructuring in the public service until 2014 (the so-called Croke Park agreement) and in the accord reached between IBEC and the Irish Congress of Trade Unions (ICTU) on the principles that should guide national economic policy and collective bargaining at firm level during 2010.

Although national social partnership was experiencing operating difficulties in the last years of its existence, its demise is significant in that it leaves the Irish labor market more or less without an elaborate institutional framework that can guide and influence the behavior of firms. More likely than not, the absence of national social partnership will accelerate the fragmentation of Irish industrial relations in which no economy-wide rules or norms exist on work and employment. Thus, Irish firms were not encumbered with any significant institutional constraints or reference points when they started to devise strategies to deal with the outset of the recession. This freedom to more or less develop the nature and extent of their own restructuring strategies was unlike the situation in many other European countries where firms were obliged to operate within the confines of national labor-market rules and laws. The absence of external institutional pressures raises interesting questions about the nature of the restructuring strategies developed by firms: Would there be any pattern or coherence to the responses, and would firms try to radically restructure their established employment models? This study will hopefully provide answers to these—and other—questions.

2.4   THE IRISH LABOR MARKET EXPERIENCE IN COMPARATIVE EUROPEAN CONTEXT

The economic crisis has been felt across Europe. Since the autumn of 2008, EU unemployment has increased by 2% age points to 9.2% as 5 million people lost their jobs. There are now 22 million individuals unemployed in the EU (European Foundation for Living and Working Conditions 2009a). Some of the member states have been worse hit by the downturn than have others. Most of the new member states have been severely affected, experiencing both steep declines in economic output and steep rises in unemployment. Of the older member-states, Ireland, Spain and the United Kingdom have been the worst affected. These countries embraced financialization more wholeheartedly than did other member states, which resulted in them experiencing relatively high economic growth through the expansion of credit. Other member states, such as Germany and France, although becoming entangled in the financialization process, helped to check credit expansion. This more restrained approach meant that when the crisis did happen these countries were not as exposed (IMF 2009).

Although the economic downturn was uneven across the EU in terms of its harshness, its effects tended to be similar across the member states (European Commission 2009). Almost everywhere men lost their jobs at a much higher rate than did women. Young people, particularly those with few skills or little experience, have also been badly hit, as have temporary workers who firms tend to let go first when retrenching. As in Ireland, construction has been the economic sector most badly hit by the recession in the EU. Manufacturing has also suffered quite severely, which is slightly different to the Irish experience where the service sector fared worse than manufacturing.

In response to the economic downturn, most member-states have adopted more active employment policies designed either to encourage employers not to lay off employees or to provide more comprehensive help for those who have lost their jobs (Cazes, Verick and Heuer 2009). Most governments have committed themselves to some form of extra public expenditure on infrastructure programs. The rationale for this type of action, normally labeled Keynesian, is pretty straightforward: in the context of fairly depressed private-sector activity, government should step into the breach and stimulate demand by funding projects with long-term economic value. Intervention of this kind undoubtedly increases government debt, but it is now seen as a fairly legitimate thing to do not only to limit the social costs of the economic downturn, particularly in terms of job losses, but also to ensure that long term damage is not done to economic structures and capabilities (Akerlof and Shiller 2009). Governments have also been reorganizing unemployment benefit systems to allow people to combine benefits with some type of work experience, training or job retention (Freyssinet 2010).

To a much lesser extent, some governments have sought to stimulate demand by cutting taxes, particularly indirect taxes. Thus, for example, the UK government reduced the value-added tax (VAT) as part of a package of actions designed to buoy up the UK economy. Using tax cuts to stimulate demand has its critics because it is seen as a policy intervention that lacks focus and is purely short term in character, which probably explains why it has not been used more widely. Some governments have provided subsidies to private-sector companies to help meet the challenges of adverse economic conditions. Some of these subsidy programs are generalized, open to all firms to promote investment and so on while others are targeted on specific sectors: the scrappage scheme to promote demand for new cars is an example of such a subsidy. These measures can be broadly described as macroeconomic interventions to help stave off the worse of the recession (European Foundation for Living and Working Conditions 2009b).

A range of measures particularly designed for the labor market has also been introduced. Wage subsidies is one policy that has been used by governments, but it is an issue on which opinion is quite divided. One influential view is that wage subsidies should not be used as a method to shore up jobs inside firms mainly on the principle that the total payment to a factor of production should not exceed its marginal productivity (Whelan 2009). The counter argument is that without wage subsidies more people than is necessary will become unemployed with adverse consequences: work incentives are weakened and a culture of welfare dependency is fostered, which undermines labor force participation, employability and employee loyalty (Phelps 1994). Both views are evident in European capitals, which explains why some governments have used them and some have not. If governments do elect to use wage subsidies, they can choose either to introduce a generalized or targeted program. Views on which program is the most effective are equally divided. As a result it is not surprising that both have been used.

Governments have also promoted work contract flexibility programs. These programs take a variety of forms. One relatively popular measure used by about 16 of the 27 member states is to provide public money for companies to introduce short-term working schemes rather than make employees redundant (Arpaia et al. 2010). These schemes are seen as having a number of advantages. In particular, they permit companies to retain employee know-how for the post-recession period and even provide opportunities for skills upgrading. It also allows employees to secure the psychological and (partial) income benefits of not losing their jobs. Schemes of this kind do not enjoy universal support because they are seen as not guaranteeing job security in the long term (Walker 2007). They are considered as providing only short-term relief from unemployment. Moreover, it is claimed that few firms take the opportunity to increase training for people employed on short-term working contracts. So far the weight of evidence appears to be that the countries that have adopted such schemes have performed better in terms of lower unemployment (EU Commission 2010).

Training has been a further measure used by governments to reduce the impact of the economic crisis, although not as extensively as might have been expected. Those member states introducing training programs have mostly targeted young people (European Foundation for Living and Working Conditions 2009b). Efforts have focused particularly on developing apprenticeship schemes that combines training with work experience. An interesting example is the adoption of the Vocational Training Act and the Youth Package in Austria in 2008. Those young people recruited onto the program are incorporated into the country's dual training system that combines an apprenticeship in a company with vocational education in a vocational school. In addition, companies are given subsidies if they recruit disadvantaged young people who in turn are supported by a special mentorship program. Since its introduction, the program has been reasonably successful, as nearly 10,000 mostly disadvantaged young people have secured positions.

The employment policy response by the Irish government to address the labor market fallout of the recession is more muted than in a number of other member states. A number of schemes have been launched to create and maintain employment. In particular, a €100 million stabilization fund was established to help vulnerable firms and a wage employment subsidy scheme was established to support jobs in the tradable sector. A work placement service was also introduced to help 2,000 unemployed people obtain some work experience. In addition, the public employment agency, FAS, introduced a number of schemes to improve labor-market matching, linking unemployed people more quickly with job vacancies, and to increase support for those made unemployed so that they could make a speedy return to employment. Until recently the government had decided against introducing wide-ranging support schemes pursued by other member states. Thus, for example, no public finance has been made available to provide greater support to companies considering introducing short-time working arrangement or providing training to employees instead of laying them off. But this stance has now changed somewhat not least because of rising unemployment levels. In particular, the 2010 budget contained a series of additional active labor-market policies to address the growing jobless problems. These measures include a work placement program and a community work-placement scheme to address mounting youth and long-term unemployment.

2.5   THE EFFECTS OF RECESSIONS ON HUMAN RESOURCE MANAGEMENT

The effect of recessions on human resource management and industrial relations during the twentieth century is a subject of considerable interest and debate in the international literature. Particular interest has been attracted to the question of whether deep and prolonged recessions, or depressions for that matter, disrupt or displace prevailing models of human resource management and industrial relations. This question of whether recessions lead to transient, if otherwise significant, changes or cause profound and lasting disjunctures in the ways firms manage human resources and relate to trade unions has proved difficult enough to resolve. Probably the biggest problem is capturing accurately the interaction between a recession and long-run or secular trends operating on the management of the employment relationship. For example, do recessions intensify the impact of secular trends on human resources and industrial relations, or do they cause such trends to change direction or character, causing the management of the employment relationship to follow a new pathway? It is difficult to assess accurately the scale and nature of change wrought by recessions on human resource management (HRM). This issue has been a recurring theme in the literature on this topic.

International Debates and Evidence

Perhaps, the best starting point to review the large literature on the topic is Stanford Jacoby's important book *Modern Manors* published in 1997. An important theme of this book is that the Great Depression of the 1930s in the United States led to the disappearance of the welfare capitalism model of managing people in many large firms that had developed from the late 19th century to the prosperous 1920s. Company unions, paternalistic employer postures and good pay and fringe benefits were core features of this welfare capitalism model. Thus, for Jacoby, the Depression had the effect of uprooting a fairly widespread and successful model of managing people at work. Interestingly, however, he concedes that the model was not completely wiped out by the Depression and that those firms that preserved the principles of welfare capitalism became the bearers of what was to become the prototype model of nonunion HRM in large firms in the United States and beyond. Thus, a secondary message from the Jacoby book is that the cumulative effect of a recession might cause an established human resource management model to metamorphose into something different.

A different and perhaps more conventional interpretation of the Depression is that it paved the way for the New Deal model of industrial relations, based on union recognition, collective bargaining and professional industrial relations and personnel management. On this account, the hard economic times of the 1930s provided the material basis for a real disjuncture with what had gone before in terms of how the American economy was governed (see Slichter, Healy and Livernash 1960; Kochan, Katz and McKersie 1986).

Of more recent vintage, much research was devoted to the effects of the recession of the 1980s on human resource management and industrial relations in the United Kingdom. Theories of labor markets and management processes commonly pointed to putative secular trends such as 'de-skilling,' labor market segmentation, the advent of the 'flexible firm,' the emergence of HRM and the advent of 'new realism' in industrial relations, that interacted with the recession and were believed to have profound and lasting effects on the conduct of employment relations (Gallie et al. 1994: chap. 1). As Gallie et al., authors of one of the key volumes in the Social Change and Economic Life Initiative (SCELI) research program, noted, "in the five or so years preceding the research, deep recession, tight monetary policies and high exchange rates had meant that, for much of British industry, survival itself required major policy changes" (1994: 11). On the whole, however, the study and the broader SCELI research program of which it was a component—while observing that it might be too soon to make a final judgment from the vantage point of the early 1990s—pointed more to continuities in employment relations models than to discontinuity. The study of employers' strategies concluded that there was "little general evidence that employers had systematically pursued such objectives as greater workforce flexibility, de-skilling, human resource management and had promoted the kinds of co-operative postures toward more compliant trade unions known as the 'new industrial relations" (Gallie et al. 1994: 28). A further volume, titled *Trade Unionism in Recession*, also questioned the view that the 1980s recession in the United Kingdom had involved "crisis and discontinuity" or a "fundamental break with the past" (Gallie et al. 1996: 1–2). The basis for the view that the circumstances and behavior of trade unions had changed radically from the 1980s was that deep recession, combined with a radical change in state policy toward industrial relations under successive legislative and policy programs of conservative governments, had interacted with secular trends involving changing product markets, rapidly changing technology and the rise of HRM (a new employee philosophy) to give rise to a disjuncture in employer attitudes to trade unions and a consequent decline in the power, influence and appeal of unions in firms and workplaces (Gallie et al. 1996: chap. 1).

In contrast with this view, Gallie and his colleagues concluded that "the general pattern had been one of very considerable continuity" (1996: 19). The picture of sharp change in employer attitudes to trade unions was found to have had little empirical basis. Only a small minority of employers were found to have had strong antiunion feelings. Nor was there any evidence from surveys of employers that union power had declined at workplace level. HRM policies in general had not been adopted with a view to undercutting union influence, and, besides, case studies revealed that firms appeared to introduce HRM in a "relatively fragmented and ad hoc way," with little impact on the underlying attitudes of employees to either management or unions (Gallie et al. 1996: 18, chap. 1). In a comprehensive review of the effects of the 1980s recession on HRM in the United Kingdom, Karen Legge (1988) reached the conclusion that for most firms, it has been a case of 'business as usual' with respect both to the practices implemented and the status of personnel professionals, with some firms practicing 'macho management' and others attempting to incorporate unions through cooperative forms of employment relations and at the same time intensifying work.

The most keenly contested interpretation of the effects of recession on employment relations concerns the effects of the deep US recession of the early 1980s—the country's worst economic downturn to that point since the Great Depression—on human resource management. Here again recession was seen by some to have interacted with secular trends to bring about a radical disjuncture in prevailing employment relations arrangements. The key disjuncture theorist was Peter Cappelli, and his main contention was that a new 'market-driven' model had been fired in the cauldron of the 1980s US recession and was set to become of wide and lasting prevalence:

> The world began to change for employers with the 1981–82 recession, the worst economic period since the Great Depression, which brought with it structural change that went well beyond the usual downturn. (Cappelli 1999b: 151)

For Cappelli (1999a: chap. 3; b) firms had responded in radical ways to the 1980s recession. Also shaping firms responses to the recession was a series of underlying secular trends. These included a more liberal public policy environment toward flexibility with respect to hiring and firing employees, wider resort to labor-market intermediary institutions, such as outsourcing providers and staffing agencies, intensified pressure to increase shareholder value, firms' growing attempts to concentrate on core competencies by divesting subsidiaries activities and pursuing outsourcing, shorter production cycles, more rapid change in products and processes and the growing popularity of new forms of work organization, especially team working. The result of firms' responses to these pressures in the context of deep recession was the increasing prevalence of the market-driven workforce and an associated market-driven model of employment relations. The main features of the new model, according to Cappelli, included the end of 'career jobs' and an overall decline in job security and job tenure, a decline in investment in training and human resource development, growing resort to 'contingent' or nonstandard forms of work like contract and temporary jobs, the disappearance of internal labor markets and career systems, the more widespread use of variable pay systems that shifted risk to employees and a move away from pension systems based on defined benefit toward defined contribution systems with increasingly stringent qualifying conditions (Cappelli 1999a; b; Cappelli et al. 1997). For Cappelli these developments were particularly salient in the case of groups like executives and managers, long shielded from adverse developments in product and labor markets.

Cappelli's 'new deal at work' was rigorously criticized on empirical grounds by Jacoby (1999a; b), who contended that the market-driven work-force model misconstrued or exaggerated some trends, while underplaying other developments that pointed to continuity with developments in work and employment during the New Deal era. Jacoby queried the extent to which job tenure had declined and questioned whether job mobility between firms had risen significantly. He pointed instead to continuity in work and employment arrangements such that the majority of employees continued to hold career-type jobs that offered fringe benefits, training and good prospects (Jacoby 1999a: 133). One significant change that had occurred, Jacoby contended, was that firms faced with more turbulent or uncertain product markets had sought to shift the burden of risk to their employees to a significantly greater degree, exposing them to a greater risk of job losses and rendering their pay packages more variable through performance-related pay, profit sharing and stock options and through growing resort to defined-contribution pension schemes (Jacoby 1999a: 135–39).

At a more general level, Jacoby cautions against the temptation to view cyclical shifts toward more market-responsive employment practices—what he refers to as the 'swinging pendulum'—as structural changes, thereby engaging in the 'fallacy of discontinuity': an "erroneous belief that the present is fundamentally different from the periods that preceded it" (Jacoby 1999a: 134). Viewed in longer-term perspective, he argued, labor-market changes during the 1980s and 1990s in the United States reflected the recurrence of a tendency toward more market-responsive employment relationships in economic downswings. Such cyclical swings were succeeded by shifts back toward more career-oriented relationships when the economy recovered and the labor market tightened (Jacoby 1999a: 131). Favoring a more gradualist interpretation of the development of the labor market, Jacoby nonetheless pointed, as discussed, to a trend toward employers shifting the burden of risk to a greater degree toward their employees as the external environment had grown significantly riskier.

The issues in contention between Cappelli and Jacoby in the United States have also anchored recent research on developments in human resource management in the United Kingdom. Of central importance here is the detailed empirical study by McGovern et al. (2007), which assessed the validity of the thesis that employment relations in the United Kingdom had become progressively marketized by examining trends over the period from the 1980s recession to 2000. McGovern and his colleagues concluded that there was little evidence that the standard employment relationship, based on full-time employment of long duration and involving internal job or career ladders, had been transformed. Temporary employment had risen during the 1980s, but by 2000 it was no more prevalent than during the 1970s. The proportion of people occupying long-term jobs had been stable, and the prevalence of job or career ladders (internal labor markets) had risen in the private sector (McGovern et al. 2007: chap. 2). Echoing Jacoby on the United States, McGovern and his colleagues (2007: 288) concluded that the marketization view of transformation in employment relations had been unduly influenced by misconstruing as 'structural change' an 'unusually severe downswing in the economy' that had involved 'short-term turbulence.' Influenced by a downward swing in the business cycle, employers had moved toward more market-responsive employment relations practices, only for the 'pendulum to swing back' toward career-type jobs, training and a concern with fostering loyalty and commitment when the economy had begun to expand again from the middle of the 1990s. The most salient feature of experience in the United Kingdom had been the "remarkable stability and durability of the employment relationship" (McGovern et al. 2007: 65). However, echoing Jacoby again, the UK researchers accepted that the adaptation by firms of employment arrangements to external pressures had involved growing employment uncertainty for employees and the more widespread adoption of performance-related pay systems. To these developments were allied the growing prevalence of performance controls and incentives more generally and other HRM practices that predisposed people to work more intensively (McGovern et al. 2007: chaps. 5–6).

Recessions and Employment Relations in Ireland

In shifting the focus to the historical effects of recessions on employment relations in Ireland, it must first be acknowledged that the detailed pictures built up for the United States and the United Kingdom through repeated representative employer and employee surveys of broad scope are lacking. Nevertheless, some significant effects of recessions on human resource management and industrial relations can be identified, especially in the case of the 1980s recession—the deepest and most prolonged recession of modern times up until the advent of the current crisis. Previous recessions, such as those of the 1920s and early 1930s, appear mainly to have given rise to cyclical effects in such areas as pay cutting, unemployment and declining union membership and density (see Roche 1997a). Significant downturns in the early and mid-1950s involved similar developments but failed to halt or fundamentally change the operation of the 'pay round' system that had begun after the Second World War.

Bearing in mind the limits to inference and generalization that arise from the relative paucity of data on employers and employees in Ireland, a case could be made for the view that recessions in Ireland have had more sustained impacts on employment relations through their influence on macro-level developments in institutions and arrangements than on micro-level engagement between employers, employees and trade unions in firms and workplaces. The deep recession of the mid 1950s is widely understood to have been a major catalyst for the 'outward' industrial policy adopted by the Irish State from the final years of that decade. This policy in turn was associated with the 'corporatist pragmatism' of Sean Lemass and his persistent concern to involve employers and trade unions in a series of tripartite institutions linked with economic planning and development (Roche 2009). National pay bargaining during the 1970s, and, in particular, successive governments' increasingly activist efforts to shore up national concertation through debt financing and an increasingly elaborate range of fiscal incentives, had been influenced by the recessions following the first and second 'oil shocks' early and late in the decade. Although recessionary conditions had acted as a spur to considerable institutional innovation at the national or central level in relations among employers, unions and the state, employment relations on the ground continued for many firms and their employees to follow the classical unreconstructed adversarial model of arm's-length, low-trust collective bargaining. The persistence of this model was commonly linked to such phenomena of the 1970s as extensive second-tier pay bargaining and pay drift, persistently high industrial conflict and doomed initiatives in 'productivity bargaining' and other ventures in cooperative employment relations (Hardiman 1987; Roche 1997b).

In large measure, the deep and prolonged recession of the period from the 1980s to the early 1990s extended this pattern of macro-level institutional innovation and transformation combined with limited lasting change in micro-level employment relations arrangements. Although the advent of the 1980s recession contributed to the collapse of 'proto-social partnership' in the form of the Second National Understanding for Economic and Social Progress, negotiated in 1980, it also contributed later in the decade to the emergence of what was to be more than 20 years of national-level tripartite dialogue between employers, unions and governments and the welter of institutions connected with social partnership. Also traceable to the 1980s, but less directly connected with the effects of recession, was a switch in state policy away from favoring employment relations based on union recognition and collective bargaining toward a more laissez-faire approach. This switch in policy, arising mainly from intensifying competition for foreign direct investment and a shift in industrial strategy toward attracting firms in sectors with little history of unionization, was to have an abiding effect on the postures of incoming multinational firms toward union recognition and the general conduct of employment relations. Beyond the multinational sector, there also appears to have been a rise in employer resistance to union recognition and a growth in the scale of the nonunion sector (Roche 2001). During the first half of the 1980s work stoppages connected with union recognition rose sharply as did the number of recognition cases dealt with by the Labour Court (McGovern 1989). However, taking the 1980s and 1990s as a whole, no pronounced upward trend in work stoppages over union recognition was evident, and these stoppages accounted for only 5%

of all strikes and 2% of working days lost during the 1990s. The incidence of recognition disputes subject to hearings at the Labor Court also peaked during the 1980s, falling back and fluctuating only moderately during the 1990s (McGovern 1989: 67; Gunnigle 2002: 236). It may, of course, have been the case that no sustained rise in industrial conflict surrounding the issue had occurred because unions had 'withdrawn from the fray' at firm level and had opted instead to focus on seeking legislative remedies to growing employer resistance to recognition.

Other than in this area, the deep and prolonged downturn of the 1980s seems to have had little lasting impact on the conduct of employment relations at firm and workplace level. As frequently bemoaned by newly created partnership institutions and as revealed in their surveys and case studies, 'progressive' developments in employment relations such as workplace partnership or the systematic adoption of modern HRM practices struggled to find acceptance in Irish businesses (Roche 2007a; Roche and Geary 2000). The employment relations landscape appeared dominated in the private sector by a sizeable, if shrinking, unionized sector, where adversarial collective bargaining continued to hold sway, by a growing nonunion sector characterized, for the most part, by traditional control-oriented or sometimes paternalistic approaches to the management of people and by small, if strategically important, pockets of leading-edge HRM or partnerships with unions. The picture in the public service continued for the most part to be one of unreconstructed adversarial industrial relations, little disturbed by successive waves of initiatives associated with 'modernization' or by the wider Strategic Management Initiative that had framed public service reforms (Roche 1998; 2006).

Some observers nevertheless viewed the 1980s as the crucible for changes that had subsequently been intensified by economic recovery and growth during the 1990s. O'Hearn (1998: 104) commented that work in Ireland had "undoubtedly become more casual and less secure since 1985," claiming that "in industry and services alike, more and more employees have flexible status, like part-time, temporary and fixed-contract work." However, employees' experiencing their jobs to be secure rose from 20% in 1989 to 24% in 2001, while those deeming it 'very true' that their job was secure rose from 38% in 1996 to 43% in 2004 (O'Connell and Russell 2007: 60–62). This trend seemed to point to growing employment security as the Irish economy recovered from the deep recession of the 1980s and early 1990s and reached virtual full employment. As regards the incidence of 'flexible' or 'atypical' work, part-time working grew sharply from the mid-1980s to the middle of the 1990s and then remained stable thereafter. Much of this was voluntary in nature: the incidence of involuntary part-time working (or underemployment) falling during the 1990s. The incidence of fixed-term employment fell from 9% of the workforce when unemployment was at its peak in 1993 to 4% in 2004 (O'Connell 2007: 45–49). Trends such as these are consistent with international evidence that forms of employment and levels of employment security follow cyclical patterns. They provide few indications of disjuncture or structural change at the micro level of work-forces or firms resulting from the effects of the deep and prolonged Irish recession of the 1980s and early 1990s.

The intensity at which employees worked appears to have risen in Ireland from the early 1990s, while levels of work discretion appear to have fallen—both developments mirroring the trend in many European countries. These trends have been attributed to secular changes in technology and work organization that increase firms' capacities to monitor and control work. These changes include the adoption of new production systems, the increased use of performance management and a general move to an 'audit culture' in private and public sectors (Green 2006: chaps. 3–5).

The following conclusions seem valid in light of this review of the established international and Irish literature on the effects of recessions on the conduct of human resource management and industrial relations:

- Deep economic downswings generally affect the conduct of employment relations by inclining employers toward more market-responsive postures that may involve downsizing and more flexible employment arrangements, less investment in training and development and general restructuring activities that may weaken internal labor markets and assured career progression.
- The immediate effects of recessions may be a poor guide to any abiding effects that may arise, and experience internationally warrants caution against misconstruing cyclical developments as radical disjunctures in employment relations models.
- If recessions during the 1980s have had any lasting effects internationally these seem mainly to have involved firms shifting the burden of risk toward their employees through regular downsizing initiatives to adjust labor supply to business conditions, the adoption of performance-related pay systems and the revision of company pension schemes.
- In the case of Ireland, recessions, particularly the deep and prolonged recession of the 1980s and early 1990s, appear to have had more lasting effects in generating innovation at a macro level in relations between employers, unions and the state than at the micro level of firms, their workforces and union representatives.
- Although some changes at national level, especially in the posture of the State toward union recognition, have had significant and lasting effects at firm level, on the whole the circumstances of the 1980s and early 1990s do not appear to have had major transformative effects on the conduct of human resource management and industrial relations at the level of firms and workplaces in Ireland.

These conclusions mean that an examination of the conduct of human resource management in the current recession needs to be approached with caution against exaggerating the significance and durability of any immediate changes or effects. But it remains important to keep an open mind. As Jacoby (1999b: 168) reminds us 'historical turning points' may indeed occur. Recessions differ in their depth and amplitude. In the case of Ireland the current recession is particularly acute and prolonged given the scale of the fall in gross national product (GNP) and the rise in closures, redundancies and unemployment. Moreover, the recession has also led to a near collapse of the banking system and to a severe squeeze in government finances, making it the most serious recession in the state's history. But even in countries where its effects may have been less acute, the recession has again provoked commentary and debate as to the nature of its effects on human resource management and industrial relations.

The Effects of the Current Recession on HRM

Judging by the volume of material on the internet, the current international recession has provoked a great deal of comment, debate and advice among HR practitioners, professional bodies, consultants and pundits as to the effects on human resource management. Much of this outlines checklists of priority areas for action: pay cuts, reduced hours, redundancies, the retention of scarce talent and the maintenance of employee commitment, among others. The CIPD has advised HR professionals on how they should manage their workforces in the recession. They are exhorted to 'think long term,' maintain employee engagement, strengthen line management capability, support employees' health and well-being, develop a strategy for redundancy, find ways to minimize redundancy if staffing reductions are unavoidable, consult with the workforce and their representatives, establish fair and objective selection criteria for redundancy, provide advice and support for people losing their jobs and plan for the future, especially by reallocating jobs and responsibilities, provide training for new jobs, and communicate with employees at all stages (CIPD 2008). In addition to prescriptive commentary, the recession has also provoked a good deal of reflection on the likely consequences for human resource management and industrial relations. Although some of these contributions are by HR practitioners or consulting houses, or by HR academics writing in nonrefereed professional periodicals, they merit consideration for any insights they provide and because they are important in forming professional opinion. The provenance of different contributions will, however, be made clear, whether deriving from professional experience, the views and offerings of consulting houses or refereed international journals.

The Recession as the Harbinger of HR Cataclysm or a New Employment Model

It is possible to identify three strands of argument in the literature. The first suggests that the recession will have a cataclysmic effect on the HR function or even on the viability of long prevalent employment models. Some such commentary is apocalyptic after the fashion encountered in commentary and analysis during previous recessions: one article proclaiming that the global crisis in the context of the ongoing globalization of businesses would decimate HR. Drawing on a consultancy study of HR in leading global companies, Pitcher (2008) suggests that numbers working in HR would be cut disproportionately compared with other support functions, whereas 'transactional' HR processes would be increasingly relocated to low-cost countries. The consultancy, the Hackett Group, active in fields that include shared services, off-shoring and outsourcing, claim in further research that the off-shoring of HR and other support functions had continued during 2009 and 2010, and that this 'mega-trend' means that major global firms are implementing hiring freezes and staff cuts in support functions in home countries. The prospect was for jobless recovery in HR and other support functions (The Hackett Group[1] 2009a; b). Contrary to this claim, research undertaken by the CIPD in the United Kingdom indicated that although widespread staff cuts were expected, more than one in five firms expected nevertheless to hire staff in HR. This was attributed to an upsurge in work linked to such developments in HR as the growth in redundancy. Some commentators on the trend nonetheless warned of a possible long-term fall in numbers employed in the HR function, while others believed that the focus of HR activity would change in a more strategic direction and that fewer would be engaged in routine transactional HR administration (Phillips 2008).

Although this line of commentary is restricted to the HR function, other commentaries point toward evidence of the 'psychological contract' at the root of the past employment model being 'rocked to its foundations by the recession' through job insecurity, less assured advancement, curbs on pay and the waning significance of employee engagement (Briner 2010). Also advanced has been the concept of a new employment deal forged in the cauldron of the current international recession. Prominent here is the international consulting firm Towers Watson (2010), which conducted a global workforce study in 2010, involving 22,000 full-time employees in 22 of the firm's 'markets.' The study contends that the recession had accelerated slow-moving and long-term shifts in the employment relationship with the result that employment globally in mature economies was in the "earliest stages of a significant workplace transformation: (Towers Watson 2010: 9, 21). The emerging new social contract or new employment deal is seen as being built on several foundations. Although relatively small proportions of employees claimed to be actively looking for other jobs at present, nearly half anticipated no advancement in their current job, and nearly 4 out of 10 believed that they would have to go elsewhere to advance (Towers Watson 2010: 6–7). This was in consequence of the career security and progression commonly provided by employers in the past—and expected by employees—being replaced by a growing awareness of the need for 'self-reliance' or 'active' rather than 'passive' security on the part of employees (Towers Watson 2010: 11). In the new employment deal, work experience and rewards were becoming more 'personalized' and employers were increasingly seg-menting their HRD and talent management effort to the roles of different employee groups (Towers Watson 2010: 14–15). All in all, employers were in the process of defining an acceptable level of risk transfer for employees.

The HR function was expected to become more agile and business-savvy as a consequence of these developments. While the Towers-Watson study presents a very general overview of the putative new employment model, backed by data from the firm's clients, strong echoes of Cappelli's interpre-tation of the long-term consequences of the 1980s recession in the United States are audible: employees were being forced to become more self-reliant, they could expect less long-term commitment from their employers (even if they still often sought an emotional connection with their organizations and were subject to employee engagement programs), their jobs were more insecure, their rewards were more contingent and their work experiences were more differentiated. Moreover, they would now benefit from talent management and Human Resource Development (HRD) programs only as long as they were recognized as 'star contributors' or 'future leaders' (Tow-ers Watson 2010: 7, 20).

The Recession as the Catalyst for High-Commitment HR Transformation

A second strand of recent commentary suggests that the recession will both increase the stature and influence of the HR function and deepen the appeal and prevalence of HR practices consistent with the high-commitment model. This model has dominated professional discourse on the features of good and effective HRM for the past two decades. Prominent contributors to this second strand are HR gurus who have given both their views on the implications of the recession for HR and their prescriptions for effective HR in recessionary conditions. Ulrich (as reported in Brockett 2010) in a practitioner conference contribution claimed that HR leaders in the best organizations have been widening their professional focus to ensure that all stakeholder groups are served—not alone employees and line manag-ers, but customers, investors and the community. HR leaders, he claimed, were also ensuring that firms were being positioned for the long term by investment in skills and the creation of a positive organizational culture and brand. Ulrich urges HR practitioners to see themselves as 'professional ser-vice groups' within their own organizations, deploying their knowledge and accessing available resources to deliver productively for clients. As he sees it—though no data are presented in support—the top 20% of organizations were already operating in this manner, 60% were moving in the right direc-tion and 20% would be incapable of doing so (Brockett 2010: 11).

Ulrich's essential idea—though expressed in a highly abstract and general manner—appears to be that HR leaders should intensify and extend the established paradigm of high-commitment management rather than regress in the recession to 'command and control.' At the same time they must also concentrate on making transactional processes more efficient and on cost cutting. The HR function should be central to this by providing professional services to multiple stakeholders and by positioning firms for the future as much as meeting current challenges. Ulrich also promulgates the need for a 'harder' HR agenda and views the economic crisis as a possible catalyst for the emergence of a business partnering model of the HR function. He is reported as advising HR practitioners to use the recession to remove underperforming staff and to recruit talent made redundant by other organizations. Costs needed to be cut and unnecessary roles removed. The HR function needed to use the economic crisis to demonstrate its capacity for making sound business decisions through 'business partnering' (as reported in *Personnel Today*, December 9, 2008).

Writing for a professional audience, Cary Cooper also adopts an upbeat posture on the implications of the recession for HR, observing that it could be the 'making of HR': challenging the function as never before and providing an opportunity for practitioners to demonstrate that they are able to contribute to managing talent. They also face the challenge of providing leadership in creating organizational cultures that motivate employees in a period of insecurity. This may also involve leadership in confronting senior management on the handling of HR issues, and being at the forefront of recovery rather than simply offering a compliant support function (Cooper 2009).

Commentary in the pages of the CIPD's *People Management* magazine by senior HR executives in the UK public sector, with past experience of reorganization and cost-saving initiatives, echo these positive assessments of the impact of the recession on the HR function. While HR would face job losses, HR directors in local government, the NHS and the civil service were reported to be 'excited' by finding themselves in pivotal positions in which they could lead their organizations in providing more efficient and effective service delivery (Pickard 2010: 19). The recession had created an opportunity for 'innovation, creativity and leadership.' This was reflected in HR initiatives in shared service provision, in interagency 'centres of excellence' that dealt with recruitment and other activities. It was also evident in the greater efficiency in HR service provision achieved by reducing HR to staff ratios to levels comparable with the private sector (Pickard 2010: 19).

Mohrman and Worley (2009: 437), writing in the top-rated US academic journal *Human Resource Management*, claim that leading global firms are developing "capabilities, including human capital capabilities, that enable them to 'thrive and survive in rough times." Again the claims advanced, supported by anecdotal examples from major corporations, are sometimes apocalyptic in tone: "during crisis, leaders must quickly introduce profound change in the way the organization operates—approaches that greatly increase the organization's capacity to leverage knowledge and employee involvement throughout the organization in finding solutions to the challenges it faces" (Mohrman and Worley 2009: 434). Although HR and related practices associated with 'profound change' are dealt with in a very general way, it is clear that the paradigm expected to grow in influence and prevalence is the high-commitment model. Thus, Mohrman and Worley speak of 'tapping into employees' energy and engagement throughout the organization and of the importance of problem-solving processes in this context. These include the involvement of employees in 'extreme strategizing' aimed at accelerating innovation in products and services. Also important was giving employees a 'sense of ownership and contribution' and the use of nonmonetary rewards and HRD as forms of recognition. The importance of communication, including two-way communication, is also stressed as a critical facet of the HR architecture for surviving and thriving in tough times (Mohrman and Worley 2009: 436–41). By making these types of changes, "during the downturn, when inertia and turf protection are clearly counter-productive and the status quo is unviable," Mohrman and Worley (2009: 443) claim that organizations "can use the downturn to introduce fundamental changes in logic and [that] will make [them] more sustainably effective through time."

Commentaries of this kind—which represent the dominant perspective among the HR commentaries—anticipate that the recession will have a benign effect on the HR profession, increasing the function's influence within businesses, through greater opportunities for leadership and business partnering. At the same time the profession's prevailing principles of good practice and associated HR policies and practices, modeled on the high-commitment paradigm, are seen as both robust and effective in recessionary conditions and growing in their appeal for businesses and thus in their prevalence.

The Recession as Contributor to Eclectic Change in HR Practice

Empirically informed academic analysis on the HR effects of the recession has been limited to date. Nevertheless, it is possible to identify a third strand of commentary, often grounded in empirical reviews, whether refereed or otherwise, which is much more measured and circumspect regarding whether changes arising from the recession are fundamental or likely to be of lasting significance. In this strand of commentary changes are often understood to be pragmatic, eclectic[2] and incremental in nature. Organizations' responses to the recession are seen to be marked by significant continuities with prerecession trends and to involve complex and even contradictory sets of measures. For example, firms may respond in ways that reduce job security and increase work intensity, while at the same time purporting to preserve or increase employee engagement. In the third strand of commentary, HRM is seen to be affected by many changes, some of possibly lasting significance, others probably cyclical or transient. But the picture put forward in reviews is that changes underway in the recession are likely to be incremental or nondisjunctive, whether with respect to HR practices, the HR function or the principles of good practice.

Articles in recent years in international journals dealing with the effects of recession on HRM draw mainly on data that predate the current crisis. Thus, Mellahi and Wilkinson's (2010) study of the effects of downsizing programs on product innovation in UK firms draws on data for the period 2000–05 and establishes that downsizing undertaken hastily, or implemented only to save costs, impaired product innovation. The scale of downsizing however had no discernable effects on innovation. Maertz et al.'s (2010) study examines the effects of downsizing, off-shoring and outsourcing on a sample of employees in the United States during the period 2003–05. This reveals that survivors of layoffs reported lower organizational performance, job security, commitment and higher intentions to quit their employing firm. Those surviving off-shoring initiatives reported broadly similar negative effects, whereas survivors of outsourcing did not reveal such negative outcomes (Maertz et al. 2010).

The limited research-based literature focused directly on the effects of the current recession on HR advances a more measured view of developments and prospects. HR is seen to have been buffeted by the recession, resulting in significant but generally non-transformative changes in the function and in prevailing principles of good practice. A commentary on HR in the recession by the UK-based Institute for Employment Studies (IES) notes that HRM prerecession had gained considerable stature from evidence that the high-commitment paradigm had delivered better organizational performance. Although the recession had tilted attention and effort toward areas such as managing redundancies, there was evidence that its effects were less dramatic than it might at first have appeared. Firms had sought to preserve employment as a first priority and often opportunistically sought out talent and recruited from people who had lost their jobs (Brown and Reilly 2009: 2). Leading firms had commonly retained a 'HR-orientated employer philosophy' in which human resources continued to be viewed as assets rather than costs. This fed through to a battery of measures designed to retain staff whenever possible and to develop HR competencies to support firms' anticipated future trajectories. At the same time, firms were focusing their HR effort and high-commitment policies on high-potential and high-performing staff. Fairness remained an abiding concern, including the retention of a sense of common purpose in which success and suffering were shared. This might find expression in reward policies, where equity in internal relativities assumed a new priority. Finally, the HR function was required to improve the efficiency of its own processes, to demonstrate its contribution to the 'bottom line' and to engage in 'proactive partnering' with line managers— eschewing any predilection toward a regulatory and remote posture (Brown and Reilly 2009: 3–6).

Griffin and Smith (2010) draw on consultancy cases and assignments in the United Kingdom to argue that the recession might provide a 'shot in the arm for HR': giving rise to opportunities for the HR function to deepen their relationships with senior management, while ensuring that the exigencies of short-term survival in firms do not preclude attention on the factors that contribute to long-term success (Griffin and Smith 2010: 17). Their prescription for HR management practices involves continuing to attend to established policies, reviewing procedures, recruiting available high-potential staff (even while downsizing), managing talent, operating well-aligned and fair reward policies, maintaining a focused HRD effort and promoting employee engagement (Griffin and Smith 2010: 18–22). Research undertaken in the United Kingdom by the CIPD revealed that the recession had resulted in firms using in-house HRD programs to a greater degree and making more use of managers for coaching. With a squeeze on HRD budgets, firms were prioritizing training that was seen to have the biggest impact on business survival (Phillips 2009).

The Advisory, Conciliation and Arbitration Service (ACAS) undertook a review of the effects of the recession on industrial relations and aspects of HR in the United Kingdom. Noting that the emerging picture is 'full of contradictions, complexities and challenges,' ACAS identified a series of what are described as 'deep-seated' shifts that have fundamental implications for the world of work (ACAS 2009: 13–14). Redundancy levels had risen sharply, though unevenly by sector and region. Short-time working had grown and agency and temporary workers were particularly insecure in the new conditions prevailing. Pay freezes and sometimes pay cuts were at the center of a growth in concession bargaining between employers and trade unions (ACAS 2009: 2–8). Although unions were observed to have adapted to the recession by adopting a less confrontational approach, collective disputes were expected to rise and unofficial industrial action to become again a feature of the industrial relations landscape. There had also been a rise in the incidence of industrial conflict involving individuals, as evidenced by a growth in unfair dismissal claims and a rise in demand for a ACAS's individual conciliation service (ACAS 2009: 9). ACAS feared that employers were reducing their levels of investment in training and that firms that had not already implemented equality and diversity policies would now be less likely to do so. Cases of intense industrial conflict between migrant and UK workers had also arisen (ACAS 2009: 11–13). There were also indications of an escalation of workloads for those at work, resulting in increased pressure and stress (ACAS 2009: 13).

ACAS supplemented this review by a further review of the data on conflict in the workplace during the recession. This supplement notes that in recessions collective conflict tends to fall while individual expressions of conflict may rise. Individual conflict can be overt, as in the referral of cases to employment tribunals and an increased volume of calls to ACAS relating to matters such as discipline, dismissal and grievances. It may also be latent: as in absences through sickness or the withdrawal by employees of engagement (ACAS 2010). In the area of collective disputes, ACAS noted that employers had often forgone a 'slash and burn' approach and unions had adopted a more cooperative posture. These postures combined found expression in concession bargaining to preserve jobs and increase employment security. Concession bargaining worked best when employers were open and honest in their dealings with unions (ACAS 2010: 3–4). Notwithstanding the prevalence of concession bargaining, union officials report many instances of 'naked opportunism' on the part of employers seeking to use the recession to worsen pay and conditions (ACAS 2010: 3). ACAS reported research showing that only 1 in 10 employees believed that they are fully informed about what was happening in their organizations. The various pressures associated with the recession (redundancies, insecurity, cost-cutting, greater work intensity, etc.) involved an increased risk of the withdrawal of engagement by employees (ACAS 2010: 9).

Thus, contrasting views are emerging not only about how HR managers are responding to the recession, but also about the impact of the recession on the strategic position of HRM inside organizations. The alternative optimistic, pessimistic and pragmatic/incremental scenarios—which are difficult to reconcile with one another—suggest that commentators are still grappling with the HR consequences of the arrival of harsh economic times. In truth, insufficient evidence has so far been amassed to permit an authoritative judgment about how HR managers have handled the recession and how they will be affected by it. By providing detailed evidence on how the recession has had an impact on people management and union representation in firms in Ireland, this study should permit a more considered view about which scenario is likely to hold sway in the coming years. To advance the investigation the chapter next reviews the types of concrete policy choices available to managers to address the effects of a severe downturn in business circumstances.

2.6   HR PRACTICES IN THE RECESSION

The literature on the HR practices used to help firms adjust to hard economic times is diffuse. Table 2.1 categorizes the main HR practices that have been identified in the literature under separate but obviously related themes, and each of these are discussed in turn.

Pay Adjustment

The literature on efforts to adjust wage rates downward inside organizations when recession occurs is dominated by the theme of concession bargaining. The term was invented in the early eighties to explain the emergence of a large number of collective bargaining agreements in the United States that involved union givebacks to management in the form of freezes or even cuts in pay and benefits (Bureau of National Affairs 1982). Concession bargaining also led to changes in wage structures so that young people started on lower salaries or new pay rates were introduced for established jobs (Craft,

Table 2.1   HR practices in the recession

Pay Adjustment	Freeze or reduction in wages, changes in wage structures, lower pay rates for new employees, limiting bonuses, changes to pension arrangement (e.g., shifting from defined-benefit to defined-contribution or hybrid pension schemes).
Employment Adjustment	Redundancies (voluntary/compulsory), early retirement, changes in levels of contingent employment (part-time, contract and agency employment), freezes on recruitment and/or promotion.
Employment Stabilisation	Redeploying employees, introduction of temporary layoff schemes, relocation of employees, use of sabbaticals or unpaid leave, in-sourcing of previously outsourced activity, managing contingent employment to 'buffer' full-time employment, training for redeployment or as investment in skill formation.
More Rigorous Management Systems	Managing performance more rigorously and tightening up on timekeeping and discipline.
Reorganisation of Working Time	Shorter or more flexible working time, limiting or cancellation of overtime.
Voice, Engagement and Talent Management	More intensive communications, talent management, employee involvement in organizational restructuring, collective bargaining agreements with specific gains for employees/unions (e.g., review clauses, financial participation or supports to union organization).

Labovitz and Abboushi 1985). Some attempts at securing concession deals have been more successful than have others. McKersie and Cappelli (1981) suggested that concession bargaining was likely to be more successful if based on the principles of openness (union access to financial information), equality of sacrifice (managers and well-paid staff accepting higher pay cuts as well as the general body of employees) and specific workforce and trade union gains (financial participation, mechanisms for reviewing pay reductions, supports to union representation, etc.).

Although the term concession bargaining relates mostly to unionized firms seeking adjustments in a difficult business environment, the underlying principle also applies to nonunion organizations (Becker 1988). Like their unionized counterparts, nonunion firms may seek to form shared understandings about how to protect the organization when commercial times get tough and freezes or reductions in pay or changes in conditions of employment become unavoidable (McLoughlin and Gourlay 1992). Again success in implementing such measures may be predicated on openness with employees when restructuring plans are developed. Similarly, the 'equality of sacrifice' principle is equally applicable to nonunion firms: nonunion employees may find a restructuring plan more palpable if it is embedded in the principle of fairness: designing restructuring plans that signal to employees that their interests are still being looked after, or at least will be in any upturn in business conditions, is seen to be no less important in the non-union firm (Estlund 2009). Under the broad category of pay adjustment might also be changes to pension arrangements triggered by the recession, such as closing defined-benefit schemes to current incumbents, introducing higher contributions for employees covered by existing schemes and initiating defined-contribution schemes or hybrid schemes, in which a greater degree of risk is borne by employees.

Employment Adjustment

Securing wage freezes or reductions is not the only option open to organizations when seeking to reduce paybill costs in a recession. Adjustment can also be secured by reducing employee numbers or by increasing working-time flexibility, or indeed by a combination of these two options (Houseman and Abraham 1995). Headcount may be reduced, at least initially, by cutting levels of contingent employment involving part-time, contract or agency workers. Cutting contingent employment might be undertaken simply as an expedient way of reducing headcount, or as part of a policy of 'employment stabilization' concerned with 'buffering' core employees against the effects of the recession (Dyer et al. 1985). Sometimes managers calculate that an economic downturn is so severe that they are compelled to make some employees redundant to avoid putting the survival of the entire organization in jeopardy. In this situation, the issue becomes whether the job losses are to be voluntary or compulsory. When job losses are compulsory the main concern is the type of criteria used to select people for redundancy. Traditionally, the seniority rule ('last-in-first-out') prevailed in redundancy situations, especially in unionized firms, although this practice has been eroded somewhat in recent times. Comprehensive objective criteria such as attendance, sickness and disciplinary records, skills, competencies and qualifications and work experience as well as performance appraisals are now commonly used to select pools of candidates for redundancies (Doherty 2009).

The advent of redundancies is traumatic, most of all for affected employees. Announcement of redundancies can also have an adverse impact on morale, motivation and productivity inside an organization. Best practice is understood to involve handling the matter more proactively by firms, employees and their representatives concluding a formal procedure on how to handle redundancies in advance of any business crisis (CIPD 2009; Schumann 2001). Formal redundancy agreements generally cover a range of issues including a transparent set of criteria to be used to establish a redundancy pool, the consultation procedures to be used in collective and individual redundancy situations, the terms of any redundancy and the assistance that will be provided to redundant employees in their efforts to obtain training or alternative work (ACAS 2009). But whatever the nature of any formal procedure the consensus in the literature is that, wherever possible, organizations are best advised to seek volunteers for redundancies as making compulsory redundancies can have severe negative consequences in terms of the morale of the remaining workforce (Bowers and Davis 2010).

Of course, at times, organizations may have no alternative but to cut jobs. In these situations, firms may seek to devise a comprehensive package for those losing their jobs (Incomes Data Services 2009). In most cases, these involve working with relevant public employment and training agencies to develop a suite of support measures. These may vary from offering individual counseling on future possible career options, interviews with training bodies to discuss reskilling and reeducation options and discussions about available employment opportunities in the locality and elsewhere. Organizations that pursue these actions usually gain the reputation of being a socially responsible employer, which makes the task of motivating retained staff easier (Cedefop 2010).

Employment Stabilization

Because job losses can have a devastating impact on individuals and their families, some firms try to find alternatives to redundancies (Baron and Kreps 1999; Cascio 2002). So-called employment stabilization measures seek to buffer the employment security of core employees by introducing practices designed to retain employees in a downturn, to lay them off temporarily, to incentivize sabbaticals or to focus on reducing levels of part-time, contract or agency employment (Dyer et al. 1985). Other workforce stabilization policies that can be used by organizations include internal redeployment and staff sabbaticals or similar initiatives (Jørgensen 2009). These policies can play a positive role in reducing staff costs. They can also be beneficial for employees. In some instances, employees may get the opportunity to perform entirely new work roles and in others they may get the chance to take a break from the routine of daily work and pursue long cherished dreams.

Of course, instead of laying off employees on part-time, temporary or agency contracts to buffer the employment security of full-time, permanent employees, some firms may respond to a recession by doing the opposite. Greater numbers of part-time and temporary workers might be employed to enhance numerical flexibility in an effort to match employment levels more closely with changes and fluctuations in market demand. A trend in this direction has been reported in the United Kingdom, where job losses among full-time employees are increasing just at the same time as part-time working is also increasing (Balakrishnan and Berger 2009).

Companies may also respond to a slump in demand by seeking to 'insource' production activities that had previously been outsourced to suppliers or to other companies (Farndale, Paauwe and Hoeksma 2009). There have been media reports suggesting that some organizations in the recession are bringing back in-house business activity that had previously been contracted out (Webb 2009). Little systematic evidence exists to indicate whether in-sourcing may be occurring on any widespread basis. For this to happen would require a departure from mainstream HR thinking which views outsourcing, and its sibling off-shoring, as legitimate policies that firms can follow to create value (Gospel and Sako 2010).

Training and employee development is another part of the HR toolbox that firms may use to try to stabilize the workforce. A common view is that the first response of firms when they enter a recession is to cut back on training budgets as part of an overall strategy of financial retrenchment: training employees in new skills and competences becomes viewed as an unaffordable luxury (Charlton 2008). An alternative perspective is that increasing training for employees represents a smart HR strategy for firms to use to cope with a recession. On this view, increased training allows firms to 'hoard' core employees in a manner that improves their skills, thus allowing them to make an even greater productive contribution when buoyant market conditions return (Felstead et al. 2010). In addition, extra training may facilitate internal staff redeployment as employees become competent to undertake a range of workplace tasks.

More Rigorous Management Systems

Some commentators on the recession have called for performance management systems to be managed more rigorously to address underperformance and to improve productivity: thus, David Ulrich's reported comment that firms should use the downturn to deal better with poor performers (Peacock 2008). In this context, disciplinary and timekeeping procedures might be managed more rigorously to address under-performance and to improve productivity. Firms might also be expected to seek other ways of reducing 'slack' and cutting costs in recessionary conditions. Work practices and shift arrangements might be changed to align production schedules with shorter working hours, or to facilitate internal redeployment measures.

Working-Time Reorganization

As an alternative, or complement, to workforce stabilization initiatives, firms may reorganize working time to avoid making redundancies or to minimize their incidence (Van Gyes 2009). Most firms experiencing difficult times, almost as a matter of course, curb overtime. If things get really bad, organizations may introduce short-time working, such as a three- or four-day week. These initiatives are attempts to ride out the worst of a business downturn while keeping organizational capabilities more or less intact. Firms in some European countries are reported to be using innovative working-time arrangements, such as annual working hours or working-time accounts to manage fluctuations in business cycles (Berg 2008; Bosch 2009; Dribbusch 2009; European Foundation 2009b).

Voice, Engagement and Talent Management

Employee engagement is an increasingly prominent concept in the HRM literature (MacLeod Review 2009). Engaged organizations are considered to have strong authentic values, with clear evidence of trust and fairness based on mutual respect and reciprocal commitments between employers and employees. High levels of trust and reciprocity inside organizations have been seen to facilitate the emergence of retrenchment and restructuring programs that take into account the interests and needs of employees as well as those of firms (Hallock 2009; Vance 2006).

Another key mechanism for maintaining motivation and commitment in recessionary times is seen to be the more intensive use of established channels for communication with the workforce. Keeping employees regularly and fully informed of the organization's commercial position, as well as management's plans, is sometimes considered indispensible to maintaining employee commitment when adjusting to adverse times (CIPD 2010). In line with this view, organizations may supplement standardized forms of direct and group-based communication such as e-mails, company bulletins/newsletters, team briefings and staff councils with special employee meetings that allow the CEO and other senior managers to speak with the entire workforce about the challenges facing the organization. Speaking openly about firm performance and managerial intentions requires managers to show how the decisions they are making are in line with the evidence about how the organization is performing (Robinson-Smith and Markwick 2009).

Some organizations may go beyond communication systems and seek actively to involve employees and/or their representatives in the formulation and implementation of organizational restructuring plans. Allowing employees to perform such a role is seen to result not only in shared understandings being created between employees and managers about the need for restructuring, but also in effective joint action to restore profitability (Glassner and Keune 2010; Mohrman and Worley 2009).

While recognizing that the recession will almost certainly pose challenges to organizations in terms of reducing surplus capacity and containing costs, some commentators have emphasized that bad economic times should not halt efforts aimed at recruiting, retaining and developing high-performance and high-potential employees. The essential message of such advocates is that the recession is no time to dilute human resource development and talent management activities, but actually presents an opportunity to intensity their use (Brockett 2010; Cooper 2009; Griffin and Smith 2010; Mohrman and Worley 2009).

CONCLUSION

After nearly two decades of uninterrupted growth and prosperity, when the issue that exercised most HR managers was how or where they would find employees to fill vacancies, many businesses are facing difficult business times. The entire thrust of people management has been turned on its head. HR managers have now to find ways to help businesses adjust to the recession. This is a demanding challenge. If HRM managers do not get their adjustment strategies right the result could be plummeting employee morale and productivity. In this situation, what economists call an adverse selection problem could be triggered: the most skilled and experienced employees, who also are more likely to have good outside options, leave the organization, and the organization is left with employees with poor outside options and with poor morale levels. Thus, when HRM managers make adjustments to explicit employment contracts so that firms are able to fend off depressed economic conditions they must take care not to disrupt, at least not to any significant extent, implicit contracts that bind employees to their organizations.

This chapter has sought to provide the groundwork for an in-depth investigation into how firms, their HR managers and employee representatives have responded to the business downturn. It has shown that the recession has had a huge negative impact on the Irish economy: no other country has experienced a sharper fall in output, and as a result unemployment has soared. The academic literature that addresses the nature of HR in recessions has been reviewed. It was found that the early literature—which assessed the impact of previous recessions on HR—suggested during the recession of the 1980s firms in major economies had burdened employees with extra risks, although it was emphasized that the enduring impact of such policies should not be exaggerated. In Ireland, previous recessions have tended to spur innovation more at the macro level of national institutions and policies more so than at the micro level of firms and their employee representatives. Contrasting views have emerged about the implications of the current recession for HR in organizations: some suggesting that the recession will throw into question the viability of already existing employment models, others suggesting that high-commitment HR policies are likely to come to the fore during the downturn, and still others suggesting that the recession will not have a huge lasting or disjunctive impact on HR either way. The chapter has also reviewed the policies and practices that are open to HR managers when they seek to respond to newly challenging business times. The rest of the study is dedicated to the task of discovering how firms and their HR managers have responded to the uniquely severe effects of the current Irish recession and how union representatives have sought to protect their members' interests in the extremely adverse circumstances that now prevail.

3 Human Resource Management in the Recession
Results of Survey of Employers

3.1 INTRODUCTION

This chapter sets out to assess the HR responses of employers to the recession. It begins by outlining the methods used to conduct the survey. It then examines the impact of the recession on firms in order to establish the commercial context for the HR actions adopted. Next, following the discussion in Chapter 2 of the HR practices that may be adopted by firms in the recession, the chapter examines the types and incidence of measures taken by firms in order to adjust to, and address, the recessionary conditions. This includes an analysis of whether firms may have adopted specific sets or 'bundles' of HR practices and what the features of these might be. The chapter also considers how HR functions in firms have weathered the recession. Finally, the chapter investigates the HR practices that survey respondents considered to be most effective in helping them manage the recession.

3.2 SURVEY METHODS

A short questionnaire designed by the research team encompassed the major themes in the literature and commentary on HR in the recession and a range of recurring themes in the HR managers' and union officials' focus groups conducted in conjunction with the research project. A draft questionnaire was piloted by being forwarded to a small number of organizations for completion and comment. This allowed for some modification and amendment of the draft as suggestions were incorporated. The questionnaire contained questions covering the following areas:

- Background features of firms
- The impact of the recession
- HR's response to the recession
- The conduct of HR
- Relations with unions
- Effective HR practices in the recession

Survey Population

The survey population comprised all organizations in the private and commercial semistate sectors with 50 or more employees. It bears emphasis that the survey profiles all such organizations that had survived or remained extant to the autumn of 2010, and that some of these will likely have instituted several rounds of measures to respond to the challenges faced. Survey respondents were selected from the Kompass Database (http://ie.kompass. com/) of Irish firms. The target survey respondent was the manager responsible for human resource management in the firm, whether that person was a functional specialist or held more general managerial responsibilities. The sampling strategy was conducted in association with the Economic and Social Research Institute (ESRI), Ireland's leading not-for-profit research institution. The survey was conducted by post. Three mail shots, two of which included the questionnaire and one letter reminder was issued, were undertaken in the case of each target respondent. There was also an option for firms to receive an electronic version of the questionnaire. Follow-up phone calls were made by the LRC, CIPD and the research team, focusing on large firms. The survey fieldwork was conducted from June to September 2010 in two waves: the first from June to July and the second during September.

Response Rates and Weighting Procedure

A total of 444 useable questionnaires were completed, representing an overall response rate of 17.2%. This is in line with both the ESRI's recent experience and with international experience of response rates in surveys targeted at firms. Response rates ranged from 8% in the case of firms with 50 to 249 employees to 28% for firms with 250 or more employees.

The achieved survey sample was weighted to compensate for differences in response rates between firms of different sizes and in different sectors. The method of weighting employed involved grossing the sample to the total number of firms in the population. Weighted survey results are reported for descriptive statistics. Standard statistical tests were conducted to check for nonresponse bias. In particular, time-trend extrapolation tests (Armstrong and Overton 1977) were undertaken by comparing the pattern of responses on key variables in first wave and second wave of survey fieldwork. The assumption is that later respondents are closest to the profile of nonrespondents, given that they had responded to the survey following more reminders and further encouragement. These revealed no serious systematic nonresponse bias in the survey results.

3.3   THE IMPACT OF THE RECESSION ON BUSINESSES

This section provides a background context for our examination of the HR practices adopted by firms by reviewing data on the impact of the recession in terms of changes in both revenue and employment numbers over the periods January to December 2008 and 2009. It also considers participants' views regarding the severity of the impact of the recession and whether the recession necessitated significant restructuring of the business.

Change in Revenue

Reflecting the severity of the Irish recession, the majority of firms in the survey (70.1% in 2008 and 84% in 2009) experienced revenue losses over the period in question. Of the remaining firms, 13.6% experienced no change in revenue, and 16.3% experienced an increase in 2008. In 2009, 7.5% experienced no change, and 8.5% experienced an increase in revenue. From Table 3.1, it is clear that more firms lost revenue in 2009. The average loss reported was 11.8% in 2008, rising in 2009 to a loss of 18.1%. When an examination of firms' performances with respect to revenue is restricted to those who experienced a loss, the average losses rise to 18.9% in 2008 and 23.4% in 2009. These data indicate the severity of the financial impact of the recession on firms in Ireland.

The average percentage change in revenue varied greatly across sectors. The sector most severely hit by the recession, in terms of revenue loss, was construction, which indicated a mean loss of 24.4% in 2008 and 37.5% in 2009. This compares to a revenue loss of 6.9% in 2008 and 12.4% in 2009 for the high-tech manufacturing sector, which showed the lowest loss

Table 3.1   Percentage change in the revenue of businesses in Ireland due to the recession

	Percentage of firms	
Percentage change	Jan. 2008–Dec. 2008	Jan. 2009–Dec. 2009
Loss of 50.0%–99.9%	4.6	9.7
Loss of 25.0%–49.9%	14.7	22.7
Loss of 10.0%–24.9%	31.5	38.9
Loss of 0.1%–9.9%	19.3	12.7
No change	13.6	7.5
Increase in revenue	16.3	8.5
Average	−11.8%	−18.1
Median	−10.0	−15.0
Lower Quartile	−20.0	−30.0
Upper Quartile	0.0	−8.0

Note: Respondents were specifically asked to state the change in revenue due to the recession. A small number of respondents indicated, however, that they were unable to state that the changes were wholly attributable to the recession.

Table 3.2   Average percentage change across sectors in the revenue of businesses in Ireland due to the recession

	Average percentage change in revenue	
Sector	Jan. 2008–Dec. 2008	Jan. 2009–Dec. 2009
Traditional manufacture	−13.4	−20.1
High-Tech manufacture	−6.9	−12.4
Construction	−24.4	−37.5
Distribution	−9.7	−16.6
Financial & business services	−14.1	−18.8
Transport & communication	−5.3	−18.6
Hotels & restaurants	−11.5	−14.4

in revenue. As is evident from Table 3.2, all sectors felt the impact of the recession more severely in 2009.

Change in Numbers Employed

A second indicator of the severity of the recession on Irish businesses is provided by the trend in numbers employed (Table 3.3). More than 6 of 10 firms experienced a reduction in the numbers in their workforce in 2008,

Table 3.3   Percentage change in employment levels attributed to the recession

	Percentage of firms	
Percentage change in workforce	Jan. 2008–Dec. 2008	Jan. 2009–Dec. 2009
Loss of 50.0%–99.9%	2.4	5.5
Loss of 25.0%–49.9%	8.2	12.3
Loss of 10.0%–24.9%	25.9	32.6
Loss of 0.1%–9.9%	27.8	25.3
No change	25.3	14.3
Increase in numbers employed	10.4	10.0
Average	−7.0	−11.6
Median	−5.0	−10.0
Lower quartile	−13.0	−20.0
Upper quartile	0.0	−1.0

Note: Respondents were specifically asked to state the change in revenue due to the recession. A small number of respondents indicated, however, that they were unable to state that the changes were wholly attributable to the recession.

Table 3.4   Average percentage change across sectors in employment numbers attributable to the recession

Sector	Average percentage change in workforce	
	Jan. 2008–Dec. 2008	Jan. 2009–Dec. 2009
Traditional manufacture	−8.2	−11.0
High-Tech manufacture	−4.2	−9.0
Construction	−22.9	−27.3
Distribution	−0.9	−8.8
Financial & business services	−8.1	−13.2
Transport & communication	−3.0	−6.5
Hotels & restaurants	−9.7	−11.6

whereas just over three-quarters did so in 2009. In both years, around one in 10 firms experienced an increase in the numbers in their workforce. The remainder of firms had no change. As was the case with revenue, the impact of the recession in terms of the change in numbers employed in the workforce was more severe in 2009 than 2008. The average change reported was a reduction of 7.0% in 2008 and 11.6% in 2009. These figures rise to a loss of 13.9% for 2008 and 17.1% for 2009 when only those firms experiencing a reduction are included.

Again, as would be expected from the trend in revenue, the fall in numbers in the workforce was greatest in construction (see Table 3.4).

Perceptions of the Severity of the Recession

A final indicator of the severity of the recession is provided by respondents' perceptions of how seriously the recession had had an impact on their businesses (Table 3.5). For almost 9 of 10 firms (87.8%) participating in the survey, the impact of the recession has been either *very* or *quite severe*. Approximately 1 in 8 firms found the impact of the recession to be *not at all severe*. It was again reported as being most severe in Construction, with almost 8 out of 10 firms (79.1%) reporting that the impact was *very severe*.

Table 3.5   Perceived severity of the recession

Impact	% of firms	% of employees
Very severe	42.7	42.9
Quite severe	45.1	44.5
Not at all severe	12.2	12.6

It was reported to be least severe in high-tech manufacturing, where more than a third (35.3%) indicated that the impact of the recession was *not at all severe*, and only 19% of firms reported the impact to be *very severe*.

The Extent of Business Restructuring

Just under two-thirds of firms (63.9%) significantly restructured their business as a result of the recession. Again restructuring was most likely to have occurred in construction firms (80.2%), followed by the hotels and restaurants sector firms (78.8%). It was least likely to have occurred in manufacturing, and in particular in high-tech manufacturing (37.4%).

3.4   HR PRACTICES ADOPTED BY FIRMS IN RESPONSE TO THE RECESSION

Table 3.6 provides details of the HR practices adopted in response to the recession, organized in line with the groups of practices identified in Table 2.1 of Chapter 2.

It emerges that sizeable numbers of firms implemented pay freezes or cuts for some or all staff. Significant numbers introduced curbs on bonuses and lower entry rates for new staff. Changes to pension arrangements were also introduced by significant minorities of firms. Deeper pay cuts for

Table 3.6   HR practices adopted by firms in the recession

	% of firms
Pay adjustment measures	
Cut wages and salaries for all staff	33.9
Cut wages and salaries for some staff	15.6
Froze wages and salaries for all staff	60.4
Froze wages and salaries for some staff	10.7
Introduced proportionally higher cuts in pay for senior staff	24.5
Introduced lower pay/pay scales for new staff	22.5
Cut bonus for all staff	38.1
Cut bonus for some staff	16.2
Introduced proportionally higher cuts in bonus for senior staff	11.5
Changed pension arrangements for existing staff	20.8
Changed pension arrangements for new staff	13.9
Employment adjustment measures	
Introduced compulsory redundancies	48.3
Introduced voluntary redundancies	29.9
Introduced early retirement	7.6

(*Continued*)

Table 3.6 (Continued)

	% of firms
General recruitment frozen	51.2
Undertook recruitment for certain grades only	19.6
General promotions frozen	14.6
Promotions to some positions only	13.3
Employment stabilization measures	
Staff redeployed to new positions or product lines within the business	43.4
Introduced 'in-sourcing' (i.e., brought back into the business work that had previously been outsourced)	5.4
Staff trained for new roles within the business	40.4
Reduced use of part-time staff	6.0
Reduced use of contract staff	14.5
Reduced use of agency workers	10.1
More rigorous management systems	
Staff performance managed more rigorously	47.2
Tightened discipline, timekeeping and attendance requirements	47.8
Reorganisation of working time	
Introduced career breaks	9.3
Introduced short-time working	42.6
Reduced overtime	63.3
Introduced flexible working hours to better match staffing levels with peaks and troughs of the business	25.5
Voice, engagement and talent management	
Communicating the demands of the business to staff has gained greater importance #	89.2
Employees have been actively involved in developing options for responding to the recession #	55.0
The business has undertaken specific employee engagement measures #	52.3
The firm undertook specific talent management measures to retain high-potential or high-performance staff	20.7
The firm has actively engaged with unions in developing HR options for responding to the recession #	61.6
By agreeing measures to respond to the recession unions have gained greater access to financial information #	13.8
By agreeing measures to respond to the recession unions have gained support for organising or representing members in the business #	7.3
Unions have secured claw-backs for their members when business conditions improve #	5.6

Note: Items on aspects of union involvement restricted to firms where unions were recognized.

Item reported is the combined percentages responding *agree* or *strongly agree*.

higher-paid staff were relatively uncommon. Headcount reductions were also commonplace, as were partial or complete freezes of recruitment and curbs on promotion.

Employment stabilization measures were mainly confined to the redeployment of people within firms, allied to training for new roles. Few firms reduced groups of contingent employees.[1] Nearly half of all firms stated that they had managed staff performance more rigorously and tightened discipline, timekeeping and attendance. The reorganization of working time was mainly focused on reducing overtime and, to a lesser extent, on introducing short-time working. More flexible working-time regimes geared better to balancing labor supply and demand in the recession were evident in about a quarter of all firms.

Turning finally to voice, engagement and talent management measures, the greater importance assigned to communicating the demands of the business to staff stands out. About half of all firms also reported undertaking specific employee engagement measures (for example, retraining staff in new missions or business priorities following layoffs and restructuring). Talent management measures are thinner on the ground, having been adopted by about a quarter of firms. Six out of ten firms recognizing unions claim to have actively engaged with them in developing HR options for responding to the recession. Other than access to financial information, which had been conceded in less than four out of ten firms, unions were reported as having gained few concessions involving the review or restoration of depleted pay and conditions (commonly known as claw-backs) when business revived or involving supports to organization or representation.

The general picture that emerges is one of firms commonly making adjustments to pay, headcount and working time, while also often introducing more rigorous work regimes. Employment stabilization measures, such as the internal redeployment of staff and related training for new work roles, are also used in significant minorities of firms. Other than the widespread use of measures to reduce payroll costs, the data also show that firms have adopted various measures geared to maintaining morale, motivation and commitment. These include assigning greater importance to communication activity and fostering ways of engaging employees. Most unionized firms claim to have engaged with unions in responding to the recession, but unions have not commonly gained specific concessions for their members or supports to organization and representation.

3.5   BUNDLES OF HR PRACTICES

Next we explore whether firms have adopted the HR practices examined in bundles that constitute different retrenchment programs. It is possible that firms have adopted HR practices for responding to the recession in so many permutations and combinations that their responses have been locally idiosyncratic or have tailored closely to their specific commercial circumstances or to their HR and employee relations legacies. To examine how firms may have combined HR practices in responding to the recession we deploy latent-class modeling. Latent-class modeling is a model-based version of cluster analysis and allows models with different numbers and profiles of clusters to be compared based on measures of model fit or adequacy (Magidson and Vermunt 2003).[2]

In exploring patterns of association within the survey data using latent class modeling, we have proceeded in a number of stages. First we considered whether patterns of HR response measures appeared to differ as between firms recognizing unions and nonunion firms—leaving aside, for the present, voice and engagement practices specific to unionized firms alone. Were this the case, it would have been best to partition the sample between those recognizing unions and nonunion firms in order to identify the features of their HR response programs. No compelling evidence was found that firms recognizing unions and nonunion firms differed systematically with respect to their overall practices for responding to the recession.[3] Second, we combined some related HR measures to reduce the number of variables (indicators of latent classes) involved in the latent class analysis. This was done with a view to avoiding broadly prevalent patterns of response being obscured by differences of detail. Cuts in wages and salaries for some or all staff were combined into a composite category, as were freezes in wages and salaries for some or all staff. Voluntary and compulsory redundancies were combined, as were the more rigorous management of performance, discipline, timekeeping and attendance—the latter providing a composite indicator of a shift to more rigorous workplace regimes. The use of specific employee engagement measures and the active involvement of employees in developing options for responding to the recession were also combined into a single indicator.

Third, consistent with the conduct of exploratory latent class analysis we estimated models with many different sets of HR response measures and numbers of clusters, taking account of model fit statistics and whether each of the specific HR measures included discriminated between clusters.[4]

Table 3.7 presents the features of a latent class model that fits the data well.[5] It reveals that firms in general fall into two broad groups with quite distinctive bundles of HR response measures. The numbers in the first row of the Table labeled 'cluster size,' are estimates of the proportion of firms in each of the clusters identified. The data in the two columns under the heading 'predicted probabilities' report conditional probabilities: these provide estimates of the probabilities that firms in each of the clusters have adopted the practice presented. The Wald statistics reported in the right-hand column of Table 3.7 indicate whether each of the HR practices examined discriminate statistically between the clusters or groupings of firms.

As Table 3.7 reveals, many firms in the cluster that comprises about half of all firms have adopted a series of payroll-focused retrenchment measures to respond to the effects of the recession. These include cuts in wages and salaries for some or all staff (89% of cases in this cluster), voluntary or compulsory

Table 3.7   HR retrenchment programs: latent classes

	Firms adopting general retrenchment programs	Firms adopting pay freeze–focused programs	Wald statistics
	Predicted probabilities		
Cluster size	0.4914	0.5086	
HR practices adopted			
Cut wages and salaries for some or all staff	0.8870	0.0852	24.92***
Froze wages and salaries for some or all staff	0.5522	0.9072	35.60***
Introduced lower pay/pay scales for new staff	0.2924	0.1479	23.24***
Introduced voluntary and/or compulsory redundancy	0.7703	0.4744	22.87***
Reduced overtime	0.7578	0.5590	8.99***
Introduced short-time working	0.6347	0.2294	11.15***
Changed pension arrangements for existing or new staff	0.3818	0.1929	32.90***
Communicating the demands of the business to staff has gained greater importance	0.89237	0.8953	0.01
Specific employee engagement measures introduced and/or employees actively involved in developing options for responding to the recession	0.7552	0.7201	0.45

Note: Model fit statistics for two-cluster model: L^2 = 392.77; indicators are statistically independent at $p > 0.05$. Unweighted survey data ($n = 434$) used for latent-class modeling.

*** Differences in parameter values across clusters significant at the 0.01 level.

redundancies (77% of cases), curbs on overtime (76% of cases) and short-time working (63% of cases). These firms can be said to have adopted general HR retrenchment programs over the course of the recession. The second group of firms have relied mainly on wage freezes (91% of cases in this cluster) and, albeit to a lesser degree, on curbs on overtime (56% of cases) to respond to the recession. These firms can be said to have adopted pay-freeze focused retrenchment programs. Firms in both clusters have attributed greater importance to communicating the demands of the business to staff and many have also instituted specific employee engagement measures and/or actively involved staff in developing options with which to respond to the recession. The Wald statistics for these parameters indicate they do not discriminate between the clusters identified, and this is also reflected in the broadly similar proportions of firms in each cluster that have adopted these two measures. Thus, most firms, irrespective of the bundles of payroll measures adopted, have undertaken measures concerned with preserving morale, motivation and commitment.

The results indicate that many firms have introduced, simultaneously or serially, multiple payroll-focused HR retrenchment practices, while many more have been able to absorb the effects of the recession mainly through pay freezes, allied in many instances with curbs on overtime. Firms in general have sought to combine 'hard' measures to control or reduce payroll costs with 'softer' measures focused on maintaining motivation and commitment.

Table 3.8 presents the detailed results of logistic regression analysis examining a range of possible influences on whether firms have adopted general HR retrenchment programs or pay-freeze focused programs. Irish-owned

Table 3.8 Influences on the HR retrenchment programs adopted by firms: logistic regression results

Dependent Variable: General retrenchment programs = 1; Pay freeze–focused programs = 0.

Influences	Odds Ratios
Irish-owned firms	1.86**
Severity of recession	1.41
Business was significantly restructured as a result of the recession	2.13***
Sectors	
High-technology manufacturing	0.42
Construction	31.09***
Distribution	0.96
Financial service	2.41
Other business services	0.80
Transport and communications	1.30
Hotels, bars and restaurants	1.32
Large firms (250+ employees)	0.50**
Medium-sized firms (100–249 employees)	0.86
Firms recognizing unions	1.06
HRM scale	0.98
Model chi-square = 111.57***	
N = 407	

Note: Reference category for sectors: traditional manufacturing.

*** significant at the 0.01 level.   ** significant at the 0.05 level.

firms emerged as nearly two times more likely to have adopted general HR retrenchment bundles than foreign-owned multinationals—a reflection of the depressed state of the domestic market on which Irish businesses are more heavily dependent than multinationals. Firms reporting that they had significantly restructured their businesses were more than twice more likely to have adopted general retrenchment programs than firms reporting no such restructuring activity. Subjective assessments of the seriousness of the recession are found to have no significant effect. This is not surprising considering, as discussed earlier, that nearly 9 out of 10 firms judged the effects of the recession on their businesses as either *severe* or *very severe*. The effects of sector are examined by using traditional manufacturing as the reference category, so enabling the fortunes of firms in other sectors to be compared to traditional manufacturing firms. The results suggest that other things being equal sectors show little significant difference in the incidence of general retrenchment vis-á-vis pay freeze focused programs, with the very significant exception of construction, where firms are a startling 31 times more likely to have introduced general retrenchment programs.

Large firms emerge as having substantially lower odds of having adopted general retrenchment programs, suggesting that they have been better able to absorb external shocks associated with the recession than smaller firms.

Whether firms recognize unions had no bearing on the features of retrenchment programs adopted. Table 3.8 tests whether the adoption of HRM practices may have affected the retrenchment bundles that were evident. Could it be that firms committed to HRM were more likely to respond to the recession by protecting employment through pay freezes and overtime curbs? Table 3.8 reports the result for an index of HRM practices measuring the degree to which firms had implemented a series of nine standard HRM practices that included performance management and performance-related pay, team working, regular team briefing and internal career progression (alpha coefficient = 0.671).[6] The results indicate that firms' commitment to practicing HRM had no evident effect on the type of retrenchment bundles they had adopted. In short, firms with more or less commitment to HRM, as reflected in these HR practices, found themselves equally prone to adopting general retrenchment programs.

3.6   RECESSION AND RELATIONS WITH UNIONS

Managers in firms recognizing unions were asked a series of questions regarding the effects of the recession on union representation and their relations with trade unions. Table 3.9 shows that the majority of firms appear to consider the role of unions during the recession in a fairly positive way. Although approximately equal numbers of respondents indicated that the unions had or had not impaired the firm's response to the recession by insisting on protracted and detailed negotiations, more respondents believed that

Table 3.9 The effects of the recession on union representation in firms

	% of firms					
	Strongly agree	Agree	Neither agree nor disagree	Disagree	Strongly disagree	Mean* score
Unions have impaired the firm's response to the recession by insisting on protracted and detailed negotiations	13.1	26.6	19.6	34.7	6.0	3.1
Unions have been realistic and constructive in engaging with the business in response to the recession	5.7	39.9	23.2	21.2	9.9	3.1
Union influence in the business has declined as a result of the recession	3.4	28.5	34.5	26.8	6.8	3.0
Unions persuaded the business to change measures initially decided on to address the recession (e.g., from redundancies to short-term working)	–	5.1	25.5	60.5	8.9	2.3

* The higher the score, the higher the level of agreement –5 = *strongly agree* and 1 = *strongly disagree*.

unions have been realistic and constructive in engaging with the business in response to the recession. Unions do not appear however to have been able to exert much leverage on managements' favored measures for responding to the recession. Only a very small number of firms (5.1%) agree that unions persuaded the business to change measures initially decided on to address the recession (e.g., from redundancies to short-term working). Opinion as to whether union influence in the firm had declined as a result of the recession is nearly equally divided between those who agreed, those who disagreed and those who felt unable to offer a clear assessment. There is little indication from this pattern of responses that employers have launched any frontal onslaught on unions or tried to use the recession to displace unions at workplaces, either in either a coordinated or mimetic manner.

We next examine whether firms actively engaged with unions in responding to the recession, whether they are given access to information or provided with other ways of improving their capacity to represent members, by conducting latent class analysis on a range of union-voice practices in combination with the two recessionary responses identified in Table 3.7 A single-cluster model, positing statistical independence between the measures examined, fails to fit the data. A two-cluster model again attains fit, and the clusters identified are detailed in Table 3.10. The results show that a minority of the firms recognizing unions (24%) nearly always claimed to have actively engaged with them in developing HR options for responding to the recession. Most firms in this cluster (6 out of 10) provided unions with greater access to financial information in the process of reaching agreement on response measures. This cluster of unionized firms might then be characterized as an active engagement group. The majority of unionized firms (76%) failed to make any of the concessions examined in their dealings with unions and nearly half of the firms in this cluster disagreed that they had actively engaged with unions in developing options for responding to the recession. This cluster might then be character-

Table 3.10   Firms' dealings with trade unions: latent classes

	Active engagement group	Limited engagement group	Wald statistics
	Predicted probabilities		
Cluster size	0.2361	0.7639	
Union voice-related practices adopted			
The firms has actively engaged with unions in developing HR options with which to respond to the recession.	0.9273	0.5500	6.18***
Unions have secured agreement on financial claw-backs for their members when business conditions improve.	0.2706	0.0093	6.34***
By agreeing measures for responding to the recession, unions have gained greater access to the businesses' financial information.	0.6101	0.0516	11.58***
By agreeing measures for responding to the recession, unions have gained support for organizing or representing members in the business.	0.3844	0.0129	6.18***
Retrenchment programs adopted			
General HR retrenchment programs	0.4488	0.4422	0.00
Pay freeze–focused retrenchment programs	0.5515	0.4422	0.00

Note: Model fit statistics for two-cluster model: L^2 = 13.58; indicators are statistically independent at $p > 0.05$. Unweighted survey data (n = 169) used for latent-class modeling.

*** Differences in parameter values across clusters significant at the 0.01 level.

ized as a limited engagement group. It is evident from the conditional probabilities and the Wald statistics in Table 3.10 that firms' overall retrenchment programs (general retrenchment versus payroll-focused retrenchment) had no bearing on their relations with trade unions. Overall the results of the latent-class analysis reveal that the majority of firms recognizing unions have made no specific concessions to unions, even where they may have actively engaged with unions in developing HR response measures. Those that had made specific concessions did so in the main by providing access for unions to business and financial information.

We undertook logistic regression analysis to examine a range of possible influences on whether firms had adopted active or limited engagement approaches in their dealings with unions during the recession. The results discounted firm ownership, judgments of the severity of the recession, the occurrence of business restructuring, sector, firm size and the incidence of HRM practices as having any significant effects on the choices made by firms. It may therefore be that employee relations legacies have been more important than other organizational or external influences in shaping the postures of firms in their dealings with trade unions during the recession.

3.6 RECESSION AND THE HR FUNCTION

What of the fortunes of HR functions in forms with specialist HR managers or departments?

As is shown in Table 3.11, about 3 in 10 firms reported reducing the number of people working in their HR functions. Although this is a significant move toward leaner HR functions in a large number of firms, considering that two-thirds of all firms reported general workforce reductions such a move hardly seems surprising and suggests that HR functions were

Table 3.11 Changes to the HR function

Measures adopted	% of firms
Decreased use of external HR consultants (e.g., for recruitment/training, etc.)	43.1
Reduced number of staff in HR department*	31.7
Restructured HR department (e.g., centralized HR services, introduced 'centers of excellence,' etc.)*	14.5
Increased use of internal staff for training and development	35.6
Cut training and development budget	50.6
Reduced the costs of HR processes/policies (e.g., in the areas of health and wellness, Employee Assistance Programs)	17.2

* Findings relate to firms indicating that they had a specialized HR department or manager.

often spared the cuts in headcount prevalent among employees in general. More than half of the firms in the survey (50.6%) cut the training and development budget, and around a third increased the use of internal staff for training and development. About 4 of 10 firms reduced their use of HR consultants (for recruitment/training, etc.). Although the proportion of firms reporting that they had restructured the HR department (about 15%) is not insignificant, compared with the proportion of firms that had restructured their businesses in some way (about 64%), the level of restructuring or organizational rationalization or reconfiguration of HR again appears relatively modest. Table 3.12 reports the views of HR managers regarding changes in the influence of HR functions within the business. More than 7 of 10 HR managers agreed or strongly agreed that the business role of HR had strengthened during the recession. There is a divergence of opinion, which may reflect a divergence in underlying experience, regarding the kind or degree of influence HR had exerted on the measures chosen by firms to adapt to the recession. Just more than 3 of 10 were of the view that the influence of HR had been restricted to the implementation of response measures adopted by the business. Nearly 4 of 10 disagreed that this has been the

Table 3.12   HR managers' views of how function has operated during the recession

	Percentage of Firms					
	Strongly agree	Agree	Neither agree nor disagree	Disagree	Strongly disagree	Mean* score
The business role of HR has been strengthened	19.2	52.1	21.9	5.8	1.0	3.8
The influence of HR has been restricted to the implementation of measures adopted by the business to respond to the recession	3.3	30.9	28.0	33.6	4.3	3.0
HR has had to learn new skills to address challenges posed by the he recession	10.8	46.1	24.9	17.3	0.9	3.5
Business pressures have meant that the issue of fairness is a lower priority	1.8	8.5	17.8	50.7	21.2	2.2

* The higher the score, the higher the level of agreement: 5 = *strongly agree* and 1 = *strongly disagree*.

case, and the rest reported no view either way. Fifty-seven percent were of the view that HR managers had to learn new skills to address the challenges posed by the recession. To what degree had the greater influence that most attributed to HR in recessionary conditions been gained at the expense of a dilution of HR managers' traditional concern with balancing the interests of organizational stakeholders to ensure that the measures adopted by firms were fair? Seventy-two percent disagreed or strongly disagreed that fairness had been compromised by measures adopted during the recession. In summary, most HR managers believed that HR had gained more influences during the recession, but opinion was more divided as to whether that influence was restricted to the implementation of firms' responses. HR managers in the main did not see their greater influence resulting in less concern with fairness in the handling of HR activities.

3.7 HR PRACTICES SEEN AS MOST EFFECTIVE IN MANAGING THE RECESSION

Survey respondents were asked briefly to describe and to rank the three HR practices they considered to be most effective in helping them to manage the recession. Respondents had scope to identify and rank the kinds of HR response measures detailed earlier in the chapter, or other measures, as they saw fit. Their detailed free-form answers were coded and arranged into categories. It emerged that HR measures aimed directly at controlling the paybill and increasing efficiency in various ways, as well as HR measures concerned with the processes and systems by which these direct measures were implemented were identified among the most-effective practices listed. As shown in Table 3.13, communications and information disclosure was listed and ranked as the most effective HR practice in helping firms manage the recession. Employees needed to be kept informed, particularly about how the business was doing. More than a third of firms (34.4%) indicated this as their most effective HR practice. In addition, where respondents gave a second and third ranking of effective HR practices, communications again came out as being very effective in a fifth of firms. Notwithstanding this emphasis on the importance of communications, fewer firms appear to have considered engaging or involving employees, or indeed trade unions, as being the most effective way to address the impact of the recession—this practice being ranked third in the rank order of most effective practices and winning the endorsement of between 7% and 12% if firms, depending on the ranking examined.

As has emerged earlier in the chapter, a central aspect of the challenges facing business was the achievement of cost reductions and productivity improvements. The results here reiterate that this challenge was being considered very seriously by those with responsibility for human resources. After communications, the next most effective area for HR to be involved was helping to create efficiencies and institute cost control measures in

Table 3.13 Most effective HR practices

HR Practice	Most effective HR practice	2nd-most-effective HR practice	3rd-most-effective HR practice
	% of firms		
Communication & information disclosure	34.4	19.1	20.0
Efficiencies and cost control	14.4	18.4	18.6
Engagement and consultation	11.6	9.5	7.0
Formalizing HR policies	11.1	15.6	13.1
Aligning HR with the business agenda	7.1	4.5	4.9
Human resources development	6.4	9.7	11.1
Managing working time	6.1	5.4	4.4
Work (re)organization	6.0	13.1	16.4
Relations with unions**	2.8	4.5	3.2
Fairness/trust	1.4	3.1	3.7

*The result for communications and information disclosure is slightly understated. Where respondents stated that communications and consultation (together) were the most effective HR practice, this was coded under engagement and consultation.

**Percentages relate to firms in which unions are recognized.

the business. The measures ranged from reviewing remuneration policies to ensure affordability to implementing cost reductions in terms of wages, salaries, bonuses, pensions and fringe benefits and redundancies. A range of measures focusing on the alignment or better alignment of HR with the business agenda also receives endorsement and emerges as the fifth most frequently cited issue in the most effective HR practices ranking.

Table 3.13 also shows that more than 1 in 10 firms identified formalizing HR policies as the most effective way of managing the recession, while similar numbers indicated this as a second- or third-most-effective HR practice. The HR policies most focused on here were performance management, discipline, absence, sickness and recruitment. Human resource development, including some specific references to talent management and the retention of high-potential and high-performance staff, was ranked sixth in importance among the most effective measures by HR managers.

Work (re)organization was considered to be the second- and third-most-effective practice in a large number of firms. The level of activity with regard to relations with unions is significant in its relative lack of emphasis in unionized firms, being ranked in first, second and third order of importance by 2.8%, 4.5% and 3.2% of firms, respectively. Adopting measures to institute or preserve fairness and trust also received little emphasis in the pattern of responses.

CONCLUSION

Consistent with general commentary on the recession and the aggregate indicators of economic, business and labor market performance considered in Chapter 2, the effects were confirmed as severe for many firms, whether assessed in terms of revenue loss, changes in employment or perceptions of its impact. Although the severity of its effects on firms varied across sectors, no sector has escaped entirely. It was also evident that the impact of the recession increased in severity in 2009 compared to 2008. Most firms reported that they had engaged in business restructuring initiatives.

Firms' HR responses to the recession reflect the severe effects and challenges experienced by many. A wide range or repertoire of HR practices was implemented across the population of firms as a whole to respond to the pressures experienced. Pay freezes or cuts for some or all firms and their employees were common, and pay rises were uncommon. Lower pay or salary scales for new entrants, bonus cuts and changes in pension arrangements were also significant in their incidence, albeit representing a second tier of responses in terms of their relative frequency. Changes in staffing levels were also pronounced: most firms in the survey experiencing redundancy for some employees and commonly instituting freezes on recruitment. Changes in working-time arrangements, involving inter alia reductions in overtime working, increased short-time working and the increased use of contingent working arrangements (part-time and contract workers) were also common. Substantial proportions of firms also reported managing staff performance more rigorously and otherwise tightening up on work regimes through a more exacting approach to discipline, timekeeping and attendance.

It is clearly important to recognize that in addition to implementing hard HRM practices aimed at cutting payroll costs and improving productivity, many firms have also implemented a wide range of softer HR practices to maintain commitment by communicating with employees and unions, by retaining HRD initiatives and by undertaking specific measures to promote employee engagement. Many have also sought to preserve jobs by redeploying staff to new positions. A significant proportion of firms—about one in five—have sought to retain high-potential or high-performance staff. About the same number have continued to recruit staff for certain, specific grades and positions and some have also continued to promote some staff. Some of these practices are assessed as among the most effective in helping firms manage the effects of the recession. In particular, communication with staff consistently emerges as a key concern of most firms during the recession.

However, symbolic measures to promote organizational cohesion, such as higher proportionate cuts in pay and bonuses for senior managers, have not been undertaken on a widespread basis. And although few firms believe that issues of fairness have been a lower priority in the recession—contrary to commentary in some circles that consideration of fairness may need to be eclipsed in responding to the recession—few ranked measures to preserve fairness and trust highly when asked to describe measures that had been most effective in helping them manage the recession.

The research revealed two broad patterns of response in terms of the manner in which firms have combined hard HR response measures focused on cost cutting and containment with soft HR measures focused on maintaining motivation and commitment. First, a general retrenchment bundle of HR practices emerged, comprising pay freezes, curbs on overtime, short-time working and redundancies. The rest implemented fewer such measures, focusing in the main on pay freezes and curbs in overtime working. Both programs included measures aimed at preserving motivation and commitment (through more effort to communicate and other engagement measures) as well as measures focused on payroll cost reduction or containment. The results of regression modeling indicated that Irish-owned firms, firms affected by business restructuring, and medium-sized and smaller firms were more likely to have adopted general retrenchment programs. Few significant differences were apparent across sectors, with the exception of construction, where firms were many times more likely than any other sectors to have adopted general retrenchment programs. Whether firms recognized unions or differences in the extent to which they adopted HRM practices had no effects on the bundles of HR practices adopted to respond to the recession.

What emerges from the overall pattern of results, therefore, is a picture of many firms attempting to balance harder and softer aspects of HR management in response to the challenges they have faced, with HR processes and systems changes accompanying hard measures directed at the immediate bottom line.

Firms that recognize unions appear to view their role during the recession in positive terms. At the same time unions appear to have been able to exert little leverage over firms' preferred methods of responding to the recession, opinion is dived as to whether union influence had declined as a result of the recession. Postures toward unions involved two patterns. A significant minority of unionized firms have deployed what was described as an active engagement bundle of voice practices, which involves unions in developing response measures and often provides them with access to business information to that end. However, most unionized firms neither involve unions to this degree nor provide access to business information. On the whole, unions seem to have achieved few specific institutional concessions in areas like organization or representation for working with firms to respond to the recession. Nor do they seem often to have been able to obtain claw-back mechanisms in concession agreements concluded with firms.

The HR function seems to have been a significant player in the response measures adopted by firms. Respondents believe that HR has become more influential in its role of supporting the business. This finding needs to be understood in the context of other survey findings. Fewer than a third of respondents believe that HR has been the biggest influence on the choice of measures adopted to respond to the recession and a similar proportion believe that the role of HR had been restricted to implementing measures decided on by the business, with a somewhat lower proportion of employees disagreeing. So there seems to be some division of views regarding the degree of influence exerted by the HR function, and specifically about the balance of that influence as between strategic leadership and strategy implementation.

At the same time as the business role of HR has been strengthened the resources available to the function have often declined, but to a lesser extent than generally prevalent levels of retrenchment in employment. Although many firms had curtailed their use of external HR consultants, fewer reduced the costs of HR processes or HR-allied services (health and wellness, employee assistance programs, etc.).

What then is the import of these survey findings for the different perspectives on the impact of the recession on HR outlined in Chapter 2. Commentators observing or predicting radical changes in employment and HR models in either of the contrasting directions outlined in Chapter 2 seek to understand inherently dynamic processes, which yet remain in their early stages—even if they sometimes seem confident to draw strong inferences from snapshot or cross-sectional surveys, such as that reported here. Notwithstanding this caveat, some indications of the effects of the recession on HR and employment arrangements can be gleaned from the survey results.

Clearly there is no evidence that HR functions in Ireland have undergone, or face, decimation or cataclysm as a result of the recession. Rather, they commonly appear to have been spared the worst effects of a general trend toward downsizing and often to have experienced a strengthening of their business role and influence.

Nor is there any compelling evidence of any transition to a new employment deal that involves jettisoning key aspects of established HR and employment arrangements in favor of a new philosophy of self-reliance. For sure, work had become more insecure for most people and career advancement, in the form of promotion, has been halted for some. It is likely also that the changes in pension arrangements identified in the survey may sometimes involve a movement from defined benefit to defined contribution schemes that shift the burden of risk toward employees. But it would be premature and indeed would involve a highly selective use of empirical evidence to posit that these types of developments represent more than a cyclical adjustment and reflect instead a secular trend involving the rise of a new model of HR and employment arrangements, especially because other changes consistent with the supposed transition to a new employment deal, such as outsourcing and the greater use of agency workers, are barely pronounced in the recession. HRD budgets—supporting investment in human capital—have been maintained in as many firms as they have been reduced, while most people work in firms that have opted to redeploy staff to new positions or product lines in the recession—presumably to avoid or stave off job losses. Beyond these features of current HR and employment arrangements, firms claim to assign greater importance to areas like communication, the active involvement of employees and employee engagement. Although the 'new deal at work' thesis is silent with respect to trade unions, no fundamental or permanent shift in firms' dealings with trade unions is evident either from the survey data. Most unionized firms claim to seek engagement with unions in the context of HR measures with which to respond to the recession, but they do so to differing degrees, and only a minority could be portrayed as committed to active forms of engagement.

Taken as a whole, these features of firms' HR practices in the recession represent a considerably more variegated profile of HR and employment arrangements than that associated with the admittedly rather vague and general thesis that the recession is the harbinger of a new HR and employment model that is likely to abide when business recovery sets in. The same variegated set of measures and responses also warrants caution regarding the view that the recession is acting as a catalyst for the transformation of HR arrangements in the direction of the high-commitment model. The views of Ulrich, Cooper and other HR optimists certainly find resonance in survey results that point to the growing business role and influence of HR. However, whether this development has provided the platform for a definitively high-commitment response to the recession is far from clear. The increased prominence of communications in firms chimes with this line of argument. But the degree to which the HR function has leveraged its new prominence to create an organizational culture that motivates employees in a period of insecurity (as per the claims of Ulrich (as reported in Brockett 2010 and Cooper 2009); positions firms for the long-term by investment in skills (Ulrich as reported in Brockett 2010); taps employees' energy and engagement, harnesses their knowledge and involvement, among other things in strategy development (Mohrman and Worley 2009), is more open to question in the light of the survey findings. And so too is the claim (by Ulrich as reported in Brockett 2010) that HR has sought to reconfigure its own activities in order to cut costs and enhance efficiency. Although insecurity has certainly increased for employees across the board, the prominence of measures that may have been undertaken to motivate employees in this context seems considerably less marked. Survey respondents' endorsement of the prevalence of specific employee engagement measures ranks 6th out of 11 statements presented to them regarding changes associated with the recession—although employee engagement ranked third among respondents' comments regarding the most effective HR practices used in responding to the recession. Active engagement of employees in developing options for responding to the recession ranked 7th out of 11 statements presented to respondents regarding recession-related changes. This seems quite a distance in particular from Mohrman and Worley's (2009) notion of employees having become involved in 'hyper strategizing' initiatives as firms seek ways of responding to new challenges unleashed by the recession. Alongside the notion of HR leaders persuading firms to engage in long-term investment in skills must be set the reality that just more than half of all firms, employing 54% of the workforce, felt the need to cut training and development budgets. Although the business role of HR gained in prominence, the incidence of reconfigured HR functions seems modest, as does the incidence of initiatives to cut the cost of HR systems and services. Finally, in respect of the conduct of industrial relations in firms recognizing unions, there is little evidence of any new spirit of cooperation, collaboration or partnership having been animated by the recession—features of industrial relations commonly highlighted in accounts of the high-commitment HR model. Unions have been conceded little in the way of supports to organization and representation, and their members have been offered few financial claw-back measures in return for the realistic and constructive postures that are recognized by firms as having been commonly brought to bear in negotiations surrounding recession-related measures. Again the pattern of industrial relations evident from the survey seems a long way from the notions of firms fostering 'a sense of ownership and contribution' as part of concerted programs to leverage the recession to shift organizational cultures and processes toward a high(er) commitment.

We are left therefore with a picture of firms often striving to balance hard and soft HR measures in HR bundles or programs adopted to respond to the recession; implementing sets of measures that involve contradictions—these perhaps viewed as inevitable or as the best that can be achieved in the conditions that prevail. The picture also suggests both elements of continuity with past practices and some reprioritization of HR measures. The new prominence of the HR function and their more pronounced business influence seems more to have been a contributor to pragmatism and eclecticism along these lines than to have provided a platform for transformation to a new model of HR and employment, however this may be conceived. These themes are explored further in the focus groups to follow and in six case studies examined later in the study.

4 Human Resource Managers
The Effects of the Recession and HR Responses

The previous chapter confirmed the seriousness of the recession for many firms in Ireland and also revealed the range of HR measures adopted in response to the pressures and challenges faced by firms. Many firms have implanted measures to control pay and headcount, changed working-time arrangements, instituted more rigorous work regimes and have sought to reach accommodation with trade unions in the context of very difficult conditions. Managers working in the HR function perceive their business role to have gained in importance and have sometimes had to work in the context of a leaner HR function, with fewer resources. In responding to what for many are unprecedented challenges they have sought to balance hard and softer aspects of HR management and to reprioritize aspects of HR in the light of the demands of the external and internal organizational environments.

This chapter and the next present the findings of focus groups involving HR Managers, casting more and deeper light on the nature of the challenges that have arisen in these areas. This chapter begins by providing an outline of focus group participants and describes the conduct of the focus groups. It next examines the effects of the recession on the wide range of businesses represented, and reviews in detail, and often in participants' own words, the HR effects of pressures on businesses in which the HR managers worked. The chapter that follows examines HR managers' understandings of what constitutes 'good human resource practice' in recent and current recessionary conditions. Each of the HR focus group chapters closes with a series of conclusions and a discussion of the implications of the findings for human resource management and for debates on how it may have been affected by the recession.

4.1 BACKGROUND OF HR MANAGERS AND CONDUCT OF THE FOCUS GROUPS

Thirty HR managers participated in the five focus groups conducted in Dublin, Cork and Galway. The participants worked for a diverse set of companies. All but one of the managers had direct responsibility for HR, the exception being a manager to whom a colleague in HR reported. Eight participating companies were in manufacturing businesses, ranging from pharmaceutical products, medical devices, food, digital products, components and children's products. Twenty-two companies were in services, including financial services, information and communication services, software development, retailing, distribution, professional services and consulting, engineering and construction, hospitality, health care and contract cleaning. All companies were in the private sector, with the exception of one commercial state-owned company and one hospital. Fourteen companies were Irish-owned (some were multinationals), and 16 were owned by foreign multinational firms. Nineteen companies recognized unions and conducted collective bargaining for some or all categories of staff, while 11 companies were nonunion. The companies represented in the focus groups spanned a wide range of employment levels from low double figures to more than 5,000 employees. In the case of foreign-owned multinationals, both large-scale and small-scale Irish subsidiaries were included. Details of the background features of firms from which focus group participants were drawn are summarized in Table 4.1.

All focus groups were mixed with respect to the sectors represented. Four focus groups involved both unionized and nonunion companies and one involved nonunion employers only. All but one focus group involved both foreign-owned and Irish-owned businesses and one focus group involved Irish-owned companies alone. All focus group participants received briefing documentation in advance on the nature and scope of the research study, instructions on the manner in which the focus group would be conducted and details of the uses that would be made of the data collected. The conduct of the focus group was structured around a small number of significant questions and issues, and these were again communicated to participants in advance of the focus group meetings. The questions and issues around which discussion was focused were as follows:

- In what ways have firms been affected by the recession?
- The implications and challenges for the conduct of HR?
- What does good practice involve in firms that take cognizance of all stakeholder interests?
- In the case of unionized firms, what good practice has been identified and are there innovative ways in which unions have sought to deal with the pressures associated with the recession?
- Are preexisting HR & IR practices being maintained, modified or dispensed with?
- Which firms seem to be involved in responding effectively?

No prescriptive definition of HRM was provided to focus group members, and focus group participants themselves identified the areas encompassed within HR practice. In addition to the areas outlined above, a series of specific HR practices that may have been involved in firms' responses to the

Table 4.1   Detailed background features of participants in human resource managers' focus groups

Firm	Manufacturing	Services	Irish owned	Foreign-owned multinationals	Union(s) recognized	Non-union
Financial services 1		X		X		X
Software 1		X		X	X	
Professional services 1		X		X		X
Financial services 2		X	X		X	
Financial services 3		X	X		X	
Manufacturing 1	X			X		X
Retailing 1		X		X	X	
Utility 1		X	X		X	
Manufacturing 2	X			X	X	
ICT 1		X		X	X	
Hospitality		X	X			X
Manufacturing 3	X			X	X	
Manufacturing 4	X		X		X	
Manufacturing 5	X			X	X	
Manufacturing 6	X			X	X	
Manufacturing 7	X			X	X	
Manufacturing 8	X			X	X	
Retailing 2		X	X		X	
Distribution 1		X	X		X	
Leisure 1		X	X			X
Newspaper 1		X	X		X	
Retailing 3		X	X		X	
Hospital 1		X	X		X	
Estate Agent 1		X	X			X
Distributor 1		X	X		X	
Professional services 2		X		X		X
ICT 2		X		X		X
Software 2		X		X		X
Professional services 3		X		X		X
Services 1		X	X			X

Note: N = 30.

recession were communicated to participants in the prior briefing material supplied. These reflected the literature on HR practices commonly adopted in recessionary conditions and recorded in commentaries on the responses of firms in Ireland. They were drawn to the attention of focus group members in the final stage of the groups' discussions. They cover the following areas:

- Wage adjustments
- Employment adjustments
- Reorganization of working time
- Workforce stabilization
- Employability (assisting employees made redundant to obtain retraining)
- Voice (new forms of employee involvement or collective bargaining)
- Process or product innovation

In oral briefings provided at the outset of the focus groups, participants were informed that the areas identified in the briefing material and those used to structure the focus groups were neither intended to be prescriptive nor exhaustive and that the researchers were willing for the discussion to proceed in line with themes and priorities emerging from discussants themselves. It was made clear that the researchers present did not necessarily expect that a consensus would emerge around these areas within the group and that there were no right or wrong answers. Participants were asked to share their own experiences and offer views based on their professional experience. Based on experience in the first focus group, participants in subsequent focus groups were asked in particular to discuss their direct experiences of the issues covered and the attitudes they have formed based on these experiences. Participants were also informed that they were not viewed in any sense as representing their own companies' views on the areas under discussion. Focus group interviews were recorded and transcribed. The transcriptions ran to more than 200 pages.

4.2 THE EFFECTS OF THE RECESSION AND HR RESPONSES

Reflecting the general business environment and the survey results presented in Chapter 3, participants identified a range of commercial pressures bearing on both their own businesses and on those with which they were conversant. Downturns in sales and profitability were widely identified as major pressures. The cost and availability of credit were also identified as a significant pressure, particularly in financial services. Share prices had fallen significantly in a number of firms. In some markets, changes had occurred in product ranges; for example, financial institutions switching from mortgage provision to deposit taking. In other instances in professional service firms, entire product areas had virtually disappeared from the market. In financial services some participants spoke in terms of a "huge loss in business confidence," although instances were related in other sectors in which investment projects had been proceeded with, even in the face of recession and falling sales. Participants also identified greater price sensitivity on the part of consumers as a significant consequence of the recession. Other firms had suffered from the effects of closures by major customers, resulting in a huge reduction in orders and no new business. A firm in the food industry supplied global markets in food ingredients and the local and UK markets in consumer foods. In the latter business there had been volume reductions and pressure on prices as suppliers sought cost cuts in goods supplied and supermarkets shifted from branded to own-brand goods. Even in sectors relatively insulated from the recession, such as medical devices, the impact was felt indirectly. For example, elective surgical procedures had been negatively affected, resulting in falling sales volumes. Also changes had occurred to product ranges with demand falling for high-end produce in favor of more generic products. These developments were compounded by changes in product purchasing strategies in major markets, such as in the United States, where centralized purchasing functions in healthcare provision meant pressure on the prices that could be charged. In one major IT and communications firm with a global reach there had been an ongoing program of change and restructuring encompassing the company's Irish operations. Here the parent firm was seeking to focus on global growth areas, and the challenge to the firms' Irish operations was to move up the value chain. Central to managing this challenge was achieving cost reductions and productivity improvements in the Irish operations.

Some businesses were significantly affected by the rising value of sterling, even where turnover had not been greatly affected by the recession. When products sourced were priced in sterling but sold in euro, "margins had collapsed."

A number of the multinational firms included in the focus groups saw the recession as exacerbating pressures already evident during the years preceding the downturn, and the major challenge they identified was the cost and specifically the labor-cost competiveness of a firm's Irish subsidiaries relative to other locations in the parent company. Irish subsidiaries were seen to be in competition for production and investment mainly with other locations in Europe, in the Americas and in emerging markets. This competition had been rendered more intense by volume reductions, pressure on product prices and sometimes by over capacity and changing tax regimes in competing jurisdictions. What were seen as the high labor costs of Irish subsidiaries were sometimes further compounded by adverse movements in exchange rates with major currencies such as sterling and the US dollar, further weakening the competitiveness of Irish plants. In these ways the recession had thrown into sharper relief the mandates of local subsidiaries of multinationals and added to the challenges of preserving, renewing or developing such mandates.

The HR managers involved in all of the focus groups held largely common views as to the implications of these various pressures for their areas of activity. In general they had experienced acute pressure on costs, especially labor costs, on headcount and labor supply in general and pressure to improve productivity. In parts of financial services, in particular, "headcount reduction and cost management has been aggressively put in place," although it was also noted that the state guarantee of loans and deposits put in place by the Irish government in late 2008 had had the effect of constraining some participating firms' reactions in the areas of cost and headcount management. Pension funds also in some cases had been negatively affected by the recession and one participant spoke overall of a 'survival agenda' having come into being in the HR area. Several multinational subsidiaries had reduced headcount significantly but had also sought to automate production to reduce their vulnerability to uncompetitive labor costs relative to other locations within their parent companies' operations.

Not all markets or firms had been so severely affected. In areas like software development and ICT business remained relatively buoyant. But even here ongoing restructuring that preceded the recession was a significant background influence. Some firms which had not been forced by commercial circumstances to adopt a retrenchment agenda, identified nonetheless what were viewed as challenges in managing staff "complacency" and of ensuring that staff did not assume that things would continue to remain as they were.

Keeping in mind that not all firms were affected to the same degree, the speed of the onset of the recession and the scale of the pressures experienced provide the context for the HR adjustments outlined by focus group participants. The main areas in which HR managers had directly responded to the pressures caused by the recession and some of the implications for the management of HR are considered in turn.

Reflecting the survey findings virtually all of the HR managers participating in the focus groups had been involved in initiatives concerned with managing retrenchment with respect to pay levels and/or headcount reductions and short-time working. Cuts in payroll budgets were widely remarked upon. Pay freezes and freezes on pay increments, on progression through salary bands and on promotions had been implemented by focus group participants. In addition, bonus earnings had been heavily curtailed in some cases where bonuses were related to sales figures. Deferred bonus arrangements were also introduced in areas of financial services.

In managing redundancies, some firms with a tradition of using outplacement service providers extended this practice to redundancies caused by the recession, seeking to "make sure that people who have had to leave us were looked after." The use of multiple measures to control pay, headcount and labor supply was common. Pay freezes and deferred pay rises might be accompanied by redundancies. The same kinds of measures might also be further accompanied by unpaid layoffs implemented on a rotational basis. Some firms had used temporary short-time working, whereas others had resorted to short-time working on a more prolonged basis. Again reflecting the survey results on the prevalence of bundles of HR practices, it was common for firms across different sectors to implement packages or programs of retrenchment measures such as combined pay freezes and redundancies, sometimes in the context of restructuring programs. In some instances, comprehensive programs were implemented involving pay cuts, cuts in bonuses or commission, reduced working time (through three-day week, part-time and career breaks), freezes in recruitment and redeployment and the rationalization of management structures. Programs of this kind also sometimes involved successive sets of initiatives where measures and priorities changed as program outcomes became clear and commercial circumstances evolved. Thus, pay reductions or deferred pay rises might be succeeded by pay freezes or agreement to pay increases due. Pay freezes might be rescinded for significant numbers of staff, and freezes on promotions might be succeeded by consenting to promotions, while other measures remained in place.

In some instances firms had implemented these kinds of measures while also continuing to make 'targeted pay adjustments' or promotions for some staff on competitive or retention grounds. Bonus schemes in other companies, linked with staff performance, also continued to operate, including one that continued in the context of freezes on general pay increases. Pension contribution payments by staff were also sometimes increased or pensions were frozen to contain costs.

Some multinationals reported that measures to control pay and headcount were implemented in the context of maintaining the competitiveness of local plants and thus securing and developing their mandates within the parent group. A specific concern of Irish management was the US parent's known 'nervousness' about a unionized site and whether the union might seek to obstruct business decisions, throwing into doubt future investment. Employees were well aware of the competition that existed between locations within the group for products and investment.

Compared with the salience of pay and headcount management, a number of other areas of HR practice received considerably less mention or attention by focus group participants. The more intensive use of communication was a major exception and the new priority accorded by many HR managers to this area are discussed later when we examine HR managers' understandings of good HR management in recessionary conditions. Here we consider several other areas discussed by focus group participants.

Recruitment and retention: Recruitment and retention had been major concerns in HR management during the economic boom of the 1990s and the 2000s up to 2008. Indeed a number of participants in the focus groups suggested that during the boom HR practitioners and departments were largely seen as being almost exclusively concerned with recruitment and selection. The dominant trend with respect to recruitment in the recession was that none was occurring, and sometimes this reflected corporate embargos on hiring by Irish or multinational parent companies. However, some firms that had implemented redundancies or other pay and headcount controls at the same time had hired new staff with specific skill sets. In several cases HR managers explained that persuading potential recruits to move to the company was made more difficult by the recession because people had become more risk averse. Surprise was expressed in these instances that people were not "queuing up at the door" to take up well-paid jobs given the depth of the recession. In other cases participants spoke of professionals displaced by the recession from some industries seeking jobs in other sectors for which they deemed themselves well qualified and meeting with considerable skepticism from HR managers who were unconvinced. Several participants spoke of a reduction in staff turnover in relatively high-turnover sectors such as the hospitality and contract cleaning industries. Staff turnover in other firms had risen, one firm reporting that some staff "can't hack it" in the more demanding environment that had arisen. HR mangers spoke of initiatives in some firms affected by general embargos on pay and promotions involving the use of bonuses and promotion to retain staff that might otherwise be tempted to move. There had been a concern to "keep the right people" in firms that were satisfied to "lose mediocre people." In a small number of cases specific 'talent management' initiatives were undertaken to "track were the future superstars are likely to be." The recession had also led some firms to shift their recruitment efforts away from traditional sources. For example, a contract cleaning firm no longer sought to recruit students, as the quantity and cost of the administrative work involved was seen as excessive. In a software firm, state training agency trainees were now viewed as a worthwhile recruitment source, whereas in the past this had not been the case.

Staff redeployment: Given the scale of the reductions sought in labor supply and the commercial environments that firms commonly faced, a number of firms seemed to have had little scope for the internal redeployment of staff or related measures. Redeployment seemed more common in nonunion than in unionized firms. In an ICT firm, affected only to a limited degree by the recession, redeployment was reported to be "part and parcel of everyday business reality." In an estate agent, where "positions had been made redundant," people had been redeployed and retrained for new positions. In responding to the closure of a plant producing a discontinued product line, a pharmaceutical firm, consistent with its HR policy, had saved several hundred jobs by redeploying staff to other jobs. In another case, a firm that had relied mainly on redundancies to adjust headcount had also resorted to a minor degree to internal staff redeployment and "moved people where we could." An engineering design firm reported that redeployment was now easier—the firm having met with "huge reluctance" from staff in the past. Another firm had sought to redeploy staff where possible but believed that the new and different skill sets it now required were better sourced through recruitment, even as some existing staff were being made redundant. Unionized firms reported more constraints on the scope that existed for redeployment. A long-established Irish firm claimed that staff redeployment was an issue with the unions. In a hospital, redeployment was something viewed as largely "voluntary" and management had adopted a "soft approach" on the issue. A retailer indicated that demarcations between different crafts and their unions had limited the scope for redeploying staff. Otherwise, the opportunity for redeployment to new locations in the context of store closures had meet with little response from staff.

Human resource development and talent management: Given the predominance of the cost and headcount reduction agenda, it is not surprising that a common—albeit not universal—experience reported was pressure on HRD budgets and activities or cuts therein. The HR manager in a professional services firm echoed a number of colleagues in reporting that it had become tougher to justify the training spend. In a hospital the training budget had been "slashed and burned," the alternative was seen to involve patients suffering, so the organization saw itself as having had "no choice." In an engineering design firm the HRD budget had been cut significantly but even then there had been a huge reluctance by managers to spend the sums allocated. One HR manager, working in a quality-differentiated service firm, indicated that there had been a cut of 24% in the training budget. This required a change in the focus and delivery of HRD from using external consultants to the greater use of internal experts to deliver training activity. The greater use of internal providers was commonly reported by focus group participants. Sometimes budget cuts and fewer staff meant a significant increase in the training burden for those involved, especially in the context of redeployment initiatives.

As well as different providers, different HRD content was sometimes evident, as in a firm that had reengineered training to gear it to the difficulties staff might be facing in managing their personal finances as a result of the recession. With changes in product ranges having occurred in some firms, staff needed to be retrained or cross-trained to undertake different operations in a more stringent environment. Staff redeployed in order to stabilize employment also required training support. In one case, where training budgets had been retrenched, the resulting budget was "remodeled" or focused on talent development and away from the more permissive policy of the past when staff had been allowed to avail of training in areas of interest to them. In this case there remained, in the eyes of the HR manager, an unchanging basic commitment to HRD but remodeled in a manner appropriate to the current circumstances of the business. Another contributor also spoke of how the recession had prompted a better balance in the HRD effort between 'soft' and 'hard skills,' with softer skills in areas such as problem solving and project management now received more attention. Skills in these areas were seen as relevant for the "cost side of the business." In another company, a change had occurred from a policy of supporting financially staff members' own training and education initiatives toward an approach where the training effort is more focused on supporting development priorities for the business and concentrated on "top talent" and "high performers." In this firm, the HR manager saw the recession as a catalyst for "better practice." There had been a significant investment also in softer skills in areas such as leadership. In a software firm, in contrast, where the budget had been cut significantly, technical training had been retained but there had been a cut in training for soft skills so-called nice-to-have skills. In another case HRD was avowed as being of continuing importance but with a "hard focus" now on the training if management were to deal with performance and underperformance.

Training budgets and the training burden had not been reduced in all cases. One manufacturing firm, committed to continuing innovation in manufacturing processes, had obtained grant aid from a state agency to continue its training effort. In this case the training effort had increased in support of the objective of up-skilling the workforce. The Irish subsidiary of a multinational enjoyed a mandate to provide learning services to the parent company and so acted as a consultant in that capacity rather than having an assigned training budget that had come under pressure in the standard way. An ICT firm, not severely affected by the recession, retained their training effort following the injunction from the CEO that nothing should be done that would have a negative impact on the "employee experience." Here external providers were retained, but the firm had sought to achieve greater consistency in the services provided. Talent management was also identified as a significant concern. A software firm that had curtailed HRD activity spoke of reintroducing HRD as a reward for staff.

Work intensity and the management of performance: A number of contributors to the focus groups indicated that employees were working harder in the recession, spurred by their awareness of the external environment and of the difficulties that firm's were facing. One HR manager felt that "people were working an awful lot harder for a lot less money." Another said that the employer and customers were demanding more and that "everyone was working harder for so much less." A HR manager in a services firm observed that staff, especially managers, were "giving more without being asked." This could involve them undertaking more hours or doing overtime without seeking payment. This development was attributed to people being "grateful for the jobs that they have." In another company the HR manager observed that people's willingness to do more carried an expectation that there would be a "payback" in the form of a restoration of pay in the future. In a distribution firm higher performance was reflected in the introduction, for the first time, of explicit performance standards for employees following an agreement with the firm's trade unions.

If work intensity had commonly increased, a number of HR managers also indicated that performance had also been managed more rigorously in the recession. A software firm was "actively managing poor performers out of the business" and was no longer prepared to accept poor performance.

At the same time, it was admitted that because pay was frozen and for the present not linked to performance there was a problem with respect to the completion rate of performance reviews generally. Apart from performance management, some HR managers indicated that disciplinary issues had not been seriously pursued in the past—this was sometimes seen to be attributable to a lack of will on the part of senior management—but these were now being pursued more insistently. Managing underperformers out was not seen as a feasible option in the public sector context of the hospital participating in the focus groups.

A related theme that arose in some focus groups concerned the formalization of policies and procedures in areas like timekeeping, discipline and grievances in the recession. In both a distribution and a retailing firm these areas had been covered in agreements with unions either reached or implemented in the recession. The HR manager for another firm noted that when times had been good, the focus had been on day-to-day concerns rather than on policies and procedures but that this had now been corrected. This principle could also extend to other areas such as consultative arrangements with staff and trade unions.

Engagement and motivation: The urgency attaching to the measures implemented to control pay and headcount and employees resulting concern with job security and sometimes manifest willingness to work harder did not mean that no attention was paid to managing staff motivation or employees' reactions to the changes that had been made. A number of the HR managers participating in the focus groups had implemented significant reductions in headcount and often in pay and bonuses while simultaneously grappling with maintaining staff motivation, morale and commitment. This might involve specific programs or initiatives concerned with promoting engagement or reengagement, or find expression in a more conventional concern with preserving or promulgating values like trust, honesty, transparency, integrity and fairness. Here we examine the theme of engagement, whereas in the next chapter we examine HR managers' abiding concern with the advocacy of HR values seen to be integral to good human resource management and with fairness.

A minority of focus group participants made reference to specific programs or initiatives for managing employee engagement and motivation. In a context in which numbers had been reduced and bonuses curtailed, one HR manager emphasized the importance of celebrating successes in such areas as outstanding sales or customer service. Others put the emphasis on managing expectations in a radically different environment to that of the double-digit growth that had been a feature of the Irish economic boom. Others spoke of the challenge of countering complacency in companies not so seriously affected by the recession, and the adoption of measures like modest pay cuts as a means of highlighting the need for continuing adaptation. Engagement was sometimes discussed in the context of how people would "remember how they've been treated over the past eighteen months or so." One HR manager spoke of his awareness of how the "internal jury" that comprised the workforce would be affected both currently and in the future by any signs of bad faith and action contrary to HR policy on the part of senior managers intent on cutting corners. It was seen as a concern of HR managers to counter any such potential damage to morale. Other HR managers spoke of the importance of reengaging staff following the implementation of redundancy programs. One HR manager felt that the preoccupation with managing the exit process meant that not enough might be being done for those who remained after headcount reductions, remarking that "you can't expect everybody to be grateful they have a job."

One firm that had instituted a significant program of restructuring and headcount reduction had undertaken a formal reengagement program that involved senior management in seeking to reassure staff that they were valued by the company and in countering distrust and fears that a further program of retrenchment might be planned. Another firm that had implemented short-time working identified employee engagement as a significant area in which HR effort was now concentrated. This involved moving toward such engagement-type initiatives as focus groups, surveys and newsletters and ensuring that follow-up occurred to any issues identified through such mechanisms. When pressed further on how engagement might be managed in the current context, the HR manager emphasized the area of communications as being of key importance. Others adopted the same focus and spoke of the need to communicate good news whenever possible. In a hotel the importance of communicating good news and seeking to balance what might otherwise be a fairly bleak communications agenda was viewed as having a direct impact on morale and thus on customer service: "our staff are meeting guests ten minutes after the meeting. If they're down in the mouth they can't go into the office and hide. They're front-line; they have to be upbeat. . . ."

In a professional services firm forced to make significant cuts in pay and headcount, staff satisfaction and morale had declined sharply in a "new environment where the paradigm had moved." Given its circumstances, the firm had continued with elements of the program, including a staff survey and performance appraisal program, but had also "put elements of [the firm's engagement program] aside" while recognizing the "need to revisit it":

> I think for us particularly the psychological contract between the employer and employee has fundamentally moved in that people no longer see us to be the once great employer of choice in that we are as prone to making commercial decisions as any other organization and culturally that is a seismic shift for an organization like ours. Now that puts a huge challenge on people like myself to try to re-engage the workforce

Some focus group participants broached the theme of employee engagement in very general terms, stating it to be an important objective but identifying few specific mechanisms, conventional or novel, as effective ways of achieving the objective: "the challenge going forward, which I think we are still in the throes of trying to work out is about motivation; how you actually build confidence and motivate people and bring them along with you."

Relations with trade unions: In general, little serious disaffection was reported in staff or union responses to the measures firms had undertaken to respond to the recession. Employees and unions in general seemed to have accepted the state of affairs that obtained and had come to expect little scope to exist for pay awards. However, some firms' insistence on renegotiating the pay increases in the *Towards 2016* national pay agreement—usually culminating in the deferred and phased payment or part payment of increases, sometimes followed by an agreed-on pay freeze—resulted in the parties referring disputes to the LRC. The hospital included in the focus group was seriously constrained from introducing changes in pay and conditions by national agreements in the sector and the long-running uncertainty surrounding attempts to conclude a national public service agreement. In consequence, cost cutting was restricted to the nonpay budget. In the contract cleaning company, terms and conditions of employment for service personnel were fixed by a Joint Labor Committee (JLC) for the sector. This constrained cost-cutting activity for this group to focus on nonpay costs, whereas headquarters staff not covered by the JLC experienced pay freezes. In other strongly unionized firms, HR managers complained about the time required to win an acceptance by staff and their unions that things had to change. Unions might also retaliate against what they viewed as excessive management measures, as in the case of a firm in which an attempt to introduce a pay freeze was countered by a new insistence on the part of staff that a Christmas bonus be paid and by threatened industrial action.

When redundancies were mooted in unionized firms, unions sought to persuade companies to opt for voluntary over compulsory measures to cut headcount, wherever possible, and otherwise sought the best terms achievable. Unions also opposed the adoption of specific selection criteria in deciding on redundancies, and sought to persuade companies simply to seek volunteers or to institute last-in-first-out arrangements. In response to a specific question from researchers as to whether unions were exclusively concerned with the terms offered in redundancy programs, or alternatively had sought specific concessions in return for agreeing headcount reductions or pay freezes, focus group participants in general were categorical that few specific concessions had been sought or agreed in their experience. Any quid pro quo that arose were of a generalized kind: as one HR manager put it, "all the staff were interested in was 'my job, my job security and my pension.' . . . and there was no request for anything, any extras or any quid-pro-quos at all." Another HR manager in a firm where short-time working had been introduced commented that "it really boiled down to maintaining jobs and maintaining membership." One firm that had implemented a series of measures to control pay and headcount had also agreed to convert some temporary positions into full-time positions, thereby delivering some more members to the union with which it had negotiated. This was seen as a measure that had somewhat appeased the union concerned. In another firm, where unions had agreed to an extension in the working week, an assurance had been sought regarding a preexisting agreement on the criteria to be applied in selecting people for redundancy. The limited degree to which unions had sought or achieved specific quid pro quo was linked by some focus group members with the manner in which firms had sought to manage recessionary pressures. One HR manager recounted the case of a firm where significant changes in the pension scheme had been announced, followed by negotiations with the union. When no agreement was secured in the negotiations, the firm had simply implemented the changes unilaterally.

The task of persuading local employees and unions to accept significant concessions was not always plain sailing, especially in Irish-owned or in non-Irish multinationals reporting good financial results at group level across global markets. Here again HR managers understood the challenge as one of persuading staff and unions to understand the specificities of the local plant's situation and performance within the multinational group. As one HR manager put it,

> we have the challenge where we are part of a very, very successful and very profitable business; our profits are very healthy on a global basis. But we have to talk on a site level and our local site profitability and competitiveness is the key. In an Irish multinational, management faced a similar challenge with local staff in a context where the global group was highly profitable and receiving praise in the press, and people can't understand why it is that we're debating with them; that we don't want to pay them [the] T2016 [pay rise].

In other cases, adjustments required in recessionary conditions were rendered more difficult by preexisting industrial relations problems or by strained relations between the parties. Preexisting good relations, as expressed, for example, in workplace partnership arrangements were also seen as paving the way for effective negotiated responses to the recession.

The HR managers had not experienced and nor did they expect any major change in unions' postures or behavior as a consequence of the breakdown of social partnership. Asked whether the collapse of partnership had led to *unions* adopting a more aggressive or adversarial posture in their dealings with firms, the HR managers responded that this had not been their experience, nor did they expect it to happen—although several thought that the industrial relations outlook had become more difficult or uncertain. In the main, as they saw it, "everybody was busy trying to make things happen and solve problems." One HR manager referred to what he saw as "interference" from the Irish Congress of Trade Unions or from union national head offices having become somewhat more pronounced since the collapse of partnership and affecting the local union representatives posture toward issues on the negotiating table. In other cases HR managers also complained about national policy issues in a general union acting as a distraction in settling issues in local collective bargaining and about the union involved being overly preoccupied with the national situation to the detriment of concluding agreements on the ground. The continuing uncertainty surrounding attempts to negotiate a national public service agreement had also compounded the challenge to responding to budget cuts in a hospital included in the focus groups. Several HR managers pointed to a skills deficit arising in the bargaining competencies owing to the return to enterprise-level pay bargaining. Otherwise, the effects, actual or potential, of the collapse of social partnership found little resonance in the HR managers' experiences or reflections.

4.3   HR AND THE BUSINESS

In some of the focus groups, participants debated whether the HR function had been fit for purpose in terms of leading firms' responses to the recession. Some thought that HR had been primarily reactive and surprised by the pace of the downturn. As they saw it, a function that had developed in an era when staff recruitment and retention often represented a major challenge had limited experience in dealing with headcount reduction, and specifically possessed little skill or experience in managing redundancies. The portrayal of the HR function during the boom as "that part of the organization that hired people and made sure that all their rights were looked after," or as a "recruitment agency" was quite widespread among the HR managers participating in the focus groups. There was general agreement that dealing with the "business agenda" in the recessionary environment presented a much more difficult challenge for HR than was hiring people, which tended to be perceived within firms as "easy and nice." As one HR manager put it, "we've gone from being a service provider to the business to the business being completely dependent on us." Another emphasized that "we've been seen as being incredibly integral to some of the things that had to be done."

The predominant view of participants by far was that HR could, and often in practice did, provide leadership in this environment and that the agenda now addressed, focusing on what one participant called "getting the business back in shape," had brought HR into mainstream business decision making. This view was sometimes articulated by participants in terms of the new role of HR as a business partner. The common perception was of the new centrality achieved by HR given the focus now on bottom-line business concerns like pay, headcount and restructuring. The general view was reflected in the comment that the "stock-in-trade for HR people had risen as a result of the recession." One HR manager spoke approvingly of HR people beginning to engage in what was described as "accounting speak" and showing a new appreciation of the business context of their work. Another echoed this view by claiming that to engage in business partnership "you have to talk the language of business."

In one commercial semistate company, there was a perception that whereas HR had been "a bit detached from the day-to-day realities of the business in the good times and perhaps a bit more interested in HR as a function" it had now become more central to "every step of every change that needed to be taken." In the same way, an HR manager in a financial services firm believed that one of the significant challenges for the function was the need to be aligned with what was happening in the business and to exercise leadership in this way. In a health-care devices firm, the HR manager was clear as to the change that had occurred. HR was becoming involved in a "lot more critical business-type issues." The situation had changed such that "whereas previously . . . at quarterly updates or management meetings, the HR update might be at the end of the agenda, over the last year we've seen suddenly it's the talking point." A participant from another multinational emphasized that the HR team "had to demonstrate leadership, not just to sit back and expect the business to tell us what we need to do." This involved "leading from the front and adopting a type of business partner model." The flip side of HR's new centrality to the operation of the business was that HR directors had to "stand up at senior level in the organization and justify your existence."

In the past in one multinational firm there had been little communication or contact between HR executives in subsidiaries in different countries and no centralized HR function or director. This has changed to a significant degree as experience of responding to the challenges of the recession, especially in achieving cost savings, had resulted in regular "HR global summits" and the collaborative development of general HR practices. One contributor felt that rather more vigorous leadership might have been shown by HR in leading change that had been predominantly focused of necessity around the cost and headcount reduction agenda. Other contributors, while endorsing the business partner model, seemed to adopt a more aspirational posture, or to view this model as an entity in the making: "the business acumen piece is where we need to add value that's of strategic importance." Others still, while stating the this model "made a lot of sense," said that they had stopped short of enacting it fully for fear that it would empower line managers to make unwise HR decisions in critical areas such as discipline and dismissals. For some the recession was seen as creating the opportunity for HR practitioners "to step up and make themselves influential" but yet they "were not sure that it was more influential." One aspect of the new situation of HR commented on by several HR managers involved high expectations by management peers of what HR could deliver. As one contributor put it, he was expected to deliver "all the changes that should have been delivered over the past twenty, thirty or forty years."

To what degree were HR managers influential in shaping the measures firms had adopted to respond to the recession as distinct from playing a key role in the implementation of measures that had been decided by other senior managers? The predominant view was that the influence of HR extended to key decisions on how firms responded to the recession. As the HR manager of a professional services firm saw it, he had been "pretty central very early, right through from the design to the execution" of the company's response. The HR manager of a contract cleaning firm had a similar view, seeing the role adopted as "central, leading, whatever way you want to look at it; but a different kind of role." The same view was articulated by the HR manager of a distribution company: "no decisions will be made unless a senior manager will come to the HR manager and sit down and discuss what's going to happen." The HR manager of a retailer was also emphatic that "we were involved from the start" with other managers, particularly operations.

The new centrality claimed for HR and reflected in these comments was seen by some to emanate from the increased dependence of other managers on HR expertise in recessionary conditions:

> There are a lot of changes being forced on companies, mostly staff changes, cut-backs on staff, reorganizing, and there are processes to be gone through and most management other than HR people don't have the knowledge of those processes.

Not all HR managers perceived their new centrality to the business in quite such vaunted terms. Some believed that their influence within senior management extended more to the implementation of business decisions largely determined beyond their reach. The HR manager for a distribution firm was categorical that the key decisions regarding HR were taken by the major retailer for which they worked: they "called the shots; they're not paying their staff, so you can't pay yours." In a long-established Irish firm, "management made the decisions and HR was involved in implementation." The HR manager of a hospital saw the situation in his organization in very stark terms: "the government decided."

When the HR managers identified skills deficits or priority areas for skills development, skills pertaining to business partnering were most commonly mentioned. These included "understanding the business and the HR competencies required to support this," "the business context of HR rather than HR for HR" and being able to present HR information at senior management meetings "in a way that the business is familiar with."

Part of the new role of HR involved providing advice and mentoring to managers on dealing with the HR implications of business decisions. When significant changes were in play, there had been more requests for advice from line management. In one ICT firm HR was central to the ongoing process of building the capability of line managers in creating a line-led HR model. Coaching and "hand-holding," sometimes of very senior executives, had been necessary in other cases given the extent and unprecedented nature of the changes introduced.

> I was very involved . . . in "hand-holding" a lot of people, through some very difficult conversations and giving them a sense of confidence, reassurance, the tools, and coaching them through some very difficult situations; trying to build their capability . . . bearing in mind that they hadn't been through this for quite some time.

In developing and illustrating the theme of HR's role as a business partner, reference was seldom made to the role of HR in positioning or repositioning the business to take advantage of economic recovery. There were exceptions. One was an IT and communications firm that had been focusing on growth areas and regions of the business on an ongoing basis when the recession arrived and continued to do so. In the firm's Irish operations, cost control was the immediate priority but "moving up the value chain" or a "higher value mandate" was seen as the longer-run imperative. Here there had been a quite explicit focus that included HR on "what the business will be doing in the next five to ten years and . . . shaping the organization to deliver that." The focus was on systems integration and converging technologies and on the competencies required in that context. This was seen to have important HR implications in areas such as performance management and improving overall performance in the workforce. In another case a hotel's decision to avoid layoffs or redundancies and to retain core staff was explicitly related to a business model in which customers expected to be served by the same staff over successive stays, and this model would be important when an upturn arrived in the hospitality sector.

Although the new role of HR as business partner found resonance in a number of Irish-owned firms as in foreign-owned multinationals, this role seemed less pronounced in a number of long-established Irish firms, where the postures of HR managers seemed more traditional in character. This probably reflected both HR managers' own understanding of their role and their sense that in established firms, where both senior managers and staff often had long service, strongly embedded expectations existed among managers and staff alike as to how businesses should behave, and these confined the role and priorities of HR within more traditional parameters. This theme is taken up again in the next chapter when we discuss the role of ethics and advocacy in HR in the recession.

The alignment of HR within firms: The researchers asked participants whether, in their experience, the balance of power between HR and other functions, such as finance and operations and between HR and senior corporate management had changed in the recession to the detriment of HR. The predominant view was that HR's area of activity or authority had not been encroached on by other management functions or by other levels within companies to any significant degree. Decisions in some cases had always been made collectively by senior management teams, and this had remained the case in the recession. In other instances HR continued to participate in business teams, and it was noted that more time was probably been devoted to HR issues in business meetings because HR issues were now to the fore. In other firms, a business partner model in which line managers were recognized as the primary managers of human resources had long been in existence, and here HR continued to support line managers in the recession. Other HR managers reported that line managers had become more dependent on HR in the recession in the sense that many line managers had little experience of managing in a downturn and so now looked for advice and coaching from HR.

Other firms pointed toward the centralization of business management or of areas of HR management that had introduced new dimensions into HR management. Prominent here was the creation by some multinationals of product-based or HR area-based 'centers of excellence' that were seen as having significant implications for the conduct of HR. These developments reflected wider ongoing processes of corporate restructuring and development rather than the specific effects of the recession. However, the new centers of excellence created interacted with the effects of the recession to subject HR management to greater levels of transparency. Irrespective of whether centers of excellence were based on product divisions or on areas of HR, such as the management of compensation and benefits or talent management, the outcome was the same: the costs associated with paying people in different locations were becoming clearer and more amenable to benchmarking and the same was occurring in areas such as the cost of redundancy. The creation of HR centers of excellence was also seen to be giving rise to more influence from corporate level in such areas as talent management and succession management. In firms not affected by these kinds of restructuring or development, experiences varied. In one multinational company, corporate headquarters in the past had involved itself little in the business or in the HR of its Irish subsidiary. In the recession this had changed as a corporation-wide hiring freeze was instituted—though not, it appears, rigorously policed.

A further dimension of how HR was aligned with other management functions and levels in the recession concerned the attention that senior management devoted to HR issues. Here participants in the main were of the view that senior management, including CEOs, were now more intensively involved in the HR agenda than in the past, and often were to the fore in leading the cost-cutting agenda.

Leaner HR functions: As well as being agents or partners in leading the HR change agenda, HR functions were also commonly objects of change in their own right. Headcount reductions often extended, or were expected to extend, to HR functions on a proportionate basis to overall staff cuts.

Sometimes cuts in HR were even more radical, resulting in the retention only of a "skeleton crew." One HR manager described a more than fourfold reduction in the numbers employed in HR as an outcome both of downsizing generally in the company and as a consequence of the creation of HR centers of excellence in the parent company and the outsourcing of HR services. In a professional services firm 4 in 10 HR positions had disappeared, responsibilities had been realigned and duplication removed, resulting in what was seen as a function that had become "more fit for purpose." Another firm had sought to centralize or recentralize the handling of HR and other support functions in the wake of a merger, and this meant the introduction of redundancies in the firm's Irish HR operation. In other cases, moves in this direction had been mooted, with resulting uncertainty within HR itself. As the HR manager of a professional services firm seriously affected by the recession put it in relation to his colleagues in the function, it was a case of "people who were uncertain, dealing with people who were uncertain."

In other cases, HR managers reported that they were expected to achieve significant cost reductions in HR processes and services as part of overall programs of cost reductions in firms. This sometimes extended to renegotiating contracts with health-care providers and other HR service suppliers. Some contributors affected by the radical restructuring of the function reported substantially more pressure for those now handling more-demanding HR activities.

4.4 CONCLUSION

Both reflecting and fleshing out the survey findings, the most striking feature of the conduct of HR in the recession, as described by focus group participants, was the extent and degree to which the main focus was on controlling and often reducing pay and headcount in response to deep and acute commercial pressures. HR responses commonly involved the simultaneous use of multiple measures to manage pay and headcount and to adjust the paybill and the labor supply in response to a sharp deterioration in commercial conditions. This hard-line or bottom-line agenda appeared to dwarf much else in its significance for HR managers and in the demands and burden it placed on them. A function that many participating HR managers portrayed as having been mainly concerned with recruitment throughout the boom was now forced to occupy new and, for many, unfamiliar terrain. Relative to the burdens of managing pay and headcount other areas of HR practice assumed less attention. Some firms participating in the focus groups continued to recruit employees for specific positions or new skills sets, and firms also took measures such as selective pay rises or promotions to retain valued staff. Some firms operated formal talent management programs, though these predated the recession. Staff redeployment was presented as a routine measure in responding to the recession in nonunion firms, but appeared to be more problematic in unionized firms, in which it sometimes cut across agreements with unions or lines of demarcation between different jobs. Human resource development budgets had been cut in many cases, and firms had responded by refocusing the HRD effort and by in-sourcing more HRD activity. In some instances HR managers believed that HRD had become more effective and better geared to business needs and even more strategic or proactive in consequence.

A number of HR managers indicated that staff had been prepared to work harder in the recession and even to concede extra hours of work without seeking payment. Firms had also sometimes tightened up on performance standards, on performance management and on workplace discipline and related procedures. Some firms had undertaken specific initiatives or programs to preserve or promote employee engagement or reengagement in circumstances in which staff had endured pay freezes or cuts, embargos on promotions and job losses. In other cases, engagement programs had been partially suspended or eclipsed while firms dealt with the management of pay and headcount.

In general industrial relations had not been turbulent, and employees and unions were seen to have accepted that commercial conditions were serious and could not be ignored. HR managers complained that negotiations continued to be too protracted, and some globally profitable firms faced particular difficulties persuading staff and unions to agree to the need for retrenchment measures in local plants. Certain issues were found to be high on union agenda (voluntary severance) and others nonnegotiable (selection criteria for redundancies). Unions had sought or been accorded few specific concessions in return for agreeing retrenchment measures. In the experience of focus group participants unions in general gained few specific quid pro quo for agreeing to concessions over pay and conditions and had to be satisfied with the prospect of better employment security for remaining staff.

The involvement of HR managers in pay and headcount measures pivotal to firms' stability and even survival was seen to have given the HR function and HR managers a new level of centrality to the business and more influence in business decision making. This was a theme on which most HR managers concurred, and which some portrayed in terms of HR having become a business partner in a more vital sense than at any time in the past. As businesses often sought to implement multiple measures to manage the paybill they had become more dependent on HR processes and expertise for their survival and regeneration. Levels of influence by HR among focus group participants varied from contributing to the choice of measures for responding to the recession to influencing the implementation of response measures. A significant development noted by a number of participants involved senior executives becoming more intensively engaged around the pay and headcount agendas and providing clearer and more decisive leadership in these areas.

The alignment of HR vis-à-vis other management functions and vis-à-vis top-level management in firms varied across the firms represented in the focus groups. No clear-cut change in the balance of power or influence as between HR and other management functions was apparent to participants. HR managers remained influential members of and contributors to senior management teams and decision making in areas central to HR and businesses more generally. Line mangers with little experience of managing in a recession had sometimes become more dependent on advice and support from HR. Cases were outlined in which the global significance of HR had been elevated by the recession, but so too were cases where corporate HR had assumed a measure of control over the conduct of HR in local subsidiaries not before evident. A general trend was that HR functions had become 'leaner' through job losses and sometimes through measures to reduce administrative costs and the costs of services provided through HR.

Of the implications of these findings for HR management the following appear most salient: first, reflecting the depth of the recession for many firms participating in the focus groups, HR has mainly been focused on hard or bottom-line measures concerned with controlling pay and headcount and on tightening up on performance standards and performance management. Softer or more developmental HR initiatives and measures, although not neglected in the experience of focus group participants, have seemed considerably more muted during the recession, as evidenced by activities in the areas of employee engagement and aspects of HRD. Second, it is this hard or bottom-line agenda and firms' dependence on HR measures to secure their survival and regeneration that has mainly brought HR and HR managers to a more pivotal and influential position in firms than ever before in their experience. It is perhaps ironic that such a degree of prominence had not been gained during a period in which more scope existed for pursuing the softer HR agenda that is more commonly associated with HR's claims to be a business partner or strategic asset. Third, HR has become a business partner in the sense conveyed by focus group participants, on foot of a mainly reactive if nevertheless vital posture and agenda. Although some firms had been involved in restructuring or business refocusing programs that preceded the recession and within which HR was a significant concern, HR managers in general seem to have been so heavily focused on immediate or short-term measures that the longer-term alignment of HR and businesses has not been—as yet—a priority or even a salient concern. In this sense, it may be important to distinguish between HR being more central to the operation of businesses and to their responses to the recession and HR being more proactive in positioning businesses for recovery or long-term growth. Although the centrality of HR to the business was a highly salient theme in all of the focus groups, HR seemed often to have remained largely reactive in this role. In few cases was HR presented as a major facilitator of the long-term positioning or the repositioning of businesses. The cases in which such a role was outlined tended to be firms not acutely affected by the recession, or in which difficulties had been experienced by Irish operations but where global operations remained buoyant and profitable. Fourth, in the light of the strong association that has been found to exist between acute recessionary challenges and the influence of HR, it remains an open question whether HR retains its newfound centrality to businesses and continues to be an influential 'business partner' when the economy recovers. Finally, the evidence of HR participants in the focus groups seems consistent with the import of the survey data discussed in the Chapter 3 with respect to whether, to what degree and in what direction models of HR may be changing as a result of the recession. Many HR managers' main focus has manifestly been on 'working the pumps' to cope with the acute commercial effects of the recession, adopting combinations of measures that seem best geared to this objective, with relatively little concern for rebuilding models of HR and employment. Indeed, the kinds of grand systemic changes identified in some of the predictions about HR in the recession seem barely salient to most focus group participants. These themes are further explored in the next chapter, which examines HR managers' understanding of 'good HR management' in recessionary conditions.

5 Human Resource Managers
Good Human Resource Management in the Recession

This chapter examines in detail the views of HR managers concerning the features of good human resource management practice in the recession. This theme was examined in a specific section of the focus group interviews that came after the discussion of the experiences of HR managers during the recession and the HR responses to business challenges discussed in the previous chapter. Although some of the themes and issues discussed obviously and necessarily overlapped sections of the interviews, many HR managers had little difficulty in outlining what facets of HR practice they believed to be particularly important in helping the firms in which they worked to deal effectively with the challenges of the recession. This chapter's examination of the features of good HR management complements the survey findings on this and related themes by permitting an in-depth exploration of HR managers' views. The HR managers' opinions on the issue point to an understanding of good HR practice articulated largely in terms of the practices and processes through which pay and headcount were managed effectively. The themes that arose in this area of the focus group interviews are considered first, and the main findings are then summarized and their implications discussed.

5.1   INTENSIVE COMMUNICATION

More than any other single theme, participants quite consistently stressed that, in their eyes, intensive communications with employees and unions were a critical aspect of managing pay and headcount reductions effectively, as, more generally, of managing human resources in recessionary conditions. Virtually all focus group participants identified and underscored the significance of this area in their experience, and the importance of intensive communications was often mentioned spontaneously in other areas of the focus groups in which good practice was not so specifically identified by the researchers as the subject for discussion.

It seemed clear that direct communications between firms and their employees was the priority concern, with communications to and via unions emerging as a secondary but not insignificant theme in unionized firms. It also appeared to be the case that one-way communications from firms to their workforces dominated the picture, although in some instances provision was also made for two-way or upward communications from employees.

The context for the greater intensity of communications in virtually all cases was the introduction of pay freezes or cuts, incentivized leave, or voluntary and compulsory redundancies. In essence, the common view of participants was summed up by the statement of one HR manager that communications with staff needed to be "honest, open and intensive." The HR managers spoke in terms of "getting the message across," "just explaining the reality," and "working through problems with people to bring them with you . . . to get an acceptable outcome." For some, effective communications were the key to managing expectations: "being very clear in our communications to people about what's happening, when it's happening and when it will end." This view was also articulated in a more negative way by a HR manager who pointed out that there was a need to "avoid paranoia." To this end the company had used staff meetings and forums. The fact that the "country was in an awful state" had not exonerated firms from the need to "go out and convince staff." Where restructuring and closure might be on the cards, staff anxiety made communications "absolutely essential" in a retail business.

The common view also was that communications had become more intensive as HR managers sought to handle the consequences of the recession, with some referring to the existence in their firms of a "communication strategy," or being a "bit more strategic about our communications." HR managers spoke in terms such as "we talked to people more," "we put a lot of effort into communications—huge" and "we tripled the amount of communications and did as much face-to-face communications as we could." Others referred to their firms having "increased the density" of communication-related activities or of communications having improved: "it's much more regular: weekly updates with staff, giving them a realistic overview of the business . . . telling them exactly where we stand." The validity of the content imparted through communications was also commented on: "we told it as it was; we said here is our position; here is what we are going to do." One HR manager described his company's approach in the following terms: "one of the things we always committed to the staff is if we know it, we will tell you." Another pointed to the importance of openness and honesty. The consistency of the message was seen to be important, involving "all managers saying the same thing about the business."

Some firms indicated that current practice in the area was a continuation of established practice: a multinational that approached control of the paybill in the context of securing its mandate, pointing out that communication has been an abiding feature of HR in the company such that staff were well aware of the importance of cost competitiveness for securing the mandate of the local plant.

For some HR managers people were more receptive to communications because they now touched directly on their primary concern for job security: "their job security is a huge issue for people; it's their greatest worry at the moment, so realistic updates and how the business stands . . . were really appreciated." Another HR manager pointed out that changes in volumes of production and the operation of short-time working had necessitated more communications with trade unions.

The communication mechanisms used were, for the most part, standard or well known in the HR field and were usually also used prior to the recession as routine aspects of HR management in the companies involved in the focus groups. Some commented nonetheless that these mechanisms "really came into their own . . . when we really needed to explain what we were doing and why." Table 5.1 lists the main communications mechanisms identified by focus group participants.

Although there was little explicit reference to the use or advisability of multiple communication mechanisms, this seems to be common practice, with the exception of smaller firms where informal methods and face-to-face communication were emphasized. Some reference was made to changes in emphasis between different mechanisms used, for example, moving from reliance on e-mail communication to communicating more on a face-to-face basis or by talking directly to people more frequently rather than making use of "impersonal mechanisms." Where multiple mechanisms were employed it was a case of "sometimes we were telling [staff] the same message again and again but reinforcing the message." Although these mechanisms are

Table 5.1   Communication mechanisms used in the recession

Communication mechanisms	
Town-hall meetings	Briefing by management
Walking the production floor	Two-way communications
Speaking to staff at regular intervals	Executive lunches with cross sections of staff
CEO and senior management addresses	Staff consultation forums (in respect of collective redundancies)
Regular e-mail—based briefings	European works councils
Meetings	Regular forums for whole organisation
Local site manager briefings	Senior management regularly facilitating meetings of staff chosen randomly
Face-to-face communications	Focus groups
Webcasts	Communication with unions
Employee surveys	Newsletters
One-to-ones	Regular 'questions & answers,' using notice boards
Joint employer—union communiqués	

acknowledged formal practices familiar in the HR field, reference was sometimes made to the use of 'informal but good' (communication) tools. Sometimes the communications engaged in were described as unofficial, as in the case of a firm that had embarked on restructuring at the European level and where local Irish management, aware that staff were gaining a sense that 'something was coming,' opted to provide local staff with an outline of what might emerge. One HR manager spoke about the significance, as he saw it, of the changed environment represented by communication channels per se. With the widespread and frequent use of texting and e-mailing by people, there was a tendency toward the "grapevine going crazy." In such an environment it was necessary for managers to be "really sharp in getting it [the firm's message] out there on time, to make sure that the message stayed pure and correct."

For the most part, HR managers discussed the importance of communications in terms of making sure that employees and unions understood the pressures facing companies and of the appropriateness of the measures to be undertaken in the light of these. In other words, the emphasis appeared squarely to be on communication from firms to their workforces. The task was to gain understanding and compliance; as one contributor put it, "if you communicate before people find out, they'll be much more agreeable." In one instance where the firm's Managing Director (MD) had been pivotal in communicating a series of measures that included a significant number of redundancies, his authoritativeness and known reputation as a tough guy was seen as a clear signal that "he was not going to turn and get turned in any way." Some contributors did point toward two-way and upward communication channels, such as focus groups, that had operated in the broader context of employee engagement mechanisms and question and answer initiatives. One HR manager in an ICT firm admitted that though the firm's communication strategy made provision for upward communication through questions and answers, this mechanism had not functioned as intended. In one case focus groups, created at the prompting of union officials, were seen as a means of "trying to create a two-way street," whereas in another instance regular engagement-related meetings with employees provided forums for attempting to resolve issues.

Some unionized firms indicated that they had adopted the same broad approach their communications with unions as to their communications with their employees. One firm had engaged in joint communiqués with its unions, involving writing to people in their homes, as a means of countering what the employer viewed as poor internal communications between and within the firm's unions' representatives and members. Another firm involved unions in a communications structure. However, other unionized firms, both multinational and Irish owned, were emphatic that direct communications were of paramount importance and even that they had sought to rebalance their communications activities in favor of direct communications with their employees and away from communication via trade unions.

As one HR manager put it, "if you are doing direct communication with your workforce, that's something that you should own as a company; you should own that line." Another spoke of how when he joined the company, "all of the communication was going through the centralized union committee." This had changed. As he put it, "we needed to rebalance this," and the mechanism adopted involved direct communications with employees on a weekly basis, in the context of an employee engagement program, with regular reports back to employees on the issues raised and the state of play regarding their resolution. Regular meetings continued with the unions, and these now involved inputs from key figures in different areas of the business who provided briefings on trends and developments in markets.

The HR managers identified a series of specific objectives guiding intensive communications. Communications were aimed at "managing people's expectations" in a radically changed environment, "trying to commandeer support and provide a bit of hope that there is light at the end of the tunnel," achieving "buy-in from unions" and winning "employee engagement." They also identified a series of specific outcomes that had been achieved in their experience. These included avoiding people being "damaged" before, during or after change initiatives and priming people to be ready "to pick up and go," such that productivity gains consequent on departures from the company could be realized. Others spoke in such terms as ensuring that the "trust and honesty that management have with employees is kept." An instance was recounted in which the acceptance without any argument of a pay freeze was attributed to communications and their effects in ensuring that there were no shocks for staff.

5.2   HARNESSING SENIOR MANAGEMENT LEADERSHIP

Closely allied with the importance attributed to communicating more intensively was the common view that HR was most effective in handling the pressures of the recession when senior managers' support was harnessed for both the agenda being pursued and for the process of communicating this agenda to employees. As discussed previously, the hard, bottom-line pay and headcount changes to the fore in HR activity were seen as cementing the centrality of HR to the business, and thus attracting senior management support and sponsorship. The HR managers were at one in their view that harnessing senior management support, sponsorship and visibility with respect to changes being sought was pivotal to their smooth implementation and acceptance by the workforce. As one HR manager put it, "when the managing director says something the company tends to stand over it." When the message "comes from the top" or from the "horse's mouth" the message was seen to carry more credibility. If HR was seen as delivering the message, there was a risk that parties affected would seek to "go over their heads" with potentially "disastrous consequences."

When the message was delivered from the top, HR remained pivotal, as one participant put it, in "conceiving and distributing the messaging throughout the firm." The approach involved "HR people perhaps writing or constructing what the managing director needs to say, but with the realization that it has to come from the horse's mouth." Sometimes this approach marked continuity with established practice: "it was always policy for HR to enable senior management, albeit that there was maybe greater use of senior management." More "focus on messages from the top" involved senior management, up to CEO level in some instances, taking "more ownership" of changes in HR practice, communicating changes, commonly leading change programs and, in the process, committing "double or triple the amount of time they might normally spend on it." Such an approach was sometimes contrasted with the more established practice of relying on HR to lead change programs: "I felt it was important that they heard from the top. That it wasn't just 'HR speak' in the sense of the kind of thing maybe they could be used to." Involving CEOs at the stage when significant retrenchment programs were being announced, or rolled out, was one approach that had been adopted. Having CEOs address staff and participate in a preliminary meeting with unions signaled that the CEO was 'leading the change.' One example of this approach in action was described by the HR manager of a multinational. The company faced announcing an unprecedented redundancy program to its staff:

> Our MD is a very strong guy anyway and he's pretty tough and ruthless and he always . . . kept the line; he never wavered. . . . He announced three hundred redundancies and he got a round of applause! Now I think that the key to it all was basically that tough decisions had to be made but there was empathy with the people who were going to lose their jobs.

In other instances it was seen as more a case of the senior management team "getting out there in dialogue with people," and this approach appeared to reflect continuity with established practice in the firm. Although the predominant model seen as successful by HR management appeared to be a CEO–leadership model or senior management–leadership model—and this model was sometimes seen as a continuation of established practice—a more team-based leadership model was also articulated, which involved HR, finance and operations managers "all being on the same page in absolutely everything we were planning to do and communicating to their respective people exactly the same message." This approach had been adopted in a context in which leadership in a multinational above the level of the Irish subsidiary was seen to have been fairly negative.

Most focus group participants related their experience of senior managers' willingness to 'stand up to the challenge' and take on a visible leadership role. Inevitably, perhaps, it was not always plain sailing. Participants signaled that competing priorities could also be part of the story, and that business leaders may not always have had the "time or the patience to comply with the best practices that HR practitioners would want to put in place, particularly around communications." It was sometimes necessary, therefore, for HR to "hold the leadership team to a commitment to this process." As for outcomes directly attributed to senior management leadership, one participant spoke in terms of a "huge impact on attitudes and morale."

5.3   ADVOCACY OF VALUES AND POLICIES

Apart from the direct leadership challenges involved in managing pay and headcount, in acting as a business partner and in adopting a proactive response to the challenges facing businesses, some focus group participants pointed to the need as well for HR leadership in other areas. The main areas identified were advocacy of HR values and policies and ensuring that managers in general operated in a fair and proper manner in responding to commercial pressures. In one focus group these themes received significant commentary from a number of contributors, whereas in other focus groups the theme was considerably more muted or even barely touched on.

When the theme received major focus, HR leadership was seen to extend to ensuring that other managers adhered to accepted or espoused HR policies and values and to curbing opportunism on the part of some line managers who may have been intent on using the recession to tackle underperformance and resolve other concerns.

Sometimes advocacy by HR might involve championing, or, as it was also articulated, 'policing,' HR policies under pressure in recessionary conditions. Such an instance arose in a firm committed to a policy of no compulsory layoffs. At senior management meetings this policy had come under pressure:

> Someone says, "Look I've got surplus people here that don't meet your needs over there; they haven't got the skills you need. Why don't we just let these people go, hire in the people we need over here, because it will take too long to train them."

Defending the continued application of an established policy in such an area was seen as "quite stressful" in "the middle of battle," "difficult" and "at times lonely." At the same time it was important to "stay on course on stuff you believe in as a core value for HR." In other instances advocacy of values was necessary when firms affected by significant restructuring sought to make adjustments too quickly and HR managers felt it imperative to "stand for what is best practice in good times and in challenging times." Other HR managers felt that "sometimes the values in an organization get compromised in the necessity to get things done quickly, pressure to do things too quickly." When this might have occurred, the appropriate response was to defend good practice: "HR has to stand up and say, '[L]ook these are our policies, these are our practices. This is the way we have done it and we are going to be doing it that way again." More generally what was described as a shift from an employees' market to an employers' market resulted in HR managers finding themselves in situations where it was necessary to be "more courageous and stand for what is right in all times, not just in good times." The advocacy of values and the championing of good practice in difficult times were seen as more than matters of ethics alone. What one HR manager described as the "internal jury" of the workforce would remember how HR and other managers managed in such circumstances and would draw their own conclusions if, as they put it, managers behaved as if all that mattered was merely "tidying things up through a little bit of bloodletting" before returning to business as usual.

In one focus group, a challenge identified by some HR managers involved in downsizing initiatives involved what one HR manager described as "trying to get control over line managers running away with themselves." The issue here was the propensity of line managers sometimes to use downsizing as a platform for addressing poor performance. This might lead to the emergence of what was variously described as "some convenient selection [decisions] justified under the guise of other processes" and what another described as "names on lists":

> Some [line managers] were of the view that "why waste a good recession," to part company with people who had been a thorn in their side.

The clear view here was that HR managers had to "stand their ground" in the face of such pressure, even though they well understood the frustrations of line managers under pressure to retain their more skilled workers, and possibly faced by last-in-first-out rules supported by unions. More prosaically HR managers had responded to line management opportunism by seeking to win senior management support for their postures and policies and by working with line managers to ensure the probity of the decisions made. This might involve making sure that they were conversant with equality and general employment law, and even going through their decisions and vetoing some of them as untenable.

For one HR manager a dilemma associated with the advent of a business partner HR model, which was otherwise welcomed, concerned the possible response of line managers:

> We haven't enacted [the business partners model] fully because we're nervous. The reality is that they're saying to us . . . the corporation are saying to us, that the HR people should be letting the line managers do their own discipline, do their own dismissals and stuff like that. But we know that on more occasions than one they would get it wrong and we'd be left picking up the pieces and have twice the work. So we're staying very active in it to be honest.

Line managers in one firm involved in implementing a modest redundancy program were seen by HR to be confusing the process with managing under-performance and had to be reminded that redundancy and performance problems were separate processes. In another firm 'reactive' line managers sought to persuade HR to follow the example of what they regarded as robust measures implemented by a "firm down the road." In a distribution firm the senior management of a major client, more conversant with practice in another jurisdiction, pressed the case for cost-effective measures that local HR believed to be unviable in Irish circumstances.

Another theme that emerged concerned the challenges that new measures or new agreements with unions posed for HR when these involved significant measures that had to be implemented by line managers and supervisors. When firms sought to tighten up on the management of disciplinary procedures, line managers who had avoided confronting discipline problems in the past now needed to be trained to better manage discipline and dismissal. In another firm an agreement with unions that incorporated new performance standards posed challenges for team managers, many of whom were viewed as good operational managers but not good people managers:

> So I have to make sure it's kind of as black and white as it can be and there is no grey. . . . The buck stops with me at the end of the day and I have to make sure that the managers are consistent in the way they're applying the procedures.

A similar challenge arose in the context of an agreement on working conditions in a retail firm in which HR felt that it needed to provide documentation 'to set out the process' for store managers in order to avoid inconsistent decisions and resulting grievances.

The perceived need, as part of good HR practice in a recession, to advocate values and defend or police policies pointed to the tensions that could arise when HR worked in closer alignment with the business agenda and with managers directly involved in implementing retrenchment initiatives and related measures. Commercial pressures on established HR policies, or the speed with which initiatives were deployed, or the opportunism of some line managers, could clash with or threaten to compromise HR values and policies, and their primary advocates and protectors, the HR managers. These tensions were highly salient to some HR managers and had been experienced by them in their firms' responses to the recession.

As discussed, this view and the concerns informing it were not universal themes among focus group members. Some HR managers had experienced few such problems, whereas others expressed the view that policing or advocacy was more important vis-à-vis senior management. When questioned about this issue, one HR manager in a significant multinational suggested that his experience had run in the opposite direction: "I think that senior management would be seen to be even more focused on HR values."

The issue of HR values arose in the focus groups in other respects than in the context of possible tensions and conflicts with managers' responses to the recession. Another values-related theme that arose concerned HR managers' empathy with staff facing job losses and concern with 'treating people well' after decisions on redundancies had been made. These responses were connected both to a general concern for people who would lose their jobs and with the provision of outplacement advice and facilities to spare staff as much humiliation as possible. Other values deemed significant were honesty, integrity, being honorable in dealing with staff and coming across as honest. Many focus group contributors also pointed to the importance of trust, and mentioned being forthright and fair.

HR managers in several long-standing Irish firms were of the view that values and ethics were shaped by expectations that were strongly embedded or institutionalized in workforces and management groups with long service. A specific culture arose in such businesses that shaped business responses to the recession and HR management in significant respects. The HR manager for one such firm spoke in terms of his company's "long-established way of doing business and of conducting itself." This spilled over into a distinctive posture toward dealings with staff:

> Most of the managers in our business would have a good understanding of what would be expected of them in terms of, I suppose, the ethics question and how that would sit with the culture of the business.
>
> Staff may expect a little bit more of these type of companies because staff with very, very long service expect a little bit more than in an 'ultra modern' company, where they're not there long and that don't expect to stay there long.

A similar view had informed the decision of another firm to engage with its unions in seeking solutions to serious commercial problems in sharp contrast with the posture of its major competitor that had sought effectively to break unions and outsource significant areas of work. Embedded expectations of this kind could even outlive the immediate context that produced them and survive as a legacy influencing a company under new ownership, as evidenced by the remark of a HR manager that the ghost of the previous proprietor was still hanging over the business.

5.4 ENGAGING WITH UNIONS

Two-thirds of the firms in which focus group participants worked were unionized. Focus group participants in firms recognizing unions were asked how unions had responded to the pressures presented to them by firms and whether unions had altered the manner in which they represented members. The predominant view was that unions had reacted "pragmatically," were conversant with the "realities of the situation," showed "more realization of the reality of the world" and had "engaged constructively." Some HR managers believed that union officials commonly appreciated problems to a greater degree than did their members, with resulting problems in "selling their message to their members" or "bringing their members with them." Relations with unions were commonly portrayed as good or positive, but in some cases it was clear that relations had been more strained or fractious— not always as a direct outcome of the recession and attendant pressures— and there had been resort on several occasions to the Labour Relations Commission or to other third parties in search of settlements to disputes. In one firm the HR manager attributed the drawn-out process of winning agreement to defer a pay rise and to change work arrangements and working conditions to interunion rivalry and conflict. In two firms, unions' negative postures were seen to have been triggered in significant respects by firms' pursuance of concessions that, with hindsight, were viewed as excessive. In one case, such a posture by a young management team with little experience of earlier recessions meant that the firm had been "open to the allegation that we were trying to exploit the recession." In a retail firm, the union's initial skepticism concerning management's search for concessions was seen as an understandable reaction in a sector that had been seen as long profitable: "so they weren't going to rush into making concessions to us as a sector when they had that perception as to how we had done during the boom."

Information disclosure and communication: The HR managers had clearly defined views on how best to deal with trade unions in responding to the pressures unleashed by the recession. One aspect of their understanding of good practice in this area involved addressing the relationship with trade unions as part of the more general concern with communications and communications strategies. Just as communicating with greater intensity was seen to be necessary vis-à-vis employees, so too was it deemed necessary to communicate with trade unions on change programs to be implemented. So information was commonly shared with unions, and sometimes this was seen as marking continuity with practice before the recession. Communications had engendered a 'strong business awareness' and had served the purpose of providing education in the pressures on the business. In one case, as earlier discussed, senior executives attended regular management–union meetings to provide briefings on conditions in different product markets. One HR manager, who had been surprised by the level of buy-in achieved from the union for a program of pay and increment freezes and changes in working hours, attributed this to the firm's strong communications strategy. Early and full information disclosure was also regarded by some as a critical aspect of good practice in engaging unions. Referring to the union as a 'key stakeholder,' a HR manager emphasized the importance of "involving them early, keeping them in the loop, working through the process and avoiding vacuums being created." Another manager was equally clear as to what was required to gain agreement on retrenchment measures. His experience pointed to the need to

> share with the unions very openly the full facts in relation to what had happened in our business; how it had literally fallen over a cliff . . . that helped with the union group and subsequently with the staff.

Others agreed that unions preferred "not to have any surprises" and to "get the information up front," even if informally, so that they could plan how they would deal with their own members. Another HR manager indicated that preparations for the introduction of a pay and increment freeze had involved the company sharing its profit-and-loss account with a small number of key union officials and representatives on a confidential basis. The information disclosed included projections of the financial consequences of not making the changes proposed. This practice not only had met with a positive response from the union, but had also elicited a reminder that the company had not been so willing to disclose information when it was profitable and a wish to see this practice preserved after the company's return to profitability! In another firm a new owner had resisted sharing financial information with their unions, leading the HR manager to insist that they had to—both with the unions and with a union assessor involved in the search for a resolution to a dispute.

In one firm a partnership agreement with unions that had been established well in advance of the recession and in a context where the firm faced significant competitive pressures was seen to have been highly effective in facilitating change in the recession "at a rate never known before." Responding to a comment by a HR manager in a nonunion firm that had they had to deal with unions they would have gone out of business, the HR manager in the partnership firm insisted otherwise:

> Some people think that a consultation process can slow things down or impede progress. That's not our experience. . . . We had a meeting of our joint communicative council at 9.30 in the morning. We met the senior managers at 10.30 and we went and met the group of unions . . . and made a joint announcement the next day detailing the pay cuts that had been agreed and that were recommended by the unions. And it was balloted on within two weeks and pay cuts were implemented [soon after]. Now, we've never worked at that kind of speed with our unions before, but I think the big thing that worked for us because we did adhere to the process [was that] it gave the union confidence that we weren't actually trying to use the recession or the downturn in a negative way.

In another firm with a history of stable accommodation of union representation, a change of ownership combined with the effects of the recession posed the dilemma of whether to involve or seek to marginalize unions in the firm's response:

> We were badly hit by the recession and I suppose there was a train of thought that we should just go for the jugular here and try to get everything we needed and not involve the unions. Or should we get the unions in and have straightforward discussions with them? We decided on the latter and we got into discussions with the unions on a raft of different proposals.

Deeper engagement with the unions was seen to have been successful from the company's vantage point and to have achieved significant outcomes, in part through renewing existing agreements. A dilemma that was identified in the area of information disclosure in another firm concerned making provision simultaneously to inform both the union and nonrepresented staff in a company, most of whom were managers. As engagement with the union was underway, the company felt it advisable to handle carefully when information would be disclosed to nonrepresented managers, to avoid being seen to 'steal the union's thunder' and so impair the relationship with the union. This approach was adopted even though it was also recognized that the nonrepresented managers were key agents in feeding and cascading information to the company's employees.

Expediting negotiations: A number of focus group participants also expressed frustration with the slowness of traditional collective bargaining in the face of rapid commercial changes that required a prompt response. Where collective bargaining was concerned there was a perception that there was a "pace and order in normal times" that would not work in the exceptional conditions that had been encountered in the recession. As one put it "we just didn't have enough time" to proceed as before, and when it came to changes involving 'money issues' this caused friction with the unions: "Unions found it difficult. They couldn't understand why we had to go at the pace we had . . . That created a bit of an issue between ourselves and the unions, to be frank." Although the pace with which employers sought to conduct collective bargaining and conclude agreements had increased, similar problems arose in a firm that had a tradition of partnership-based working with unions. The traditional partnership approach was portrayed as slow and tedious, and this presented a challenge in responding to external change that was now "so rapid in its impact"; "the same ground-rules would not work in bad times as in good." An attempt to speed up the pace and intensity of engagement through partnership had also given rise to tensions with the union. In another case reported in the focus group, a firm had been prepared to impose a "guillotine" on collective bargaining: bringing the process to an end and acting unilaterally if an agreement could not be secured within the requisite commercial time frame. As discussed in the previous chapter, the HR managers could identify few specific quid pro quo sought by, or accorded to, unions in return for agreeing pay freezes or headcount reductions. Sometimes this reflected a reality in which, as one HR manager put it, firms had "absolutely nothing to give back."

Having regard to fairness: Echoing a long-running theme in human resource management and industrial relations, a number of HR managers stressed the importance of having regard to fairness in formulating and in negotiating concessions in response to the recession. Concern with fairness was not restricted to HR managers in unionized firms, but the theme was developed more fully and concretely in that context. In one firm, cost reduction measures presented to different categories of unionized and nonrepresented staff had been broadly similar because, in the words of the HR manager involved, "we tried to be fair across all these." Seeking fairness in this sense was understood as having important practical consequences. Nonrepresented salaried staff had been "much easier to deal with," but the firm was aware that treating them unfairly "might move them to organize themselves." Fairness also dictated the need for awareness of parity of treatment of different categories whose agreements terminated at different times. Sometimes firms found themselves seeking different concessions from different groups, some unionized and others not, and here the challenge was seen to involve educating staff to understand why certain issues were covered in existing collective agreements and could not be altered without successful renegotiation. In another firm, fairness was seen to be best served by implementing disproportionate cuts in pay at the highest salary levels with tapered cuts at lower levels and a salary threshold below which no cuts would be made. To the surprise of the HR manager involved, some thought the threshold arrangement unfair, and it was removed in a subsequent round of pay cuts where cuts affected staff at all levels. In other cases graduated cuts had been accepted by employees. HR managers also commented that fairness was best served by implementing redundancy programs at all levels— including senior and middle management—rather than confining job losses to lower staff categories. A HR manager involved in implementing reductions in working hours also underscored the importance of fairness and consistency in this aspect of working conditions and the need to confront staff resisting concessions made by their colleagues. One HR manager displayed a jaundiced view of the extent to which unions sought to act in a fair way, citing their insistence on the last-in-first-out principle, which was seen to work to the advantage of union members and staff with seniority, and "sacrifice" newer staff.

A number of focus group members were of the view that good preexisting relations with unions, whether through collective bargaining or through workplace partnership, had been an asset in their attempts to engage unions in responding to the pressures of the recession. Although unions had been realistic and pragmatic in their response to company retrenchment proposals they had also had their "own agendas" and nonnegotiable issues. Prominent here was the priority accorded to voluntary over compulsory measures for reducing headcount and a complete unwillingness to negotiate over severance criteria other than seeking volunteers or operating on the last-in-first-out principle. Some focus group participants were heavily critical of unions for, as they saw it, prioritizing pay and conditions over jobs. They observed that it had been their experience that unions were extremely reluctant to negotiate downward adjustments to pay and conditions as a way of preserving jobs and significantly more willing to countenance redundancies and other measures to cut labor supply. Some also felt that unions should have been more amenable in their dealings with companies that had been willing to recognize them and to provide good pay and conditions to their members.

Unions and innovation: In general, the HR managers viewed unions as reactive to management proposals for dealing with the effects of the recession and believed that they showed little capacity to provide innovative options for responding to problems. In one instance, union officials had prompted a company to opt for short-time working as its main response to the recession. In another instance, a union had sought company support for the holding of a general training program for activists on the company's premises. Another company had been asked to allow staff that had been laid off to come to work to gain experience in the operation of a new piece of equipment in order to improve their overall skill level. Other than in instances such as these, however, there was a clear sense that, as one HR manager put it, "the company creates the initiatives and the unions respond." One company had presented a series of costed options for responding to the recession to the unions representing its unionized staff categories and to its nonrepresented staff. It had also indicated to the unions involved the company's willingness to consider counter proposals from the unions themselves, with some constrains on what would be entertained. In the words of the HR manager involved "they came back with nothing, absolutely nothing," opting instead to engage in constructive dialogue around the options presented by management. One constraint on innovation identified was the concern of some unions with the "national agenda" and on ensuring the local agreements were consistent with their posture thereon.

Spontaneously mentioned in one focus group as something that could cause difficulties was what one HR manager referred to as unions' "not wasting a good recession *phobia.*" In their view, this reflected a general concern within the trade union world. HR managers denied that using the recession to achieve desired changes in terms and conditions had been a feature of adjustment programs in their own companies. They believed that unions would quickly see through such a posture and that it would make the business of finding accommodation and reaching agreement more difficult. They were emphatic that in their experience "this is about getting through a period" and that there were no disguised agendas revolving around "trying to rebalance the playing field." As one HR manager, seeking to articulate the view of the whole group, put it, "We are all trying to navigate our way through a recession here and coming out intact in the best possible shape as far as everybody is concerned." A case was cited where a reassurance was articulated in an agreement with the unions that it was not the company's objective to bring about a permanent diminution in terms and conditions of employment. Opportunism was seen as something that pertained mainly to individual managers, to echo a theme discussed earlier in the chapter.

5.5   PROFESSIONAL AND PERSONAL NETWORKS

A theme introduced spontaneously by the HR managers in one focus group when discussing good HR practice was the greater use of professional and personal networks to share information, provide briefings in key areas such as handling downsizing and redundancies and to identify models of good practice. The theme was examined by the researchers in subsequent focus groups with broadly similar results. Networking activity seemed of greater significance to HR managers in the capital, possibly because some formal networks met more regularly or frequently. Some of the networks had long existed either on a sectoral basis or under the aegis of employer bodies. But there was agreement that they had become more important in the recession in developing knowledge and skills in areas like downsizing, where HR managers had acquired little experience over the past decade. There was agreement that regular meetings of these networks or 'forums' had become significantly better attended in recent years and that they had been "proactive" quite early on holding meetings to address issues such as redundancy. The modus of these networks was described by some as "very informal" but allowing for a "lot of information sharing." IBEC was one of the bodies that facilitated networking of this kind. As well as drawing more intensively on professional networks, some pointed to the greater importance in recent years also of personal networks, usually comprised of colleagues and contacts working in the same sector and conversant with the same kinds of challenges. As one HR manager put it, "on a personal level I would have had more contact with my HR counterparts . . . in the last year than I've had for a number of years. So there is a lot of contact, a lot informally, but nevertheless very meaningful." In the regions, networking appeared less in evidence in dealing with the challenges of the recession or was not seen as playing such an active role in HR managers' responses. This was not because networks were not in existence: sector networks and CIPD were offered as examples of professional networks to which people had resorted. A HR manager in one multinational indicated that the internal network, represented by colleagues in different territories, was the most useful and its use was not related to the recession. The HR manager in a hospital saw formalized metrics in HR that allowed comparisons across health service units as a functional equivalent of networks. Another HR manager viewed the periodical IRN as a more general provider of such benchmarking information.

5.5   CONCLUSION

When HR managers were asked to discuss their views of good or best practice human resource management in the recession, they focused mainly on
a series of clear themes. The most prominent of these was the importance
of intensive communications with staff and unions regarding the commercial pressures confronted by firms and the responses deemed appropriate.
Reflecting and expanding on the survey results in Chapter 3, HR managers
indicated that they and their firms had communicated more intensively with
employees in the recession than ever before. The communication mechanisms employed were well familiar, and few clear trends were apparent in
their relative usage. For the most part, the emphasis was on communication from firms to their employees and to varying degrees to their unions.
Two-way communication or upward communication seemed considerably
less pronounced. The balance of communication activity seemed to be
tilted toward direct communications with staff rather than communication
with staff representatives. There were instances of joint communiqués with
unions and of the use of management–union communication structures, but
their use seemed to reflect attempts to deal with unusually fractious relations
with unions or arose from preexisting partnership arrangements.

Again reflecting the survey results, HR managers also commonly indicated that senior management had been harnessed to the task of communication more than in the past. This strategy was adopted to add credibility
to communications and to the measures communicated to employees and
unions. HR continued to play a role in formulating the communications
fronted by senior executives. There was more to this development than simply prevailing on senior managers to deliver the message to employees or
unions. The key development involved harnessing senior managers in leading HR responses to the recession.

A number of HR managers spoke of the importance of advocacy by HR
managers of policies that might have been challenged, strained or undermined
by the recession and, more generally, that pointed to the abiding importance
of values seen to be at the core of good HR management. Although the
degree to which HR policies or values may have been strained or under
threat varied across firms, a number of sources of strain were identified.
Line managers, focused single-mindedly on meeting commercial challenges,
might sometimes try to cut corners and use the recession to resolve problems
of underperformance or discipline, or may sometimes simply have lacked
the skills, experience and training to enact the roles required to implement
HR measures. Overlapping this issue but also a distinct concern was the
importance of underscoring values of abiding concern in HR management:
values such as honesty, integrity, transparency, trust and fairness. Values
like these were palpably of concern to HR managers and were understood
as abiding features of good HR in the recession, as in other conditions. In
long-standing Irish firms, staff and managers, often of long tenure, were

seen as having particularly clear expectations as to how firms should do business and treat employees, and these expectations were adjudged to be of continuing significance.

HR managers in firms that recognized unions had clear ideas about effective engagement with trade unions in recessionary conditions. In general, reflecting the survey results, unions and their officials were portrayed as constructive, realistic and pragmatic in their dealings with firms. Firms commonly avowed the importance of sharing information, including financial information, with unions. Experience in negotiations with unions in the recession appeared more mixed. Some HR managers expressed frustration with the time taken to revise agreements and reach accord on new measures. The general view was that it was necessary in turbulent or uncertain commercial conditions to expedite negotiations with unions and that the traditional model of collective bargaining was no longer viable. Unions were seen for the most part as reactive in their responses to the recession and were not generally seen as effective in proposing innovative responses to the challenges of the recession. Good preexisting relations nonetheless facilitated engagement and agreement.

A concern with fairness in the treatment of different categories of staff was also underscored as an aspect of good human resource management, and this theme was developed in particular in relation to staff in unionized firms.

A number of HR managers indicated that they had made more use of personal and professional networks as sources of advice, intelligence and support in handling the HR challenges of the recession. HR metrics and other sources of information useful for benchmarking practices and performance had also been used in some cases.

These findings have a number of implications for our understanding of good human resource management in the recession, of current ideas of good HR in general and for debates on the future of HR and employment arrangements. First, HR managers' views of good HR in a recession largely echoed the received view as to how good HR in general should be understood. When the researchers sought to provoke focus group participants by asking baldly whether the HRM textbooks needed to be rewritten to incorporate the effects of recessionary conditions on HR practice, the common response was that long-standing principles and practices remained relevant and robust. Some were of the view that, at most, some modification of these principles and practices might be required, but what this might involve was not clearly identified. The corollary of this position and the import of our findings in general is that little striking innovation is evident in the practices or approaches adopted by firms and their HR managers in response to the recession. Many of the established tools in the HR toolkit appear to be regarded as 'fit for purpose' by HR managers with deep experience of responding to the serious and acute commercial challenges unleashed by recessionary conditions. At the same time, some changes in the relative importance or priority of different areas of HR practice were clearly evident.

Besides the enormous effort devoted to managing pay and headcount, the overriding significance HR managers attributed to intensive communications was striking; managing underperformance and discipline was noted as a new development by a number of HR managers; recruitment had ceased to be a major concern, and HRD effort had been significantly reduced in many firms. What emerges here is a reprioritization of familiar areas of HR practice in recessionary conditions rather than any profound challenge to the underlying HR and employment paradigm, much less any signs of any paradigm shift.

The theme of employee engagement also seemed considerably more muted in practice than might be expected from the burgeoning recent literature on this area, or indeed from the survey findings. For sure, firms and their HR managers sought to grapple with hard as well as soft aspects of HR management: motivation, commitment and values continued to matter for many even in the face of acute pay cuts and headcount reductions. But specific programs for engagement or reengagement, or specific initiatives in this direction, were not commonly in evidence. The firms that underscored the continuing importance of this area most of all, seemed to be those least seriously affected by the recession. One firm acutely affected by the recession that had operated a formal engagement program indicated that it had to turn aside from this, while maintaining some specific initiatives in the area, but that it also intended to return to the theme. Rather than the kind of proactive and vigorous harnessing of employee (or union) involvement in identifying and implementing business options—supported by two-way communications and multiple involvement initiatives—commonly canvassed in the engagement literature and in arguments about the transformative effects of the recession, what was encountered more often was quite different. The dominant pattern involved in the main one-way (top-down) communication, increasing the intensity of work regimes, a new concern to manager underperformance and discipline and the suspension of profit sharing or performance bonuses. For the most part, the values that continued to matter for HR managers in delivering commitment, or at least compliance, were values of a conventional kind: trust, honesty, transparency and fairness supported in the main by rather conventional HR practices. In the same way, to reprise a theme developed in the previous chapter, HR seemed to have become more central to businesses mainly in terms of a harder agenda focused on pay and headcount control and management. HR had not gained this ascendancy around an engagement or high-commitment paradigm that had been made more urgent and compelling by the most serious commercial crisis of modern times.

6 Trade Union Officials
Representing Members in the Recession

Survey results in Chapter 3 and the HR focus groups in Chapters 4 and 5 point to a quite mixed picture with respect to managers' views on the representative activities of unions during the recession. Firms in general and HR focus group participants view unions in the main as having adopted a realistic and pragmatic posture in the face of the pressures experienced by employers. Managers claim as a general rule to have engaged in some way with unions in negotiations over HR response measures, albeit that such engagement varied in depth and only a minority of firms actively engaged trade unions. Some managers believe that unions have retarded their firms' responses by insisting on detailed and protracted negotiations. Firms and HR focus group members underline that few supports to organization or representation were traded for union cooperation in agreeing response measures. Financial claw-back arrangements for union members when business conditions improved were also rare. These data point toward most firms' willingness in one way or another to accommodate unions rather than to launch any frontal onslaught against union representation during the recession.

Absent from the story so far have been the views and experiences of union officials themselves. This chapter examines the views of union officials who participated in a series of focus groups that took place in Dublin, Cork and Galway. The 17 participants in the union focus groups, 16 of whom were full-time union officials, represented employees working in the private, commercial state-owned sectors and, in some instances, in the public sector. They worked with the following unions: the Services, Industrial and Professional and Technical Union (SIPTU); Mandate; the National Union of Journalists (NUJ); the Communication Workers' Union (CWU); Unite; the Technical, Engineering and Electrical Union (TEEU); and the Irish Municipal, Public and Civil Trade Union (IMPACT). Between them these unions account for 62% of all trade union members in Ireland. They organize and represent members across a wide span of Irish industry and services in both the private and public sectors.

The focus groups were set up in the same way as those of the HR managers. Participants received briefing documentation on the nature and scope of the research study in advance of the focus group meetings. This documentation asked them to reflect on the following issues:

1. The ways in which firms and unions have been affected by the recession
2. HR's response to the recession and the challenges their response posed for union representatives
3. The constituents of good HR practice in firms that take cognizance of all stakeholder interests
4. Union priorities in representing members during this period
5. The focus of collective bargaining and whether any concessions were made by unions in return for job security, or more influence or other gains

In addition (again, as was the case with the HR managers), a series of specific HR practices, identified in the literature on HR as being commonly adopted in recessionary times, were also included in the material for their consideration. These HR practices covered the following areas:

- Wage adjustment
- Employment adjustment
- Reorganization of working time
- Workforce stabilization
- Employability (assisting employees made redundant to obtain retraining)
- Process or product innovation
- Voice (new forms of employee involvement or collective bargaining)
- Content or focus of collective bargaining

At the start of the focus group, participants were made aware that the areas identified in the briefing material and those used to structure the focus groups were not intended to put a limit or boundary on the issues to be discussed. Participants were asked to share their own views based on their professional experience and were informed that they were not viewed in any sense as representing their own unions' views on the areas under discussion. Participants were given instructions on the manner in which the focus group would be conducted and on the uses that would be made of the data collected.

This chapter first looks at union officials' views on the effects of the recession on both their relationship with employers and with their own members. Following on from this is a discussion on the nature of collective bargaining in the recession. Unions then give their viewpoint as to the features of good HR practice and the drivers of good practice. The chapter ends with a brief account of union views on the public sector (related only to those parts of the public sector represented by the focus group participants, i.e., the health sector including voluntary agencies funded by this sector, local authorities and higher education institutions).

6.1   THE EFFECTS OF THE RECESSION

As union officials, the focus group participants were involved with firms that had been severely affected by the recession in terms of falling revenues and market pressures. Although it was business as usual for a number of firms, in that both unions and management sat down together and attempted to work out how best to solve the difficulties facing them, all the focus group participants highlighted significant new difficulties and challenges that have arisen for them as a result of the recession.

A major negative impact of the recession for many of the focus group participants was the change in the union's relationship with the employer. Where good relationships had existed between both parties in the past, in that the union "would be contacted properly and a sequence of meetings would take place . . . to discuss possible changes," unions were now being bypassed in a number of firms: "HR are by-passing the process and instigating change from the floor . . . now you're getting a call from a shop steward or a member saying that they're just rolling in these changes." This has obviously created a problem for unions, in that much of their energies had now to be taken up by trying to get the employer to the table in the first place. This issue is discussed in greater detail under the heading of collective bargaining.

A number of different factors contribute to this 'new' relationship with some employers according to the focus group participants. A primary driver is the current state of the labor market. Buoyed up by the strong available labor supply, focus group participants were of the view that some employers were being opportunistic when it came to implementing change in response to the recession. They claim that employers were taking advantage of employees' fears: "People are terrified now because they're saying the unemployment rate is going up and up. If they don't bow to whatever pressure is put on them . . . sign this piece of paper and accept a ten percent cut or your job is going . . . then they could be out there as well without a job." Employees had therefore been agreeing to any pay cuts or changes that management wanted. Unions were having difficulty convincing members to stand up to employers given the background threat of losing their jobs. The focus group members told how some companies have "acted unilaterally and they have gotten away with actually a lot really because of the climate of fear that's out there."

Another factor contributing to the breakdown of 'normal' relations between employers and trade unions, as perceived by the focus group participants, was the speed with which the recession has developed and the consequent perceived need for immediate cost-cutting action by businesses. The union representatives present stated that they found themselves in a position where they were forced to react:

> You're reacting to an announcement by a company that they're going to downsize, whereas previously they might have been in and they would be talking to you in advance about it and you'd have an opportunity to

make or put forward an alternative. [Now] you're being given less and less time to do it.

Companies did not want long negotiations, according to the union representatives. HRs have told the unions that they are under too much pressure to give the unions time:

> They abandoned the chance of a good deal for . . . speed and because you go to the Labour Court doesn't automatically guarantee you a resolution. That's very frustrating, so if HR managers were to commit to adequate time it would certainly lead to better deals, better agreements.

Some companies "want implementation with immediate effect," leaving unions little time to tackle the issues and develop a strategic approach or consult with their members. The push for urgent and speedy change was seen as being a contrast to the traditional way unions and employers did business.

A third factor contributing to the undermining and destabilizing of the traditional union–employer relationship according to the focus group members, has been a change in business culture and ideology. Business at national level has pulled back from social partnership, and this, in the unions' view, has given employers license to 'do their own thing.' For some it was seen as a signal from the center to go it alone:

> My view is that social partnership was an ideology that suited employers for the twenty odd years that it was in vogue and as soon as it didn't they were pulling away from that . . . it suited employers because it was a way of regulating wages and in fact during the boom years when there were huge profits being made . . . it was wage restraint and it allowed employers to pay minimal pay increases and to take huge profits.

The unions believe that there is a strong antiunion ideology abroad now, often supported by the media (it was pointed out that many newspaper groups were now owned by big corporations) and that this antiunion ideology has filtered down as far as HR in some firms:

> We've got employers now who traditionally would have gone through the procedures of local meetings, going to the LRC and going to the Labour Court. Now they're saying we're not participating in that. Why? Because they don't have to and they're following the lead of other employers who have done the same . . . so and so didn't do it so we're not doing it either.

Union focus group participants bemoaned both the loss of the predecessor to the human resources manager, that is, the personnel manager, "[who] generally speaking, was somebody who had come up through the company, who had a relationship with the employees . . . because he was deemed to be responsible for their wellbeing within the company," and the traditional way of doing business with the employer, that is, where the personnel officer "negotiated with the union because there was a relationship with the union official." They point to a change in focus: "there is no real attention (now) being brought to the way business is done and should be done . . . there is a different focus . . . away from the welfare type toward the HR manager being a company representative." The participants pointed out the "general lack of importance attached to the union-management agreement, whereas, going back fifteen or twenty years . . . the union management agreement was your bible. . . ." Now, the union representatives claimed, the focus for HR professional training is on the needs of the firm, that they have become business managers: "the role of the HR function today is less about developing relationships with the union official and more about delivering a shareholder bottom line . . . we are viewed unfortunately, as an impediment or some sort of obstacle." However, whatever reservations or problems the focus group members were having with HR, they did point out that a company with some kind of HR structure is better than a company with none: "in weaker, smaller companies, where employees are more open to the vagaries of whatever change might be taking place in their sector and where HR is needed to be most proactive and innovative, it's rarely if ever there."

Among the focus group participants, there was a view that there was a serious shift in the idea that employers wished to retain staff. "In good times, a good employer's agenda is driven by a desire to retain people," where as now "in the recession the only responsibility employers have taken is to survive and be competitive and others are rowing in behind that to pursue a maximum, long term profits agenda." "People at the top now see their staff as a liability, who could be replaced from an open market much cheaper than they're being paid." They wanted to get rid of the staff "brought in when times were better." Some of the participants compared the current recession to that of the 1980s, where, it was claimed, there seemed to be a more human attitude taken to job losses:

> If an employer came in and said I've got to cut jobs, they felt nearly that they were failing and letting down the people that they had brought in . . . whereas nowadays it's like, people are not people, people are just commodities or numbers. An awful lot of the management is done at arm's length and seen as numbers rather than any kind of personal added-value being given to a company.

A number of the focus group participants called for a strengthening of the existing industrial relations legislation to help address, what they perceive to be, the current power imbalance between unions and employers. Given the essential voluntary nature of collective bargaining in Ireland, the system relies, to some extent, on the honor of the participants. Because employers were now no longer honoring existing agreements, according to the focus group participants, current legalization needed to be strengthened: "I think at the moment within the current system we have dispute resolution that's voluntarist, and it is being largely ignored by employers, and that's a problem. So two things have to happen, it either has to be strengthened legislation-wise or the employers have to step up and fulfil their responsibilities in participating."

The focus group participants also called for the resources of the Labour Court and conciliation services to be increased because of the demands of the recession. "Cases need to be speeded up. People don't want to hang around for six or eight months and particularly where jobs are threatened, there's going to have to be some fast track method of dealing with the most, the next urgent case as opposed to which one it is and where it is on the list."

One further change that has come about as a result of the recession relates to the nature of the relationship between unions and their members. Prior to the recession, according to focus group participants, "there were a number of things that removed you from your membership." During the time of social partnership, the union representatives stated that their members did not see the link to the work that the unions did on their behalf at national level. This had helped to bring about an attitude of entitlement among workers: "I've heard on numerous occasions, sure we are entitled to that anyway." Annual pay increases negotiated at national level, according to some participants, were seen as government increases. Other factors have also contributed to the distancing between union officials and their members: "You would walk into a factory, you would walk down, chat on the factory floor stuff, now it's all signing in, ID cards, the plastic things that you pin on and there is this barrier." According to the focus group participants, the recession has highlighted the need for them to review their relationship with their members and to try to engage more directly with them in the workplace.

One obvious impact of the recession is the major loss of jobs and some not just temporarily. Although this was felt across all sectors, the loss of manufacturing jobs in some traditional industries such as rubber, plastics and clothing was very keenly felt. This was the case both because of the availability of cheap replacement imports and because of the fact that some of these industries were linked to the declining construction sector. It was also stated by the focus group participants that the impact of the recession was hidden in the retail sector. The reason for this was to do with the large numbers of part-time workers in this sector in addition to workers on minimum-hours contracts. The hours are being cut back, but as the contracts have not been broken, the union did not have any avenue to challenge this "even though the amount of hours taken out of a particular shop is the same as a factory closing." Against this backdrop, matters relating to the collective bargaining process were explored.

6.2 COLLECTIVE BARGAINING IN THE RECESSION

In broad terms, employers were predominately pursuing adjustments to varying degrees that would bring about reductions in employment costs. These were mainly in the areas of wages and benefits, overtime, headcount and/or working hours, according to the unions. Unions, for their part, have focused on protecting jobs and preserving terms and conditions of employment. They were 'trying to hold onto as much as possible . . . to avoid compulsory redundancies by way of reduced working weeks and a voluntary redundancy package.' On the positive side, where engagement has been meaningful with the employer, unions believed that they had managed to influence the agenda away from compulsory redundancies, to talking about reduction in hours, in addition to changes in contracts and additional flexibility. For some employees, (such as employees with long service) and in specific sectors (for example, the construction sector) rather than face massive change in their workplace and their work practices, voluntary redundancy packages have been taken up, and unions have tried to facilitate this.

The focus group participants indicated, however, that the recession had brought out different responses from employers in terms of both 'good' and 'sharp' practices. Good practice involved the union being called in by the company and being asked to work with them to achieve a solution. All of the focus group participants gave examples of companies that came to the table and with which they had completed deals, involving pay cuts, pay freezes, redundancies, and so on. They had also "tried to engage on alternative cost savings and productivity measures."

Whether meaningful discussions actually occurred, however, in the eyes of focus group participants often depended on a number of factors. For some unions, the very process of negotiation itself was hampered by what they considered to be the "serious lack of expertise and experience from a HR point of view." This lack of negotiation experience was often compounded by the fact that many HR managers were either not aware of the existence of an agreement between the employer and union or did not know the detail of the agreement, according to union representatives: "I'd have to say the response back from an awful lot of the HR managers is—what document is that?" Another factor believed to be hampering the negotiation process was the quality of the advice given to HR practitioners: "the advice that they get tends to be: . . . 'just do it,' even from their own organisations, 'take a chance, sure its bad out there, but the workers will wear it.' And that causes a lot of adversarial reaction that isn't needed." The cutbacks in the HR department itself also meant, in some instances, that the HR person with whom the union had developed a good working relationship was no longer with the company. The outcome of this was that

> there is a serious lack of someone who knows how people actually think, who knows how to bring people along with them and who knows how to do a deal with a union official at the end of the day.

The unions also found that HR staff were often just as worried as everyone else about losing their jobs.

Another factor affecting negotiations with employers was the attitude from corporate headquarters according to the focus group participants. With certain sectors or industries, it was "recognized that you had to do business with the union." However, even in the cases in which a good relationship may have existed with HR in Ireland, instructions on how to proceed in the recession may have come from outside Ireland, for example, corporate headquarters in the United Kingdom or the United States. The non-Irish parent organization, working from a different agenda and with little knowledge of industrial relations in Ireland, often wanted their decisions to be implemented with immediate effect and often unilaterally. HR's commitment to staff in Ireland had then to be overruled. The notion too, that "things are done differently in Ireland" was easier to sell to nonunionized UK and US companies and multinationals in a time when doing business was profitable and labor shortages existed, according to the focus group participants: "now that's turned around . . . and therefore any ability to influence parent companies or financial controllers . . . is gone and that, I think that's a key difference." An example quoted by a focus group participant illustrates this point: "Ireland is now seeing a drop in the level of redundancy payments . . . whereas in the past the level of the redundancy settlement sent a message to staff that the company would look after them."

With regard to the sharp practices (mentioned earlier), the focus group participants stated that in certain companies, normal industrial relations processes and procedures were being ignored. "Most disputes have arisen because employers have broken pre-existing agreements":

> I was in the LRC some months back where company X was being brought to task and there were I think something like between thirty and forty Labour Court recommendations across all sectors of employment that they had agreed to implement, which they didn't, and they sat opposite us and admitted that they hadn't.

The focus group also stated that disciplinary procedures were being ignored:

> In the past somebody might have been counselled, you know, if you got a verbal (warning) in an unofficial capacity by a supervisor or manager. Now it's—sure there are four hundred and twenty odd thousand people on the dole, give them a final written warning. If they step out of line in the next year they're gone, we can get somebody else in.

There was a view among the focus group participants that companies were looking for reasons to dismiss people because they could not afford to keep them anymore. Companies "were managing [people] out of the company," a case of "catch me if you can, take me to the wherever you want, and . . . I'll settle if I have to at some point." Given that the length of time it might take to get a meeting with a Rights Commissioner for an Unfair Dismissals case could be up to two years, it was alleged that this suited employers and that if they (the employers) lost, the penalties did not have any detrimental effect. The focus group participants also stated that they saw an increase in the severity of the penalties being meted out to employees: "the penalties are way more severe, what you might get a slap on the wrist before, you are actually getting a formal warning for or no warning. Something you previously get a warning for, you could actually get dismissed for now."

An obvious knock-on effect of these sharp practices has been the erosion of trust between management and employees. In describing one situation, a focus group union participant referred to a meeting that day with an employer to discuss 250 job losses. She wondered whether it was really 250 job losses or was it because

> this particular company has tried to erode every term and condition of employment that is in being in the particular firm. This firm took over another one about four years ago and recognized everything at the time under previous agreements. Just in the last twelve months it really doesn't like what it signed up to in 2006 and hasn't progressed their agenda of cuts and so now has decided that the best way of cutting is to say 250 people are going to lose their jobs.

The focus group participants were having difficulties in deciding which companies were really in trouble and which were "trying it on," whether the motivation was "repositioning for a recovery or to dilute wages." Some employers were using the recession, according to the focus group, to cut costs to unnecessary levels and to gain back concessions negotiated during earlier times. There were some companies in the retail sector, according to the participants, who were looking for major concessions while at the same time "declaring straight up they were making huge profits." Other companies threatened to close if unions did not agree to drastic changes, even going so far as to announce a possible closure to the media. One union official described it as the employer "looking for one permanent hit at the union, while they are weak and while the workforce is scared." Given the condition of the labor market and what was happening in other organizations, employers have been able to challenge and avoid their trade unions, even in sectors that were still profitable, according to the union representatives. When unions do not have density in an organization, a fear was expressed that there was little they could do about this.

The focus group participants discussed the negative implications of employers taking an opportunistic stance. They agreed that it usually ended up leading to more difficulties between unions and employers, generating more of an 'us and them' conflictual-type engagement. If the employer asks for too much, staff are often aware of this and hold back and do not want to cooperate: "people are just saying—'not going there' even though there might be a genuine need to make some savings but because it's perceived that they're looking for more than is fair and reasonable then everybody pulls completely back. So relations then would go downhill." The focus group participants stated that they believed they were not always being given the full truth. Unions felt that "when you dig deep into it you find on many occasions it's not the situation that's being put to you, you're not being told the full story. Sometimes it's a company that are making an awful lot of money . . . using it as an opportunity to cut back on conditions."

The success of collective bargaining is seen to be predicated on both unions and employers recognizing the process as the principal means of organizing dealings between workers and employers. According to the focus group participants, this recognition by employers, in some instances, has not been forthcoming:

> Whereas in previous recessions the collective agreement was always sacrosanct and there was a decorum there, let's be honest, among representatives, either IBEC or SIPTU or any union, that we will get a heads up on these things, and I have seen now the last two years, many examples where the heads up is not occurring, we are not getting the phone calls in advance and you could certainly take a very dim view of that, that the intention is to put us under pressure from the beginning as opposed to embracing I suppose an open discussion about this being a shared problem.

Unions were finding it difficult both to get employers to come to the table, and to resist unilateral action being taken by them. A number of unions complained of the necessity to ballot for industrial action just to get an employer to engage with them:

> The vast majority of my ballots for industrial action in the current environment are to stop unilateral actions being taken and I have to take that step because in the initial engagement the employer said, "I don't want to talk to you, you've no significance for me. If your members want to be part of a trade union that's their own affair, I don't have to recognize you." And that's the stance that they take which puts me in a position as an official of having to go back to my members and say look, we're going to have to do something here to even get them into talk. And that's, I see that as fifty or sixty percent of my workload in the current environment, being honest about it . . . that's a huge hurdle for us . . . a lot of negative effort.

Union representatives added that even though they might not have been involved in the initial stages of consultation, they were "still expected to manage the impact of the decisions made" and to deal with the questions and concerns of staff.

When management did call in the union, it was often the case that they wanted to address the difficulties of the recession by cost cutting, with *immediate effect*. Immediate effect meant that unions were not given any opportunity for either real engagement or time to consider alternatives. It was mentioned by a number of the focus group participants, that when unions were being contacted, it was often only to rubber stamp cost-cutting measures already decided by management: "More often he will say, he'll make an announcement to tell people this is what we're doing and they might allow the union an opportunity to influence some minor change or some minor alteration to it . . ." In other cases, companies were going directly to the staff on the ground and "just being told there's a problem. We must take this action or you won't have jobs."

There was a sense too among the participants that some HR practitioners had adopted a short-term view of employee relations in the recession: "I've sat in meeting rooms with HR people and they have their 'mission values' and it's all this wonderful speak about, you know, consultation, consideration and our people are our best asset, all very plausible points that they have stated but the reality is that in these times . . . they look at the short term. You have all these wonderful concepts . . . the benefits have been shown in previous studies but Irish business just doesn't seem to grasp that." Some focus group participants also had negotiations with HR people who complicated things in a way that was not helpful:

> They are trying to do stuff they should have done years ago anyway and that tries everybody's patience and takes their eye off the ball. Somebody saying our productivity is down, our costs are up, how do we manage it? But they have a raft of other stuff that is antagonistic towards the people we might be selling it to . . . Reposition of the company, that's management by crisis and that is, I suppose an understandable thing to do but I think if you are in a true crisis, you manage for the true crisis, not the incidentals that you should have been doing anyway.

The union officials also agreed that there had been a change in the focus of their day-to-day work, in that there had been an increase in the number and amount of time they were spending on individual issues: "twenty years ago, the workload of an official would have been divided or split sixty percent in terms of representing groups and forty percent in terms of individuals where it is now reversed where sixty percent of an officials work now is dealing with individual cases as against forty percent which is dealing with group issues." This, they stated, had implications for the overall system of collective bargaining.

Terms and Conditions of Employment

According to one focus group participant, "it's nearly open season on everything from an employer's point of view you know, that anything that's there that's been negotiated over the years is now on their agenda to cut." One union representative stated that she had "never used the Payment of Wages Act so much, ever. There are employers who are cutting workers' pay without their agreement."

Although recognizing that cuts in headcount and so on were often necessary, what some focus group participants found difficult to accept was the fact that just because the business was not making as big a profit as in the past, it now wanted to cut employees' terms and conditions of employment. What employers were forgetting, according to the focus group participants, was that "these are not terms and conditions of employment that were given without strings attached to them, they're terms and conditions of employment that were negotiated where the employer got something as well." In certain sectors, employees did not even benefit during the boom years when huge profits were being made according to the focus group participants:

> We didn't make many gains over and above the national wage agreements because anytime we went to try and make gains on foot of huge profits we were told all those profits were being put back into the companies and therefore there was nothing to spare and anyway it was cost increasing and outside the terms of whatever wage agreement was in place.

For those companies that have implemented redundancies or early retirement or have introduced atypical working arrangements, the focus of the union's work has been on those employees who have been left behind and the regulation of their workloads. They have been looking for recognition of the temporary nature of the extra work people have had to take on:

> Somebody will change what they're doing but only if they can drop something else and we are trying to force employers into a position where it reserves some structures for people so that at the end of the whole thing there will still be promotional outlets for people, there'll still be a career and they won't be so driven into taking on more and more work.

Companies were adopting an ad hoc approach to reducing headcount according to the focus group members. In some sectors, where voluntary redundancy or early retirement schemes were offered, there appeared to have been little long-term consideration of the implications, relating to either the loss of skills and/or the distribution of work among the remaining staff. In contrast, another focus group participant gave information from the printing and publishing sector, where companies wanted to "keep their stars," and staff had to reapply for their jobs.

> That had terrible consequences for the people that lost their jobs. We were arguing it should be fair, there should be voluntary redundancy, to be based on "last in first out" but I think the response that we got from HR

was, this isn't a factory making widgets, these are highly skilled people and we can't afford to allow the ones that we think are more skilled than others to take a voluntary package and go, so we're doing it this way.

A different approach again was adopted in a financial services company, in which the focus for management in relation to employees working atypical working arrangements was "if numbers are to fall they [management] want to have as much control over it as possible, over who goes and who stays." They did not want a situation in which "staff were being enabled to decide who was reducing hours."

A worrying aspect of collective bargaining currently mentioned by the unions was the fact that some companies who had already implemented wage cuts, were coming back for a second and third 'bite of the cherry.' "Once the idea that a wage cut is a solution they come again for another bite and another bite." Participants shared the fear that this could become a 'downward spiral' that would not foster recovery in the long run, because more and more money was being taken out of the economy.

In response to a question posed by the researchers during the focus groups, the union officials agreed that their role can mean that they can feel pulled in two different directions. In the first instance they feel the need to support their members and to get the best deal for them at the table. However, they may also see that the company needs to make changes in order to survive, and the union may want to cooperate with the company, even though this may mean some workers losing their jobs.

Other issues brought up by the focus group participants included concerns about the minimum wage: "the message quite clearly to us is that the minimum wage is next to be targeted, there's no question about that. The employers' agenda is very straightforward here . . . to get that minimum wage down, which will increase their profits, and all the rest that goes with it and this Government seems to be amenable to that approach."

A number of focus group participants indicated that they were in discussion with employers around pensions, in particular with regard to the cost of defined benefit pension schemes. The outcome of negotiations has usually resulted in "either an increased contribution by the employees, or in some cases, a dilution of the benefits. While in other cases we have seen companies that have unilaterally implemented changes to the pension schemes." Union representative were also involved in agreements that saw the closure of defined benefit schemes to new entrants. Although it was acknowledged that the pensions issue had been under discussion for some time before the recession, one participant stated that the trend is his sector (financial services) was to dismantle pensions. He stated that

there seems to be a concerted attempt to dismantle them because workers are accepting serious diminution to pensions before they can afford to take pay cuts. So there was a bit of an attempt to contain pay or slightly reduce it, it was massively resisted but their approach of dismantling good pension schemes might have been costed at twenty five percent of salary replacement then. It's much more easily pushed through and that's happening sometimes because it needs to be done and sometimes because it's opportunistic to do it, or because the competitor is doing it to remain competitive.

According to the focus group participants, there was little evidence of innovative responses to the recession. It was more a case of "just the basics." One participant stated, however, that the union had negotiated an annualized-hours agreement (which particularly suited the sector involved) to avoid staff having to work a three-day week. In another case, the unions (more than one union was involved) cooperated with an initiative taken by the managing director, who instead of redundancies, introduced a 'one week off in five for a period of months.' Now the company is doing well and employees are back on full-time work. According to the union representative, "early intervention was critical and I may not have been as early making the intervention if it wasn't driven by management. I'd like to think we facilitated the arrangement and we got there eventually."

Concessions Gained by Unions

For the most part, few reciprocal concessions were gained in return for cost-cutting measures, according to the focus group participants. Unions themselves have focused on "consolidating what we have" on saving jobs and consolidating the rates of pay of their members and getting this written down into an agreement. The unions were also focusing on getting employers to sign agreements that the "company will not implement changes unless going through a negotiated agreement with the union."

In the retail sector, unions have managed to have profit sharing written into some agreements for the future, when the upturn in the economy comes about. This would be dependent on continued financial transparency. In a financial services company the union sought a commitment from the employer on bonuses in the future. The union was looking for a commitment that when the good times returned the company would give workers an opportunity to achieve a bonus of up to 25% (based on company performance indicators), that had been available only to the managers up to that point. But they found it very difficult to get that particular agenda moving.

In the printing and publishing sector, the focus was to enter into short-term arrangements of reduced working weeks in preference to having redundancies. This kept staff on the books with good standards of pay and conditions that, unions hoped, would be maintained until the economy recovered. There was a view that if staff were let go now, any new contracts in the future would not be as good. There was also the threat that other employees would do their job for less money.

Again in the printing and publishing sector, one participant stated that they did manage to get agreement on a claw-back mechanism:

> We have made concessions in terms of pay but we've sewn into agreements that there is a claw-back mechanism. Where it has been an adjustment in pay we've got a corresponding increase in leave which means the pay per hour rate hasn't changed and we've got agreement that when things improve that there'll be a refund of what workers have sacrificed now.

In the same sector in another company, where management did open up their books to the union and a pay cut was implemented, the union set up review forums that will review how the company is doing on a quarterly and annual basis.

One gain made by unions in this recessionary period related to their being able to organize workers. Some have managed to grow density in companies in which they were working and in new companies. In one case in the hotels and catering sector, the union worked closely with management to bring a company out of examinership. In return for pay cuts and other concessions, the company agreed to look at a partnership agreement with the union, and, as part of the process, workers would be actively encouraged by management to join the union. The union expected to substantially build on their original 20% density in the company. In another company in the construction sector,

> in return for a twelve month suspension of a portion of the rates of pay, (the union) gained union recognition in the twenty six counties with the company and also there was a review period built in, that was to be examined every six months and further to that, it was index linked, so that if those house prices on those specific sites raised, that the rates of pay would increase *pro rata*.

One other potentially positive outcome of the current situation, according to the focus group participants was, by having engaged and worked with the employer and come up with survival plans or alternative solutions to the problems being faced, that this has set a precedent of sorts for the future, where the unions could hope to expect the same level of engagement with employers, particularly if the solutions found had proved to be successful. Some of the focus group participants stated that they were now more engaged with employers on an ongoing basis, given the uncertainty of the recession. This, in turn, had the knock-on effect of having more discussion with their members, both in terms of keeping them informed and onside, and on being more prepared for changes in the future.

It appears however, that for some of the focus group participants, the recession caught them off guard and unprepared for the level of its severity, not having experienced anything like it before. This was further complicated by the cessation of the national pay agreements, in which during the previous 20 years unions "have had the pay issue resolved . . . we didn't have to have this open discussion on what pay should be." In the early stages of the recession, the focus, according to the unions, was on "keeping the headcount as long as they could . . . there was a genuine hope in the company at the time that business would pick up. . . ." However, as the economic crisis deepened, certain commercial realities also set in; for example, the company may have lost orders and realized that they were lost forever. This, in turn, lead to the emergence of a different bargaining agenda, related to such changes as short-time working, redundancies and pay freezes and cuts. One focus group participant talked about his union being "late converts to the discussion about downsizing and changes and modernization." After repeated attempts at survival plans over a long period, unions accepted that the business was in trouble. In order to keep the business going they had no choice but to engage in cost-cutting measures.

Another participant stated that although "it's easier for trade unions to go and just have industrial action in a lot of cases you know because it's what we've always done," but that now when companies provide the union with financial data, the union is in a better position to sell an agreement to their members. In one case, mentioned by a focus group participant from the retail sector,

> what we've never done before with companies, we've sent in our own financial advisors and the company have quite willingly cooperated with that and it would have been a help, it would certainly have been a help where you're talking about cuts, nasty cuts in some cases of members' terms and conditions of employment when they hear from somebody that, you know, has been engaged by the union, paid for by the union that is there to advise them on their behalf.

6.3 OFFICIALS VIEWS OF THE FEATURES OF GOOD HR PRACTICE

In response to a request that they identify the features of good practice from their perspective, the focus group participants mentioned the following issues or aspects: honoring existing agreements and procedures, meaningful consultation and willingness to explore alternative solutions, communications, access to valid data and financial transparency, a business plan and agreed mechanisms to allow for future reviews of agreements. Each of these aspects of good practice is addressed separately.

Honoring Existing Agreements

There was a broad consensus among the focus group participants that they "have collective agreements which are being ignored" and that employers were also trying to move away from a collective approach toward individualizing the employment relationship. The participants highlighted the need for employers to honor existing agreements and not to impose unilateral change.

Meaningful Consultation and Willingness to Consider Alternatives

According to the focus group participants, where workers or their representatives are meaningfully engaged with the employer, then even though the staff will not like having to make changes or take cuts in their terms and conditions of employment, they are much more likely to remain committed to the employer than if they were left out of the consultation process altogether. For the participants, real consultation "is a mixture of things" and takes place where there is "a shared problem" and a willingness to look for "a shared solution." Meaningful consultation is about "bringing people with you" and that "the change is agreed." It is about being able "to see the real situation in the company and about being allowed to come up with realistic alternatives." As one official saw it,

> when an employer says—things are bad, you can have a look at my books, say that what they want to do is keep the business going, keep people in employment and that they are prepared to look at alternatives. I mean if you get all of that then I think workers generally will buy into it . . . because they feel they are a part of it, they feel that they're contributing to saving their own jobs and livelihoods and all of that.

Meaningful consultation also meant local and timely engagement for the focus group members: "consulting with unions at an early enough stage that the whole procedure can be exhausted both locally and into the third party. Very often companies are coming and saying we need this yesterday" . . . "there's a lot of shock tactics being used by employers, like you know, we're in a crisis and we have a meeting with our bank on Friday and it's Wednesday. We'll meet you tomorrow for half an hour and people feel that they're forced into a corner. . . ." According to the focus group participants, "there should be adequate time given for the negotiations to occur . . . people see change as a threat . . . it's difficult to change that mind set into an opportunity."

According to participants, unions want the company to ask for the union's help and advice and not to just "go through the motions," presenting the unions with what they intend to do and calling this communication consultation. What companies often do not know, including HR, according to the focus group participants, is "how work practices on the ground can be changed, how flexibilities can produce far greater savings in the long term than a sheer economical decision to cut pay or whatever." At the end of a process where meaningful consultation has taken place and employees feel they have been listened to, there are multiple benefits for the company in terms of, first, discovering better ways of doing things, and second, there is

a better chance of "keeping people on board and buying into the notion—
I'm a part of this company—and not apart from it just as a source of labor."

Another component of meaningful consultation was seen to be the
employer's willingness to engage with a third party. "A willingness to engage
with a third party which is seen by workers as being fair where there might be
a lack of trust with the employer or their motives. Even a willingness to even
engage with a third party even if what it delivers is what they're looking for,
is seen as being fair and acceptable because somebody else has endorsed it."

Communications

The participants were of the view that if HR wanted to develop not just
trust with unions but also trust with staff, then good communications were
essential. "If there is bad news coming down the track, the first thing is to
communicate that in advance and give people an honest outlook as to what
the future might hold." One participant also mentioned the importance of a
good communication channel with the union "overtly confirming the union
as a stakeholder."

Financial Transparency

Union officials in the focus groups were of the view that a willingness on
the part of the company to provide financial transparency, to open up their
books to the union or allow the union to appoint somebody to look at
company accounts would indicate a positive HR response. When this has
happened, unions have found that it helped to get members to buy into
agreements because they have the facts and figures with which to make
an argument. There was a view also that when companies were willing to
provide information in the recession, then they will also need to do this in
the good times in the future. In cases in which companies did not provide
financial information to the unions, "and were basically asking us to follow
them in the dark," it would be less likely that workers would cooperate on
such a deal. However, it was also acknowledged by the unions present that
the disclosure of financial information could also be a double-edged sword
in that the burden of dealing with the information was being transferred to
the union. There was also the issue of a company having publically declared
a profit in the case of multinationals but at the same time was asking locally
for some form of cutback in earnings (e.g., overtime payments). This was
often a difficult situation for unions to deal with.

Viable Business Plans

When the crisis started the assumption among the workers was that the
company had a 'grand plan' to deal with what was happening. In many
instances, according to the union officials, this did not appear to be the

case. Allied to the notion of financial transparency, the focus group participants expressed a view on the importance of the company having a good business plan for the future. A business plan for two to three years down the road, they indicated, would help to ensure confidence that the company was not just taking a short-term view but knew what it was doing:

> If there is some light at the end of the tunnel it's very easy to do a deal, a short term deal for a year or eighteen months, but for us to buy in, the key for us would be that after that twelve or eighteen months that there actually is a business plan that makes sense, because the last thing you want to do is get onto a spiral that's just a downward spiral.

An Agreed-On Mechanism to Allow for Future Review of Agreements

The focus groups indicated that they found that management did not often want to make any commitments concerning the future. However, they felt that "if workers by agreement are prepared to take some pain now during this difficult time, then there needs to be a recognition that when the good times come back whatever they've given has to come back with it." The groups indicated that some commitment should be written into agreements whereby what was given up by workers could be refunded and that if this was the case, there would be greater buy-in from workers:

> There are very, very few employers saying take a pay cut now or reduce premiums for overtime or unsocial hours premium and this will be reviewed and reinstated at a later time . . . If an employer is genuine, will work with you, wants to alter an agreement but commits to when we turn this country around again, no matter how long that's going to take, when it comes back, when the company is able to pull itself up, stand on its own feet, that there will be recognition of that contribution and that things will be reinstated.

Focus group participants stated with regard to the retail sector that when bonuses were given up during the recession, profit sharing of some kind in the future should become a feature of agreements.

6.4 DRIVERS OF GOOD PRACTICE

The focus group participants were asked to describe the features of organizations that supported good HR practice. Their responses identified the following features.

The Existence of a Robust HR Structure, Strong HR Policies and Leadership

Focus group members stated that HR had an important role to play regarding the prominence of good IR/HR practices in a firm. They generally agreed that where strong HR structures and policies were in existence, coupled with a strong HR leader being able to stand up to diktats from finance or other areas of senior management, a better chance for real negotiations and cooperation existed. Otherwise, according to the focus group participants, HR are "just there to mop up any decision that is already taken by people higher up the organisation." The union representatives stated that they also needed HR to uphold existing agreements in the face of challenges and to both authorize and corroborate the union's role in these. "The influence or the priority given to whoever is on top of HR" is also extremely important according to the unions.

Recognition of the Union as a Stakeholder

The focus group participants stated that a good HR manager would be someone that "recognized the trade union as a stakeholder in the organization and that its members are employed in the organization and are coming to the table." This recognition or acknowledgment of the role of trade unions in an organization could also be reinforced by chief executives when they address staff. The participants also mentioned the importance of respect from the employer to the input of employees and their representatives:

> I suppose ideally what you would say it that there would be respect by the employer for the input of the employees and their representatives and if you have that then you will get an open-minded attitude to the savings that are not just the ones the employer has come up with but that they're prepared to look at alternatives.

The unions, on more than one occasion, highlighted the example of two organizations doing the same thing, for example, reducing headcount. They pointed out that the two organizations end up doing the same thing; however, one does it by opposing (the union) and the other one does it by consulting and reaching an agreement with the union: "The outcome will be that the one who does it by consulting and agreeing will have a staff who are more likely to remain engaged in that organization, whereas the other will have a staff who are very seriously discommoded and won't have a long term commitment."

Related to the current difficulties in the financial services sector, one participant highlighted how two organizations took two different approaches with employees and their representatives. One of the organizations gave a guarantee of no compulsory redundancies for a period of 18 months, in exchange for pay moderation and a contribution to the pension scheme, by both the company and the union. The agreement was accepted by 95% of employees on a vote. The second organization did not give any guarantees or concessions in return for pay and headcount adjustments, even though they were in a position to do so, according to the focus group participants. The outcome is that in the first organization employees and management have "a very good working relationship, well relatively in the circumstances between staff and they're all heading in the same direction, sorting out problems." In the other organization, employees no longer trust their employer, and commitment levels are low.

Embedded Collective Bargaining Practices and Facilities

The preexistence of good relations with unions in an organization, along with embedded practices for consultation and collective bargaining, contribute to good practice in employee relations according to the focus group participants. When there are structures in an organization that allow for representation, including basic facilities for the professional conduct of representation on the shop floor (such as access to a phone, a computer or a room for meetings), it is harder to ignore them because people have an understanding and a day-to-day appreciation of their function. They are a good visible indicator that there is a reasonable relationship between management and unions, and it is more difficult to dismantle such structures at local level than at national level:

> I also think where you have maybe good and embedded kind of policies or ways in which you deal with things within organizations . . . it's harder to dismantle that from the point of view of the influence and it's easier to use that and you can use that very effectively very quickly.

The Existence of a Culture of Trust between Employers and Employees

In distinguishing between good and not-so-good employers, the union representatives highlighted the importance of building trust between employees and the employer:

> If that trust isn't there, or if it was there in some semblance or other and has now disappeared, then we all have a major task in terms of trying to bring people back into a space whereby they all recognize the difficulties and the problems and they all work toward a solution or a resolution of those difficulties and problems.

When a company is looking for agreement on a headcount reduction or on shorter hours, to get the trust and cooperation of staff, according to the union representatives, other issues would need to be addressed, for example, for employers to stop opposing all individual claims on a point of principle and referring them to a third party: "where everything goes to a third party and everything is confrontational an employer can expect a proposal to reduce the working week, reduce pay or reduce headcount to be equally confrontational."

Supportive CEOs and Organizational Cultures

Another factor influencing collective bargaining in an organization is that it can "depend on the personality at the top of the organization and their attitude to staff." When the CEO's attitude is respectful and caring toward staff, according to the focus group participants, this will have a positive influence on the status of collective bargaining in an organization. An example of this was provided by one of the focus group participants:

> I think it's the attitude of the person at the top again that it comes down to, I mean he [the CEO] would come across as having concern for staff . . . So he set a structure in place that allows everybody to have an input, that's the whole idea, that they have an input into what goes on. It's been helpful, you know, because where there have been redundancies and there are ongoing redundancies . . . they're all on a voluntary basis and everything is being done on the basis of 'if there's an alternative to redundancy, the alternative is done.

A participant also observed with evident exasperation,

> We had lots of problems two years ago and again it was down to the fact that the chief executive at the time had the totally opposite view and went out of his way to make sure that the trade unions weren't involved in anything and I mean we had three or four major agreements negotiated entirely by the Labour Relations Commission, one taking six months. Six months spent on one change agreement that there was no discussion of at all, that went from a position where for the whole of six months both sides never met to accept the rules and you can't do business that way you know.

The focus group participants also mentioned the importance of the CEO personally addressing the workers and delivering good news (should there be any) in addition to the bad news.

Union Organization

There was agreement among the focus group participants that one of the key factors enabling workers to "stand up for themselves" and to not allow the union to be bypassed is high union density, that is, when a significant proportion of the workers were organized:

> The normal practice would be in certain industries, the electrical industry, the building industry, that the density of people who were there, there was recognition that you had to do business with unions and most of the employers reaction was that you know, there was a consequence, a stoppage, a strike, whatever it was, a penalty somewhere along the line, they were going to lose as a consequence of not doing business with the union, not meeting the collective arrangements.

Local Embedded Business

When business is embedded in the local community and links exist not just with workers and their families but also with local schools and local community groups, this can be a feature of an organization that contributes to good practice according to the focus group participants:

> Where the business is local, management have a dilemma in that they can't separate themselves from the community. It would be highly embarrassing for a local family owned newspaper [for example] that's embedded in the community, to have a row with the local workforce when they're all neighbours and friends basically you know.

6.5   THE PUBLIC SECTOR

A number of the union officials present at the focus groups represented members from both the private and public sectors. Their representation in the public sector covered the health sector (including voluntary agencies funded by this sector), local authorities and higher education institutions.

Impact of the Recession

Some issues that arose for unions as a result of the recession were common to both the public and the private sectors. Public service unions were not exempt from being marginalized by employers "with the Government walking away from agreements," according to the focus group participants, nor was the notion of sharp practice absent from this sector. Even though high union density existed and the structures of social partnership were in place, the focus group participants were concerned about the impact of the message emanating from public sector management. They were of the view that the message from the center was to "consult the unions and then do what you want." In reality, unions felt that they were being pushed out of the picture. They were also concerned that agreed practices and procedures were being manipulated in some areas of the public sector: "there is a directive operating within the [department's name withheld] at the moment whereby any cases that are referred to a rights commissioner by the trade union side are to be rejected in the main by the management side . . ." and that the union

> ends up then referring the matter to the Labour Relations Commission and ultimately into the Court. But to a large extent and this is a very silent kind of a position that has been taken, right, where they will agree to have a case heard by the rights commissioner service, so you are put through the ropes in terms of having to operate all of the procedures while at the same time you have the employer side . . . just ignoring the thing to a fairly large extent.

As was the case in the private sector, some unions stated that this gave them only one option in terms of doing meaningful business with their employer and that was to "walk in with a ballot mandate in your pocket . . . Otherwise it's a case of waiting for the court to issue a recommendation by which time, the nub of the issue has been decided one way or the other anyway." One focus group participant accused HR of 'breaching the law' irrespective of the consequences:

> The claims that I would deal with have escalated in the area of temporary or fixed term contracts, where workers have been faced with proposals that clearly breach legislation, so the number of referrals that have gone in, have rocketed and that's because temporary workers are so vulnerable, I mean four thousand have been lost in the local authority sector, that's actual people across the country. Many more have been told we may renew your contract but it will be at a lower grade or on fewer days a week.

Overall, and similar to the private sector, unions were concerned that what was being tapped into was the general fear of loss of employment and that high union density, while assisting unions with their work, was not proving to be any kind of guarantee that management would adhere to agreed processes and procedures.

The union officials perceived the biggest single impact and challenge of the recession in the public sector as being the effect of the employment control framework and its impact on the delivery of a service by a smaller workforce. When HR was operating in a positive way, one focus group participant described the public sector employer's approach to this issue, as one in which efficiencies and the elimination of duplication on service delivery were explored, as were flexibilities. In other cases, agreements have been reached that members would take a percentage (an example of 10% was quoted) of the work of a vacant post. The unions were concerned about balancing the extra amount of work that a staff member would take on, to avoid increases in workloads leading to stress and sickness absences. In general, however, the focus group participants were dissatisfied with what they saw as the public service's unplanned approach to early retirement and redundancy selection and the lack of consideration of the consequences regarding loss of skills and distribution of work among the remaining staff. One union representative stated that applications for early retirement in the public service were being blocked by local management, only to be over-ruled and agreed on at the central or department level, with no regard for consequences:

> There is no value on who is leaving, no attempt to get any understanding of the impact it's going to have or the effects, or what services are going to have to diminish as a consequence of that. That's a purely financial decision by the Department of Finance section that deals with money and is now taking over the running of the company, Ireland Inc. . . . money first and then we worry about the consequence afterwards and that sends out a message to people left behind, particularly ones that are trying to patch it up.

They were also concerned about "attempts to change terms and condi-tions of employment." Staff were being organized on a team basis, which, although this gave greater flexibility to the organization, it also made it "dif-ficult to identify grade levels and differentials."

There was also some level of agreement among the union officials with regard to the lack of HR influences both in the private and the public sec-tors, where HR is perceived as "just picking up the pieces." A number of the focus group participants regarded the public sector as having "very poor HR practices" and that "any business that is being done is totally contingent on the individual that you deal with . . . some individuals who actually will try to do some business and sort things out and you will make headway there but the vast majority aren't of that frame of mind." The unions pointed to the local authorities where "people just tend to go in spend a few months or a year or two and move on, they have no real experience or expertise from a HR point of view." One participant observed that to manage HR depart-ments in large public sector organisations in Ireland you need no qualifica-tions what so ever. There is no industry standard where you have to have a certificate, a diploma, a degree or a master's in HRM at all. Some of the participants claimed that "HR isn't valued . . . it's basically a troubleshoot-ing role, it's a penance that people have to put up with during the course of their public service careers."

One major difference did exist between the public and private sectors, according to the focus group participants. They saw workers and their rep-resentatives in the private sector as having at least some autonomy with which to act or react, whereas in the public sector, "because of decisions that have been taken by Government, literally public service employees are frozen in terms of what they can or can't do." This was also the case for voluntary agencies, which were in the main funded by government: "we are seeing external pressures being applied on the voluntary agencies . . . and indirectly by the government in terms of ensuring that the pay cuts follow through there as well." The public sector has been "driven by government rather than by any decisions it may want to take itself."

The focus group participants also stated that unions themselves were having difficulties in the public sector dealing with the expectations of their members and the union's ability to deliver: "there is a [mismatch] between the expectations as to what trade union members expect their unions to do during a recession to protect them and what they can actually do." Public sector unions have therefore been engaged in damping down expectations, according to the focus group:

> The situation has switched very quickly from unions dealing with claims for greater pay increases, shorter hours, grading claims, looking at someone over there who has got something, I want that too. We had to very quickly change, or try [to] change the expectations of members to a more realistic outlook, to say that these gains that would have been available in the early part of the last decade, are not necessarily there now and that change in perspective and damping down expectations continues to be a difficult task.

This problem was further reinforced, according to the focus group participants, by the fact that this was the first major challenge that most of their members working in the public sector had ever experienced, in terms of their rights and their pay and conditions.

6.6   CONCLUSION

The views of union focus group participants on the actions and postures of firms in the recession are considerably less sanguine that those that emerge from the management survey and focus groups of HR managers. Although again no picture of any concerted onslaught against union representation emerges, the officials nevertheless portray unions as often encountering great difficulty in representing members and in securing their terms and conditions and jobs in the recession. It is evident from the focus group participants that the onset of the recession instigated a period of considerable turbulence for trade unions, in particular in terms of their representation and negotiation roles. In traditional collective bargaining, unions aim to mobilize members to improve or maintain their terms and conditions of employment while also holding on to their jobs. In the current recession unions are not only trying to do this, but they also appear to be struggling in some cases for their own survival as part of the collective bargaining process. They claim their roles are not being facilitated as they have been in the past. Many claim to be operating in a hostile environment following the breakdown of national social partnership (which they had relied on for over two decades to provide guidelines), and all this against a background of the most severe recession Ireland has ever known.

As the recession progressed, unions have had to adapt themselves to new realities. The precariousness of some firms, in terms of their basic survival, has meant that the unions have had to come to terms with a wide range of factors, such as understanding financial data, working against the background of the real threat of company closure, dealing with both honorable and opportunistic employers (and knowing the difference between the two) and, in the end, being party to decisions that may have a negative outcome for many of their members. As the recession has developed the scale and duration of the process has also had an impact on unions. The work of union officials has become very challenging, not only with regard to employers but also in terms of managing the demands and expectations of their own members.

On the other hand, the union officials also believe that employers have been too quick to abandon what they view as the hitherto successful collective bargaining process, and have underestimated the concerns and potential contribution of staff in this crisis. They claim that when the real issues are identified, staff and the unions are quite capable of coming up with alternative proposals or even the acceptance of proposals, however unpalatable, that have to be implemented.

It was clear from the focus group discussions that social partnership has left a mixed legacy. Although it decided the issue of pay for over two decades, there was a view that the process had not only demobilized shop stewards, but also left unions members with a lack of connection and understanding of the work unions did on their members' behalf. This has provided the unions with an agenda for the future with respect to how to maintain and foster an appreciation of their own role and relevance.

The focus group participants voiced concerns about the breakdown in some instances of established rules and processes of industrial relations, where some employers have changed the rules of engagement in an opportunistic way. The union officials have accused HR of having a prescriptive response to problems generated by the recession, which the unions have sometimes tried to counter by securing employment and growing density in the firms concerned. In this connection some spoke of the need to get back to some shared and common understanding of the 'business' of industrial relations between trade union officials and HR managers.

In terms of the import of the findings for the contrasting views reviewed in Chapter 2 as to the nature, depth and likely persistence of change in HR and employment arrangements, the following conclusions appear warranted. There is little evidence in the views and experiences of union officials that firms have generally sought to achieve more cooperative or collaborative relations with unions better to respond to the pressures of the recession. Preexisting cooperative or partnership-based relations have in some instances been sustained and have assisted the parties to reach accommodation when faced with acute pressures. But the more common pattern appears to have involved employers and HR managers seeking to bypass unions, rescind or ignore collective agreements and change the rules of the established game of collective bargaining and industrial relations. Against such a background union focus group members have sought to articulate and underscore a largely conventional understanding of good industrial relations and human resource management rather than sensing the outlines of any better or more appropriate model for the times and conditions that prevail. As previously discussed, the argument that HR and employment arrangements are changing in the reverse direction to the established concept of high commitment is silent with respect to expectations regarding relations between firms and unions. Nevertheless, the data presented here might suggest that a fundamental recasting of relations with unions is underway and one that 'tears up the rule book' of either traditional or high-commitment management. Indications in the trade union focus groups of a new relationship between unions and employers, of a breakdown in the normal relationship and of employer actions undermining and destabilizing the traditional union–employer relationship all appear to point in this direction. But other indications of union officials' experiences warrant caution against interpreting such changes in terms of a fundamental shift in employer–union relations likely to abide beyond the acute phase of the recession. Most union officials appeared to hold the view that changes in posture of this kind were dictated by 'short-termism' and 'opportunism.' Although short-termism and opportunism could, of course, congeal into a new settlement between the parties of a lasting character and one in which unions become marginalized and excluded, the changes experienced by union officials seem to be more often understood by them as being opportunistic rather than programmatic or systematic. And this appears to tell against the rather apocalyptic idea of a new employment deal unleashed by the recession but that is likely to displace established HR and employment relations when the effects of the recession have passed.

7 Containing Job Losses and Staying on Course
Irish Life and Permanent, Sherry FitzGerald and Dublin Airport Authority

This chapter and the next examine a series of six cases of responses by companies and unions to the pressures unleashed by the recession. This chapter outlines the rationale for case study selection; examines the first three cases, which involve the introduction of measures to minimize job losses in three major firms; and presents a series of conclusions on the issues that emerge. The next chapter examines three additional cases that involve other challenges associated with the recession. Each of the case study chapters presents conclusions on the set of cases examined.

7.1 THE SELECTION OF CASES

The series of cases examined are regarded as instances of good practice in responding to different sets of recessionary pressures, often incorporating significant innovative features. They are regarded as cases of good practice by meeting a series of criteria. First, the parties to employment relations succeeded in all cases in securing or strengthening the businesses affected by finding accommodation commonly involving significant changes to the operation of businesses, to terms and conditions of employment and to work practices. Second, many of the cases were viewed as good or exemplary practice in the industrial relations or general news media. Third, a number of the cases examined were recommended to us as good practice when we canvassed expert opinion for instances of exemplary practice in handling the recession. Fourth, some cases were familiar to us through other strands of the research study and seemed to us to warrant deeper examination through case studies. Finally, the cases involve some or many of the principles and practices advocated as good practice by participants in the focus groups.

Potential cases for study were thus identified in a number of ways. Industrial relations reportage, especially in the weekly specialist periodical *Industrial Relations News* (*IRN*), was systematically examined for instances that might repay study, and journalists working for *IRN* were interviewed for other possible suggestions that may have received less coverage. Our own knowledge of developments in the area and that of professional staff of the

LRC was also used to corroborate or extend the list of possible cases, as were comments and suggestions from the Board of the LRC. The project steering group, comprised of members of the LRC, CIPD, IBEC and ICTU also provided guidance as to possible cases and endorsed the list of cases on which we chose to focus.

Having generated a list of potential cases for study, our next step involved examining the features of these cases on the list, such as were evident from the various sources of information available to us, to determine whether it was possible to classify or 'cluster' the cases in terms of the types of recessionary pressures they involved. 'Stratifying' the list of cases in this way would allow us to study cases that reflected a range of recessionary pressures and scenarios, thus allowing us to generalize our case results with more confidence rather than simply randomly selecting cases. An examination of cases on the list led to the identification of a set of clusters, as set out in Figure 7.1.

One of the original clusters identified appeared to relate less to pressures generated by the recession than to ongoing processes of restructuring or rationalization that predated the recession and did not decisively experience an impact from recessionary pressures. Another cluster appeared to involve general attempts to foster or preserve good industrial relations, again in circumstances to which the recession seemed of rather marginal significance. We thus decided to drop these clusters from consideration. This left us with the clusters outlined in Figure 7.1.

The first cluster, which accounts for the majority of cases known to us, involves companies concerned with responding to the recession mainly by instituting programs to contain job losses by undertaking initiatives aimed at controlling or reducing payroll costs. The second cluster identifiable involved companies that implemented HR programs in the context of either declared or de facto survival plans. The third cluster comprised the Irish subsidiaries of multinational companies that sought to preserve or renew their mandates through enhancing the competitiveness of their Irish operations. The fourth cluster comprised companies that sought to preserve pay and conditions through involving employees or unions in other cost control measures. The fifth cluster comprised companies known to deploy classical or 'textbook' HRM practices and that had undergone significant global restructuring or reorganization. Here the focus would be on how human resource management was conducted in the Irish subsidiaries of these companies.

The sets of cases in the clusters identified are not distinctive in all respects or overlap in various ways, and there is room for debate both in determining the defining features of the clusters and in allocating cases to each one. However, it appears to us that the clusters identified represent a valid and useful means of portraying the spectrum of conditions generated by the recession, as reflected in cases of good practice, either documented or drawn to our attention or both. Clearly we do not claim to have identified here all sets of recessionary conditions having an impact on firms or their unions, nor even

Cluster 1
Containing Job Losses
▪ Pay cuts/freezes, increment freezes, deferred rises ▪ Alter pension arrangements ▪ Voluntary redundancies &/or career breaks or self employment options ▪Sometimes 'claw-back' arrangements
Aer Arann AXA Insurance Dublin Airport Authority * DHL Educational Building Society Focus Group Company Irish Life & Permanent * National Irish Bank RTE Sherry Fitzgerald *

Cluster 2
Survival Plans (Declared or Effective)
▪Pay freezes ▪ Changes in working hours or shift arrangements ▪Redundancies ▪Sometimes 'claw-back' arrangements ▪ Sometimes partnership
Aer Lingus Superquinn * Tara Mines

Cluster 3
Mandate Renewal & Competitiveness
▪ Pay freezes or deferred rises ▪Voluntary Redundancies ▪Some rehiring and re-skilling
Focus Group Company Medtronic *

Cluster 4
Preserve Pay and Employment & Engage Staff/Unions in Cost Control Measures
▪No pay cuts or redundancies ▪Possibility of short-time working ▪Possibility of partnership
Focus Group Company

Cluster 5
Classical HRM Firms Undergoing Global Restructuring
▪Employment stabilization ▪ Undertaking measures to promote employability
Ericsson * Focus Group Companies HP IBM Intel

Figure 7.1 Recessionary conditions and case study clusters

Table 7.1 Clusters of firms and their responses to the recession

Clusters	Case studies selected
1: Containing job losses	Irish Life and Permanent
	The Dublin Airport Authority
	Sherry FitzGerald
2: Survival plans (declared or de facto)	Superquinn
3: Mandate renewal and competitiveness	Medtronic
4: Classical HRM-based firms undergoing global restructuring	Ericsson

less all cases of good practice that fall within our defining criteria, as outlined previously. There are obvious sources of bias in a list of potential cases for study generated in the manner outlined. For example, large prominent companies are more likely to become known and reported, as are initiatives undertaken in unionized companies.

Having identified the clusters and their associated cases, we next sought to identify and gain access to cases for study. Here we tried to arrive at an overall set of cases that would contain as much internal diversity as possible with respect to such features as operating in the private sector and commercial public sector, indigenous and multinational ownership, manufacturing and service industries and unionized and nonunion status. Second, we sought to prioritize access to cases that appeared to provide the richest experiences of responding to the circumstances associated with each of the clusters. Only one of the companies approached declined to participate and this was a case located in the fourth cluster: companies seeking to preserve pay and conditions by engaging staff or unions in other cost-saving measures. As the other case identified in this cluster, Aughinish Alumina, is already very well covered in the general literature on Irish employment relations we decided also to exclude this cluster from consideration in the final choice of cases for study.

This left us with the following set of case studies, listed with their associated clusters in Table 7.1.

Although the selection appears to us to represent a good spectrum of cases that are also reasonably diverse by sector, ownership and union status, the set of cases cannot, of course, be viewed as representative in any statistical sense of all instances of good practice in responding to the recession.

Methods of Data Collection

In each case selected for study, available background reports and documents were reviewed prior to the conduct of interviews. Key management and union officials were interviewed in all cases. Interviews lasted for a minimum of one hour and often extended to several hours. The interviews were recorded and transcribed for analysis. In many instances our interlocutors provided additional internal documents and agreements for review. Draft cases were submitted for comment by interviewees, when this was requested (usually by managers), and their comments were taken into account in finalizing the text. Specific queries were also presented to research interlocutors where issues remained unclear. To permit cross-case comparison, the case studies are reported under a common set of thematic subheadings.

COST CONTAINMENT AT IRISH LIFE AND PERMANENT

Context

Financial institutions were in the maelstrom of the Irish banking and economic crisis as the industry was beset by the global credit crunch and domestic specu-lative lending to property developers. In September 2008 as insolvency loomed in the country's main banks and financial institutions, the government guaran-teed deposits and borrowings. Irish Life and Permanent (IL&P) experienced a significant impact from the Irish financial crisis. In responding to the crisis the firm sought to institute new arrangements for the conduct of industrial rela-tions with the trade unions representing its employees, to operate through a unitary HR function (then in the process of being created) and to win agreement on a series of cost-saving measures. Its efforts to find accommodation with its unions and employees were affected and constrained by a legacy of adversarial, low-trust industrial relations and by established organizational structures. This case study charts the ebbs and flows of efforts in IL&P to adjust to the onset of the financial crisis in Ireland, culminating in measures that included incentiv-ized career breaks, a voluntary redundancy program, agreed pay rises and the freezing of service-related increments.

IL&P has its origins in the coming together of three of Ireland's oldest financial institutions, Irish Permanent, Irish Life and the TSB. Irish Per-manent was established in 1884 as a building society and by the mid-20th century had evolved into the largest mortgage lender in Ireland. Providing finance to people seeking to buy their own homes was the mainstay of its business, although in 1992 it established a new subsidiary Irish Permanent Finance to offer personal and car loans. Two years after that move it changed its status from a mutual building society to a publically quoted financial institution. The history of TSB stems back to the creation of the first Irish Savings Bank in Waterford in 1816. After further savings banks were set up across the country, the government of the day introduced the Savings Bank Act in 1863 to bring the multitude of banks that had been created under government control and to restrict their activities to savings accounts. These restrictions stayed until the 1960s when they were lifted, which enabled the savings banks around the country to expand the range of financial products and services they provided. In addition, during the 1980s a wave of mergers occurred between different savings banks, which created a more streamline organizational structure in this part of the finance sector: the TSB Bank, which was created in 1992, was a by-product of this merger activity. Irish Life was formed in 1939 as a result of a decision by nine different companies that had been active in the Irish insurance market to merge. When the new company was formed the Irish government decided to take a stake that increased steadily until it acquired effective control in 1947 by owning 90% of shares. By the 1960s Irish Life had become the largest life insurance provider in the country. Since then the company has pursued an ambitious business strategy. First of all, it got involved in banking activities by taking a 25% stake in Irish Intercontinental Bank. Then it systematically went about internationalizing its insurance business by entering other European as well as US markets. The culmination of these expansion activities was the company's privatization in 1991.

The process of integrating these three companies started in 1999, when Irish Life and Irish Permanent merged to create IL&P and ended in 2001 when the new company acquired the TSB Bank from the Irish government. Bringing together these three companies resulted in the creation of the third-largest financial institution in Ireland. There are two main components to the business. One is Irish Life, which has more or less continued to focus on the insurance and pensions markets—it remains the biggest provider of life insurance in Ireland, with a 20% share of the market. Irish Life carries out its activities through six subdivisions, which specialize in different market niches. The other is Permanent TSB, which offers a full range of personal banking products and services. This banking arm operates more than 110 branches and 65 agencies throughout Ireland and is the country's largest provider of home mortgages. There are other aspects to the business; for example, the group has a minority interest (30%) in the third largest nonlife insurer in the Irish market, Allianz. Overall, however, Irish Life and Permanent TSB are the mainstays of the business.

The formation of IL&P brought together three organizations with different cultures and industrial relations histories. For example, merging Irish Permanent, a mutual building society, and TSB, a state bank, brought a range of challenges as each organization operated in distinctive ways. However, the need to integrate fully the three disparate organizational cultures was mitigated by the decision to allow Irish Life and Permanent TSB to act separately in two different market segments of the financial sector. Each organization also brought its own industrial relations history to the new company. Historically, each organization would have experienced periods of relatively stable industrial relations punctuated by spells of industrial action. The decision after the merger to keep apart Irish Life and Permanent TSB meant, for all intents and purposes, these two parts of the organization functioned separately on industrial relations matters. Each has its own bargaining structure to conclude agreements and different negotiating agendas frequently emerge in the two parts of the business. For example, in Irish Life, management engage with only one trade union, Unite (formerly Amicus & ATGWU), whereas employees in Permanent TSB are represented by three trade unions, Unite, SIPTU and Mandate. This probably makes Permanent TSB a more complex environment to conclude agreements.

Although the decision was made to allow Irish Life and Permanent TSB to operate relatively autonomously, the new organization, as the third-largest financial institution in the country, faced pressures to follow organizational practices that approximated to best in class: its internal structures and processes had to be of a similar level of sophistication to those existing in its main rivals so that it could recruit and retain highly skilled employees and could signal to the market that with a workforce of about 5,000 it had the competence to be a big-time player in the finance industry, particularly in Ireland. Thus, although the new organization was separated internally into two main operating units, the pressure to modernize structures, processes and practices was company-wide. To enact organizational change and modernization, IL&P felt obliged to recast it HR function inside the organization along the lines of the business partner model developed by David Ulrich.

According to Ulrich (1997) creating a high-performing organization involves dividing the HR function into three broad activities. First of all, strategic business partners need to be created, which involves senior HR professionals working closely with business leaders to influence and steer strategy and strategy implementation. Although this role was seen as varying across organizations, it was anticipated that strategic partners in the HR team would work on such matters as organizational- and people-capability building, long-term resource and talent management planning and using business insights to drive change in people management practices. Secondly, centers of excellence are considered necessary to create small teams of HR experts with specialist knowledge of leading-edge HR solutions in discrete policy areas such as pay and recruitment. The role of centers of excellence was conceived as delivering competitive business advantages through HR innovations in areas such as reward, learning, engagement and talent management. The last part of the jigsaw was creating shared services—a unit or units set up to handle all the routine 'transactional' services relating to HR across the business. A shared services center typically provides resourcing, payroll, absence monitoring and advice on the simpler employee relations issues. The main remit of shared services is to provide low-cost, effective HR administration.

IL&P created a business-relevant HR architecture along the lines of the Ulrich model. At the group level, the HR function was reorganized, which led to the creation of centers of excellence and central services. A number of strategic HR projects have been launched by center of excellence teams in such areas as talent management and learning and development. In addition, the central services unit has made a series of changes, particularly in the area of IT, to improve the delivery of transactional HR functions. Some moves have been made toward HR developing a more strategic role by developing new ideas about how internal structures and processes could be adapted to achieve better value for money. But the organization has probably yet to diffuse a fully integrated, fully operational business partner model. The experience of the central HR team is that a business partner HR model cannot be created overnight. It must be seen as an organizational process that involves adapting structures and mentalities over time. The HR functions in both Irish Life and Permanent TSB possess considerable autonomy to negotiate separate agreements.

Because there has been little attempt at harmonizing or even coordinating industrial relations across the two parts of the business, the HR agenda in the two divisions is shaped as much by the legacy of past events as any current initiatives. For example, in 1996, before the merger, Irish Life experienced a difficult 16-week-long strike over the reduction and redeployment of sales managers. This left a legacy of bad feeling and mistrust inside the organization, which management almost immediately set out to address. Since 1997 a battery of initiatives has been launched to improve employee–management relations. Employee engagement efforts have probably not been as concerted in Permanent TSB simply because its industrial relations tradition is different. The distinctiveness of employment relations in the two divisions is reflected in and reinforced by Irish Life not being an 'orbit of comparison' for Permanent TSB and vice versa. Although each side of the business has followed broadly separate employment relations pathways since the merger, neither experienced serious industrial relations problems for the most of the 2000s. The prosperity prevailing during this time allowed the company to pursue attractive reward schemes as well as other generous HR policies that kept industrial relations problems at bay.

Although relations between management and unions were stable, both tended to view developments in the company in different ways. For their part, managers were of the view that unions continually opposed proposals for organizational change, thereby delaying necessary business modernization. They frequently were frustrated with union tactics of stretching out negotiations on proposed reforms, effectively seeking to filibuster any change initiative. A further irritant for managers was the inability to conclude agreements internally. For managers, too many proposed agreements failed to be ratified in ballots, and there were too many visits to the LRC and Labour Court. Although these tactics exasperated managers, they recognized that patience and perseverance were key attributes they had to retain in pushing forward the agenda of business improvement. Ideally, they wanted greater cooperation and harmony with the unions. Unions had a different perspective on developments inside the organizations. The result was the creation of an organization in which structures were too cumbersome, which prevented closer cooperation between unions across the company. Unions also thought that management were too aggressive in their pursuit of organizational change. In addition, although the unions did not regard relations with management as excessively adversarial, it was recognized that there existed limited 'shared understandings' between the two. For the unions, it was their first responsibility to represent their members' interests in a robust manner, and they were not overly preoccupied whether a 'unity of purpose' existed with management. Of course these views were not held evenly across the organization. Relations between managers and unions were perhaps warmer in the Irish Life side of the business than in Permanent TSB, where more suspicion reigned between the two sides.

7.2   THE IMPACT OF THE RECESSION

The benign business environment that had kept industrial relations stable inside the organization in the years after the merger changed rapidly in 2007 due to the worldwide financial crisis. Irish banks were particularly severely affected by the crisis and pushed in some cases near to the abyss. Although the recession adversely affected IL&P, its impact was not nearly as crippling as on other Irish banks. This is because the organization did not get involved in lending large sums to property developers; even at the height of the Celtic Tiger the company stayed with its main lines of business—providing mortgages to homeowners and pensions and other forms of insurance to individuals. At the same time, the company did not get off lightly. Sales of some its finance products and services fell by about 50%. Concern started to emerge about the impact on the business of nonpayment of loans by some clients. There was even a worry given the turbulence of financial markets whether the banks would have access to sufficient credit to ensure liquidity.

7.3   DEVELOPING A RESPONSE STRATEGY

To counteract this downturn in business fortunes, the company adopted a more cautious approach to lending. It introduced an economy drive across the organization to reduce operating costs and to make processes more efficient. In early 2008, the company was able to reduce costs by introducing a ban on recruitment and not renewing about 30 short-term contracts. But after these initial cost reductions were realized, it became apparent that it would be difficult to achieve further savings without making permanent employees redundant or cutting particular parts of the operation. A series of in-house HRM brainstorming meetings was organized to discuss how costs could be reduced with only minimal negative impact on organizational activity or employee morale. At one of these meetings, a HRM manager made an off-the-cuff remark that the company could pay some employees to leave the company. This remark was picked up by another manager who suggested that it may not be such a far-fetched idea to give employees some form of remunerated sabbatical for a particular period. It would allow the organization to save on staffing costs at the trough of the recession, but would ensure that employees returned when business conditions were likely to be better, thus ensuring that the organization did not lose the investment it had made in these people. For employees, such a scheme would allow those inclined to do so the time to depart and fulfill some ambition beyond the job, in the knowledge that a job was waiting for them when they chose to return.

The more the HRM managers talked about the idea, the more it appealed to them because it appeared a win–win initiative that benefited both the organization and employees. Detailed plans were developed on how such a scheme would work in practice, and once it became apparent that it was feasible, the scheme was launched. In November 2008 Permanent TSB announced that it would be offering employees the opportunity to take a career break. Employees were offered up to €20,000 to take a two-year career break and up to €35,000 for a three-year break. Employees taking the incentivized career break would be offered up-front payments to a maximum of half their annual salary. Those wanting to avail of the offer had to agree to a number of conditions. They would have to sign a noncompete clause to ensure that they did not take a job at a rival bank during the break. In addition, they had to accept that they might not get their own job back on their return—which was in line with the company's general policy when people left the company for a time. Instead, the company committed itself to placing returning staff in "an equal role in the same general geographic area" (Interview). The organization thought that the scheme would be particularly attractive to its younger employees, who could use the career break to travel or return to university to upgrade their skills. The proposal was positively received by employees. A total of 140 employees out of the bank's total workforce of 2,500 took up the offer, most coming from Permanent TSB; only a small number came from Irish Life—the higher incidence of atypical work in this part of the organization made the scheme less attractive to employees there. The employees taking the career break were a mix of all employees: men and women, Irish and non-Irish, some who had worked for the organization for 3 years and others for more than 20 years. Thus, it was simply not young people taking the opportunity to leave the organization for a short time.

Although the incentivized career break signaled to employees that the organization was committed to retaining staff, if at all possible, during the recession, it was not enough to shield the business from the harsh impact of the downturn. In 2008, the company was included in the government's guarantee scheme that was designed to safeguard all deposits. Although the company did not have any serious systematic bad loans, being covered by the guarantee was perceived by employees as the financial crisis taking its toll on the organization. A massive drop in profits in 2008, when the company notched up losses of €437 million, only confirmed this impression. It became immediately apparent that more had to be done across the organization to achieve a better balance between revenue and expenditure. In particular, management was emphatic that discretionary expenditure needed to be reined in across the organization, future spending commitments scaled back and organizational efficiency improved by introducing more rigorous performance schemes.

The HR team accepted that it had to contribute fully to this consolidation effort. To signal that concerted action was needed it was decided that senior managers would receive no bonuses. However, because bonuses were an important part of the remuneration structure for some employees, it was decided to pay bonuses to more junior staff at 25% of normal levels. In conjunction with the business the HR team also decided to increase the level of communication with employees. There was a concern that unhelpful rumors were beginning to circulate about the recession imperiling job security, pensions and employment benefits and rewards. The business wanted to put out the message that nothing would be decided about employment and working conditions without careful deliberations and in-depth discussions with trade unions. At the same time, the business as a whole realized that it had to do something on pay and rewards to help the organization contain costs and restore competitiveness.

The business decided that it would need to introduce a pay freeze in 2009. In a move that departed from established practice, the HR team sought to create a single bargaining process within the organization to obtain union agreement for the pay freeze policy and other related matters. Established procedure was for each part of the organization to conclude separate collective agreements. The HR team considered this change in practice was warranted by the severity of the decline in company fortunes. The various unions were kept fully informed of developments and appreciated that the company was experiencing difficult times. They realized too that expectations about rewards and benefits would have to be tempered: room no longer existed for the generous deals that had been concluded in the early part of the decade. Moreover, the trade unions understood the calculus that helping the organization respond effectively to the recession would be the most sure fire way of advancing the interests of their members. At the same time, they were not prepared to roll over and simply cede to company demands. They were eager to gain full information about the extent to which the company was unable to award any pay increases and to obtain guarantees about job security and other working conditions. They were suspicious of the decision to establish a single bargaining process and only reluctantly decided to join.

In proposing a single bargaining process, management was hoping that it would secure an agreement with the unions on a series of measures to help the organization counter the harsh business environment it was experiencing. This was not the only strategy open to management. Technically, Toward 2016, the national pay agreement, was still in operation and although this provided for a 6% wage increase for employees during 2009–10, it also contained an inability-to-pay clause, which allowed firms experiencing financial difficulties to opt out of paying the increase, subject to a verification process.

Management at IL&P could have elected to follow this procedure, which almost certainly would have resulted in them not having to deliver any pay award. But it chose not to do so at that time in early 2009, deciding instead to travel the more difficult route of creating an internal procedure to build a company-wide consensus about the need for a pay freeze and other measures.

7.4   IMPLEMENTING THE RESPONSE STRATEGY

The first move made toward the single bargaining procedure was the creation of a facilitation process to allow for a full exchange of information and views. The company, with the agreement of the unions, appointed an external third party expert to manage the facilitation process. A hotel in the center of Dublin, away from the company, was selected as the neutral venue for the discussions. When the facilitation was under way, it was immediately evident that a lot of work would be needed to ensure that the process was a success. The lack of trust between the two sides was palpable at the beginning. Moreover, the process was a challenge to the unions because it was one of the few times they were obliged to forge a common view on company-wide issues. Thus, the process got off to a hesitant start, but the facilitator did an enormous amount of behind-the-scenes work to soothe anxieties that existed on both sides. He was also able to craft an agenda that was widely acceptable. Without this initial work by the facilitator, the process may not have got over the first hurdle.

In the ensuing three to four weeks, intensive meetings took place, about eight in all, involving all the parties. The unions challenged management to provide full information about cost and reward structures as well as the company's financial position. In response, management provided the unions with an unprecedented level of information on a broad range of topics. The company's finance director made a presentation that contained so much sensitive information that trade union representatives were required to sign a confidentiality agreement at the start of the session. Unions were also provided with a lot of information about the company's ability to deliver pay increases. In effect, the company opened up the company's books to the union during the facilitation process. These efforts by management to highlight the difficult commercial circumstances that the company was experiencing paid off as a new openness and candor developed between the two parties. Slowly but surely it appeared that union and management were now closer to being 'on the same page' with regard to the company's predicament.

Yet an agreement with the unions on a consolidation plan for the organization proved elusive. Unions were extremely reluctant to enter an agreement that would in all likelihood involve their members making concessions. Union representatives were sensitive to the fact that no other agreement had been concluded in the financial services sector in the aftermath of the financial crisis. They were aware that any agreement they entered into would be the benchmark for similar deals that needed to be done elsewhere in the industry. As a result, they were determined to get the best possible deal at IL&P. Moreover, the union representatives calculated that although their members were fearful for their jobs and pensions, they were also annoyed, if not angry, that they were being asked to make sacrifices to indemnify the wildly profligate actions of a handful of irresponsible property dealers and financiers. Thus, the union officials were in a precarious position: although they empathized with the difficult times faced by the management of IL&P, to retain their credibility with their members and with other employers as a negotiating force, their representatives had to adopt a hard bargaining stance throughout the facilitation process.

Ultimately, although the facilitation process led to high-level information sharing and a lot of positive interaction between the management and union teams, the gap between the two sides was simply too large to bridge. As a result, the facilitation process ended without any agreement being concluded. Although it could be said that the process aimed at securing agreement had broken down, the relationship between management and unions did not descend into acrimony: the facilitation process nurtured cool, dispassionate heads on both sides. Of course, both management and unions reflected internally to assess whether they had followed faulty tactics during the course of the facilitation process, but this was done behind closed doors. For the company, although some positive things came out of the facilitation process, the bottom line was that it was still without an agreement on pay and working conditions. In the absence of any agreement, the company introduced a pay freeze for 2008 and made no profit-related pay bonuses because there were no profits to share. Management concluded that it would be best to avail of the services of the LRC in its efforts to secure a deal with the unions. But it waited nearly 8 months before starting this third-party process so that a better climate existed for the negotiations.

In early to mid-2009, management along with the unions decided to begin the LRC process. However, these talks did not prove successful. In the aftermath of this first round of facilitated talks and in an effort to prove beyond doubt the difficult financial circumstances facing IL&P, the company decided to trigger the inability-to-pay clause of the national social partnership agreement, Toward 2016. An investigator was appointed to examine the financial state of the company. This assessment was conducted at a time when, if anything, the business conditions facing the company had worsened. Before the facilitator announced his decision, management and unions met once again and agreed to recommence the LRC talks. This decision to restart facilitated talks led to the inability-to-pay process being put on hold. The hope was that the LRC would be able to broker a deal between the company and the union. Although the ability-to-pay decision had formally been parked, it nevertheless acted as the ghost at the negotiations convened by the LRC. Knowing this decision lurked in the background, the unions decided to temper their demands. Moreover, LRC staff used the decision to encourage the unions not to pursue overly ambitious bargaining demands. In a sense, the inability-to-pay process was the lubricant that was needed to free up the stalled negotiations.

Yet the negotiations that the LRC managed to get going between management and union were anything but easy. Marathon sessions were needed to make slow progress through a long, complex agenda. Finally, after protracted exchanges and endless support from LRC staff, a deal was hammered out with which both sides were relatively satisfied. In terms of content, the agreement was nothing exceptional, which belies the complexity of the negotiations. On pay, the company agreed to give employees a 2.5% increase in 2009 and 2010. However, the company would give no salary increments or profit-share bonuses in these two years, which would have been valued in excess of 6% on average. The 6% set out in the national wage agreement was also set aside. The company committed itself to making no compulsory redundancies in 2010, but did not make any commitments on job security beyond that date. For its part, the union agreed to engage in a review of the company's defined benefit pension scheme until an agreement was reached. In November 2009 the staff accepted the agreement, bringing to an end a protracted process. The result was a big boost in morale to both staff and management alike as the agreement restored stability to internal industrial relations.

7.5   OUTCOMES OF THE STRATEGY

Since the endorsement of the agreement, relations between management and unions have been constructive and positive, which is fortuitous because business conditions went from bad to worse in the early part of 2010. With the downturn in commercial circumstances, management were forced to propose harsher measures than hitherto had been the case. In particular, it put forward a voluntary redundancy program for the Permanent TSB side of the business. Business conditions were considered too acute for a simple rerun of the incentivized career-break scheme. This proposal for voluntary redundancies was agreed to quickly and painlessly by the relevant unions. The implementation of the program went smoothly and resulted in 200 employees leaving the organization. Our assessment suggests that the new, more constructive relationship between management and unions is also reflected in the progress that has been made in the discussions about restructuring the organization's pension provision. It would be wrong to say that a fully cooperative system of industrial relations now prevails in the organization. But both management and unions have emerged from the long, arduous process of reaching a collective agreement trusting each other more. This new spirit of constructive engagement will be needed as the company continues to face tough market conditions.

Like other parts of the business, the HR function has had to cut back on its planned activities. Parts of a recently formulated learning and development strategy, for example, have had to be put on hold. More use is now being made of internal trainers instead of external providers. The organization is still committed to the Ulrich model, but the context for its use has radically changed. The financial crisis has caused IL&P to review its business priorities, and this agenda is currently dominating the work of the HR function both at the group level and in different parts of the business. Thus, HR managers are busy leading discussions on the reform of the organization's pension scheme and engaging in scenario planning to make the organization more flexible by recasting internal structures. Throughout the organization, members of the HR team are advancing the idea of value for money: they want employees and teams to think about how they can improve the value in what they do. Thus, the HR function is advancing the business partner model through the policies that are being enacted to deal with the recession rather that by creating structures and systems consistent with this model.

A number of interesting points emerge from this case study. First of all, IL&P adopted some innovative HR policies in response to the economic crisis. Offering incentivized career breaks to employees was widely lauded as a creative way temporarily to adjust employee numbers in inclement business conditions without permanently losing the company-specific skills and knowledge possessed by these people. Very quickly after introducing the scheme, it was being mimicked by other organizations, the acid test of whether a HR policy is widely considered to be well designed and useful. Second, almost immediately after the start of the financial turbulence hitting Ireland, the organization cranked up its communications with employees. Senior management was eager to keep employees as fully informed as possible about the impact of the recession on IL&P, not least to allay employee fears and anxieties about their jobs and livelihoods; apocalyptic rumors had spread like bushfires on the arrival of bad business times, and management sought to do everything to counteract these. Management was also eager to establish an open and constructive dialogue with the unions to establish consensus on the need for cost containment. This resulted in the unions gaining an unprecedented level of access to financial information. This strategy was not fully successful due to what might be called the initial conditions prevailing in the organization.

Third, inevitably when the new company was formed it was not starting from a clean sheet, but with a series of inherited legacies. One of these legacies was an industrial relations culture characterized by a lack of trust and shared commitment between employees, their representatives and management. These characteristics existed to a lesser or greater degree in each of the organizations that came to form IL&P. To use old-fashioned language, the initial conditions in IL&P, at least in terms of industrial relations, was a them-and-us mentality. Because it was decided not to integrate fully the new business, but allow different parts of the organization to operate autonomously, HR found it difficult to develop a coherent pan-organization strategy to promote a more consensus-based approach to industrial relations.

The differentiated corporate structure that was put in place made it difficult for the HR team to promulgate a distinctive uniform set of values based on consensus and unity of purpose across the organization. The relative absence of this normative structure made the task of developing a common approach to the crisis all the more difficult. Nevertheless, the facilitation process that was launched was relatively successful in bringing the two sides closer together than ever before. Both management and unions realize that the task now is to build on this success and to move more decisively toward a consensus-based industrial relations model. The general point is that developing shared understandings between management and unions cannot be done overnight. Departing from relatively adversarial industrial relations requires sustained and ongoing efforts.

The fourth interesting point that emerges from the study was how cooperative and competitive forms of bargaining and negotiations coexisted at the same time in the negotiation and facilitation process. The lesson from the case study is that to obtain more mutuality and shared understandings between unions and managers, especially in times of crisis, organizations, in particular those with a complex legacy involving variable forms of industrial relations, almost inevitably have to accommodate both cooperative and competitive forms of bargaining.

MINIMIZING JOB LOSSES AT SHERRY FITZGERALD

Context

If the boom in property values was synonymous with the Celtic Tiger economy, the slump in the property market has been one of the cardinal features of the Irish recession. An indication of the scale of the decline in property values is that in mid-2010 house prices nationally were 34% below their (2007) peak and 42% below their peak in Dublin. House prices had returned to their 2002 levels. The cumulative fall in the price of new houses by the end of 2011 was projected to be close to 50% of their peak. Trends in activity in the housing sector also reflected a severe downturn. At the end of April 2010 new house completions were 50% down on April 2009 (ESRI 2010: 18–19; Bank of Ireland 2010: 2–3). Rents for private dwellings fell by 27% from their peak levels (Daft 2010: 6). In the commercial property sector, capital values underwent a cumulative decline in the downturn of 56% (Bank of Ireland 2010: 11). These trends mark Ireland out as an outlier internationally and have had significant implications for businesses in the real estate sector. In 2010 some analysts believed that the recession in the sector was bottoming out (Bank of Ireland 2010; Daft 2010).

Sherry FitzGerald is Ireland's leading estate agent, with a strong brand identity and commitment to customer service. The firm has both residential and commercial property arms (the latter being partly owned by DTZ International) and has an international presence through its Marsh and Parsons business, which engages in residential sales and lettings in central London, and through its affiliation with Christie's Great Estates, which is involved in the sale of high-end properties in many countries. In addition to its direct employees and international activities, the firm also operates a network of franchises throughout Ireland through local estate agents. The firm has grown significantly from its foundation in the early 1980s, acquiring a series of real estate and related businesses and expanding beyond its original Dublin base. The company went public in 1999 but became a private company again in 2000 under a management buyout. In early 2008 Sherry FitzGerald employed 315 staff in its Irish operations and about 177 in its London property business. The company's business represents upward of 20% of the Dublin residential market branch network, and its commercial arm is in the top five in the sector. The company does not recognize trade unions or engage in collective bargaining.

7.6   THE IMPACT OF THE RECESSION

The case study focuses on HR responses to the recession affecting those directly employed by the firm, primarily in its residential and commercial property divisions. Like other firms in the sector, Sherry FitzGerald was significantly affected by the recession, the associated credit crunch and the slump in the real estate market. In mid-2006, the company anticipated the fall in the residential property market, which was particularly pronounced in Dublin. The fall in the commercial property market occurred at a lag of about 18 months. With a shift occurring from a sellers' market, the company began to consider the implications for how the business was configured and the role of HR in supporting the business. Those directly involved in top-level management "saw a correction coming in the marketplace but did not [at first] see the tsunami coming" (Interview) represented by the Irish banking crisis and the deep and prolonged recession that was to ensue. In the residential market the volume of transactions fell by some 40%, and their capital value fell by some 50% from the market peak to 2010. The volume of the new homes sales fell by about 70%. In the commercial property division the market trend led to a change in the product mix with more emphasis on the provision of professional services and less on the agency function.

During the boom, fees had drifted downward in the industry to an all-time low because property was selling so quickly and customers placed little value on service quality. As the volume of transactions fell away and property values collapsed in the recession, Sherry FitzGerald determined that it could not remain in business with its present fees structure. In the very difficult prevailing market conditions, and against the industry trend, an increase in fees placed a premium on service quality, and the company's need to add more value to services was supported by more focused learning and development activities as well as the addition of a customer insight function to the business.

7.7   DEVELOPING A RESPONSE STRATEGY

As discussed earlier, Sherry FitzGerald anticipated changing market conditions in 2006 and had begun to rethink the manner in which the business operated and the role of HR in supporting the changes that seemed warranted in the light of business trends. HR is a group service function, providing support to all divisions of the business in Ireland. The function, including HRD, employed five people at the outset of the recession. The numbers employed changed thereafter, but not significantly. During the period of sustained buoyancy in the sector, HR priorities focused on recruiting and retaining staff. From 2006 onward the focus was to change toward restructuring and retraining.

As conditions in the industry began to change in 2007, HR was engaged in reviewing the type of people the company needed and the competencies they should possess. Other HR practices and systems such as performance management and succession planning were also subject to review. It was decided to restructure the reward system better to reward individual high performers, as the existing system was seen to reward average over 'star' performers to too great a degree. A quarterly bonus system linked to teamwork at branch level was also part of the reward system, and this was now to be more closely aligned to data emanating from customer insight research. The company sought to achieve a balance between individual and group or team aspects of the reward system, both to recognize individual sales and fees income and to preserve a team culture. In particular responsiveness to customer service was recognized as integral to the brand and increasingly important to business success. More difficult market conditions were also seen to warrant the removal of a variety of fringe benefits.

In the summer of 2008, Sherry FitzGerald resolved that significant further and new changes in HR were warranted. Staff could no longer be insulated from developments in the market. Turnover had declined substantially, and losses were expected for 2008 across the business. The firm decided that its chief HR priority in adapting to the worsening downturn would involve employment protection and job security. Faced with the imperative to cut costs significantly, the company initially resolved to engage in salary cuts in its Irish businesses as the 'primary platform for change' rather than to institute immediate redundancies. Salary cuts were to remain in place until market conditions improved significantly. Any redundancies that might be deemed necessary in the future would be kept to a minimum, and the company declared that there was no plan to close any branches or departments. Career breaks and flexible work options such as reduced working weeks were offered to staff. Although voluntary, these measures were nevertheless targeted at staff in particular roles or at individual staff members, who were asked to consider their situation in the company. Some use was also made of staff redeployment within the business, as a recruitment embargo was also in operation. With the onset and the deepening of the recession, a significant number of staff that had joined the company during the boom chose to exit in the more difficult market conditions now prevailing, and with pay cuts now in place. Often longer-serving staff appeared better able or more willing to adapt to changes in the market. Although the company lost some high performers in this way, the general posture was that some who left had taken a sensible decision to exit the firm or sector.

The strategic decision to prioritize job security was understood and was communicated as appropriate to a business and culture that emphasized teamwork and as consistent with Sherry FitzGerald's brand and reputation. For senior management it was seen as a case of "Sherry FitzGerald being all about our people working together in good times and bad times" (Interview). It was understood that some staff would have preferred to keep their salaries and see colleagues let go. But the company's decision was to reinforce the culture by instituting cuts to protect jobs.

7.8   IMPLEMENTING THE RESPONSE STRATEGY

Sherry FitzGerald's strategy was communicated to senior managers and staff in July 2008, and the first round of pay cuts came into force in September. The plan involved introducing cuts in base salary on a sliding scale, with the heaviest burden falling on the highest paid staff and with protection for staff on the lowest pay, whose pay was not reduced. The scale of the cuts introduced was significant involving reductions from the top down of between 33% down to 5% for those affected. All fringe benefits—specifically car allowances and employer pension contributions—were also suspended. The approach adopted was seen as both fair and well aligned with the company's culture.

To roll out the first round of salary cuts, Sherry FitzGerald used a program of intensive communications. Staff were informed of the measures to be introduced by the company in a series of town-hall meetings, undertaken between managing directors and people employed in the business's different divisions. The ground for these was carefully prepared. Senior managers and HR met to agree and 'script' the substantive communications, which were then led by senior managers. The town-hall meetings were followed by one-on-one meetings between line managers and their reports, and HR provided support through a dedicated service informing staff of the effects of the salary cuts on individuals. Staff could also seek information or voice their views through the company's open-door policy. The approach adopted was understood as to be transparent, and this was seen as critical to the preservation of the trust of staff in senior management and the company. Although no structured assessment of staff responses was undertaken, informal feedback and feedback received from line managers indicated that staff in general felt that the measures undertaken were unavoidable and fair. Nor did the changes result in any litigation or significant level of grievances. The changes in Sherry

FitzGerald were being undertaken in an industry where competitors were making people redundant and closing down branches, and staff reactions were also affected by their awareness of developments in other companies.

With no easing of market conditions, the salary cuts implemented were not sufficient in terms of cost savings, and in late 2008 compulsory redundancies were seen as unavoidable. In total 31 redundancies were implemented across the Irish businesses. Although it was hoped that this would be the final necessary cost-saving measure, in April 2009 the company implemented a second round of cuts in salaries. This round again involved cutting salaries based on a sliding scale, although this time the reductions were introduced across the board with no protection for those on the lowest salaries. This arose from staff feedback that it was felt that insulating any groups from the pay cuts was unfair.

Besides reductions in salary and offering a variety of reduced and flexible working time options, the company also changed some other HR practices and systems. Once the program of salary cuts and related changes in work and working time options was implemented, HR resumed the review of HR practices and systems that had begun in 2007 but had been overtaken by the severe effects of the recession on the business and the demands on HR and senior executives in responding to these. There was a concern to retain and motivate high-performing staff and to prevent them being head hunted by competitors in the short or medium term. Competences were also again addressed in the context of how the business might evolve. Talent management and succession planning were again considered.

There was a concern, in particular, for streamlining the performance management system and adapting to the prevailing business conditions, but a determination at the same time by HR to maintain the performance management process in the face of skepticism from some in management as to whether much could be gained given the more difficult conditions in the marketplace and the reductions in bonuses that commonly followed. The management of performance, both through twice-yearly formal reviews, and more generally on a day-to-day basis, now occurred in the context of formal metrics in place in the business. These included key performance indicators, fee income, conversion rates in turning property valuations into sales, market share and customer satisfaction data arising from the company's customer insight process. These metrics were employed both at the branch and at the individual level as appropriate. The company also now adopted a more rigorous approach to managing underperformance, with less tolerance being shown to underperforming staff than during the property boom. There was no greater resort to disciplinary processes, however, with any problems in this area confined to verbal warnings.

Sherry FitzGerald maintained its HRD effort but reduced its spending— HRD activity now also became considerably more focused and proactive. During the property boom the company had been willing to respond to staff training requests. Now HRD activity was more closely aligned with business imperatives, which included fostering cross-learning between the company's divisions and business activities and supporting marketing messages with service attributes valued by customers. Training was now used to a greater degree to change staff behavior and was seen as having gained considerably in importance in consequence. It had been intended by the company to focus on employee engagement and to assess staff attitudes and satisfaction on a structured basis, but this activity had been set aside due to the pressures of handling the effects of the recession. Employee engagement was identified as a significant area of future activity.

The HR function was seen as central to and influential within Sherry FitzGerald's response to the recession. HR managers were required to devise responses to new business realities, as interpreted chiefly by senior business unit managers. To this process they brought their expertise, knowledge of employment law and professional appreciation of the importance that response options and their implementation needed to be perceived by staff as reasonable and fair. HR was seen as operating in a partnership role with senior managers in devising the company's response to the effects of the recession. This was seen to have occurred as much through informal as formal processes, although the degree of informality/formality varied across business divisions in reflection of their somewhat differing cultures. Those involved in general management and HR positions believed that handling the effects of the recession had elevated the status and stature of HR, because HR had become more involved in the business, in contrast to the period of the property boom when it seemed often to be preoccupied with recruitment. It was also clear to people involved in the function that HR had needed to become more conscious of the importance of delivering value and delivering solutions as distinct from simply informing other managers of problems and constraints. Although strategic competence was important, operational processes also remained central and people involved in HR had to be comfortable in working at both levels and in moving between each.

7.9   OUTCOMES OF THE STRATEGY

Sherry FitzGerald has retained its position and brand identity in the industry during a period of severe and unprecedented contraction and has preserved and indeed reinforced its culture. The company's operational cost base has been reduced by some 48%. Minimal compulsory redundancies have been instituted and there has been a satisfactory level of take up of reduced and flexible working-time options. Employment has fallen to 214 in 2010, a drop of about 32% from the start of 2008. Natural attrition, including retirements accounted for 70% of the fall in employment and compulsory redundancies accounted for 30% (representing a fall of about 10% on the employment level in early 2008). Staff experienced significant cuts in pay and the curtailment of some fringe benefits.

As senior managers see it, the company has experienced no significant decline in morale, and staff in general appeared to have formed the view that changes introduced in pay and conditions were unavoidable, appropriate and fair. No litigation or rise in grievance activity arose from the changes made to terms and conditions of employment. Of course those who exited the company may have included employees unwilling to accept salary cuts, curtailed opportunities for bonus earnings or other changes in the company's HR regime.

As management perceives it, the combination of anxiety resulting from recessionary conditions in the industry, pressure on the business, the systematic use of metrics and the more rigorous application of HR processes, such as performance management, have meant that staff are now often working more intensively or feel under more pressure than in the past. A fear factor has also come to exist in the current environment, notwithstanding the company's concern to reassure staff that any developments in the business with implications for pay, conditions or job security have been and will continue to be communicated openly to all employees.

Like other firms in the sector, Sherry FitzGerald experienced a severe impact from the recession and the slump in the Irish property market. The company resolved that only by achieving cost reductions could it remain in business and secure the maximum number of jobs. Sherry FitzGerald's approach to unprecedented commercial pressures was well aligned with its culture, brand identity, mode of conducting business and business strategy. Leadership, trust and teamwork are the values seen to be of major importance to the success of the business, albeit balanced by a focus on individual performance and sales. The focus in managing the effects of the recession was on maintaining teamwork and, more generally, on preserving commitment to the firm by preserving the maximum number of jobs, cutting base salaries—initially through larger proportionate pay reductions at higher salary levels—stretching performance, focusing HRD and changing behavior in the direction of better service quality at a time when fees were being increased.

Intensive communications, conducted for the most part through established mechanisms, in particular town-hall meetings and one-on-one meetings between line managers and their reports, were seen to be a highly significant and effective component of the company's approach to implementing changes in terms and conditions. These mechanisms were backed up by information on the effects of the changes on individuals provided by HR and through the company's open-door policy.

The firm had begun a review of HR systems, processes and objectives with a medium- to long-term focus at the outset of the recession. This review was initially overtaken by the cost-cutting program, but more recently HR has returned to concerns such as the core competencies required to support the evolving business, succession planning and employee engagement—areas seen as central to position the company for its future development.

The changes introduced met with little resistance from staff, although some people not willing to countenance lower salaries and revised terms and conditions more generally may have left the company as a result. For those remaining work pressure and performance expectations have been higher in a work and business environment in which metrics relating to hard (conversion rates, fees income, etc.) and soft (customer satisfaction, service quality, etc.) dimensions of performance are more systematically deployed in the management process at both the individual and the branch level.

HR is seen as acting as an effective and valued business partner to the senior managers involved in developing and implementing the response program in different divisions of the business. The function is seen as influential, but is also expected to contribute solutions to business problems. HR is seen to have gained in stature through its contribution to securing the firm in the most severe crisis ever experienced in the Irish property market.

THE COST RECOVERY PROGRAM AT THE DUBLIN AIRPORT AUTHORITY

Context

The Dublin Airport Authority (DAA) is responsible for operating the main Irish airports at Dublin, Cork and Shannon. The DAA also has an international division, ARI, which is mainly involved in airport retailing activities. The DAA was established out of the reorganization of Aer Rianta in 2004, an initiative undertaken to provide greater strategic and operational autonomy for each of the airports. Aer Rianta/DAA has a tradition of orderly and progressive industrial relations and human resource management. The company is highly unionized: union density standing at 95%. The unions representing staff are SIPTU, Mandate, IMPACT, UNITE and the TEEU. SIPTU accounts for 70% of staff. The negotiating and dispute resolution procedures in place when the company and its unions responded to the recession were standard, involving provision where deadlock existed, for resort to the LRC and the Labour Court.

From the mid-1990s to the early 2000s Aer Rianta and the majority of its unions were party to a radical and innovative partnership arrangement, known as Constructive Participation (CP). This involved a series of structures and joint arrangements designed to involve unions and employees in decision making from the level of day-to-day work to business units and corporate commercial strategy. The CP initiative chalked up some significant achievements, especially in areas such as the adaptation of airport retailing following the abolition (in 1999) of duty-free sales for passengers on flights within the EU and in the development of a joint strategy for the company's future development (in 2000). However, the partnership model proved unsustainable and decayed under the weight of a series of internal and external pressures—leaving in its train a complex legacy that combined negative and positive experiences and assessments by management and unions. By the time of the onset of the recession, HR and IR at the DAA had reverted to a standard pattern for Irish commercial state-owned enterprises, and few of the figures who had been prominent in CP remained involved on either side. Thus, the legacy of the company's and unions' foray into cooperative industrial relations was both variegated and depleted when the parties faced the new and unfamiliar challenges of a contracting business from 2008. Yet both the emergence and some of the achievements of CP also indicated the capacity of the DAA and its unions to adopt innovative postures toward the conduct of industrial relations and to develop innovative solutions to commercial challenges.

The airports, particularly Dublin Airport, are classical occupational communities. Staff frequently reside in areas contiguous to their work. Family ties and intermarriage among staff are also common. Terms and conditions of employment have traditionally been favorable relative to other employments. Although no work stoppage had occurred at the company for a decade, the airports were vulnerable to industrial action and closure, especially in areas such as security and the fire service. Measures such as compulsory redundancies or unilateral pay cuts were viewed as anathema or likely to be staunchly resisted in the commercial semistate employment and industrial relations culture that prevailed at the DAA. If the unions had the capacity to disrupt or close the airports, it was less clear whether the government would sanction management proposals that might provoke work stoppages and disruption.

7.10   THE IMPACT OF THE RECESSION

Airport charges at the DAA had been regulated since 2001 by the Commission for Aviation Regulation. The recession began to affect the DAA in the third and fourth quarters of 2008. Over the year as a whole, passenger traffic declined marginally by 0.6% to just under 30 million. Passenger traffic had fallen by 6% in the final quarter of the year. Group profit for 2008 fell by 28%, and credit rating agency Standard and Poor's changed the DAA's rating from A to A−. The DAA projected that 2009 would bring significantly more difficult trading conditions and involve the first significant decline in passenger traffic for two decades. In 2008 the DAA employed just over 3,000 full-time equivalents (FTEs), 2,668 of these worked in the DAA's Irish airports. A ban on the recruitment of permanent staff had been in place since 2007 pending the outcome of a competition for the right to operate a new terminal under construction at Dublin Airport. Some 300 employment contracts were rolled over on a month-to-month basis by the DAA.

Business conditions did worsen significantly during 2009. Passenger numbers declined by just under 13% and turnover also fell by 13%. The DAA's Annual Report for 2009 recorded that group profit declined by 51%. After provision for redundancy payments, this resulted in an after-tax loss of €13 million in 2009, compared to a profit level of 47 million euro recorded in 2008. Consistent with its posture toward the industry and developments at the DAA, Standard and Poor's further reduced the DAA's credit rating.

The group's response to the effects of the recession on its businesses was to launch a cost-cutting plan with significant implications for staff costs and industrial relations, as is examined in the following. During 2009, as the DAA sought to secure agreement on its cost-cutting plan, the outlook for 2010 progressively worsened. Early in 2009 the company projected that payroll cost savings of €25 million would be required in the light of the anticipated earnings shortfall for 2010. This was revised upward to €55 million in June of 2009 in the context of an expected earnings shortfall now estimated at between €60 to €70 million. The DAA had borrowings of about €1 billion in 2009, mainly arising from the ongoing construction of a second terminal at Dublin Airport and related infrastructural development.

At the same time as the recession was having a severe impact on its business the DAA was anticipating the opening of the new second terminal (T2) at Dublin Airport in 2010. T2 was designed to accommodate 12 million passengers annually (compared to the 24 million passengers accommodated by Terminal 1 in 2008). The government had declared its intention to open the operation of T2 to a competitive tender process. The DAA thus faced the prospect of having to compete to operate its own new terminal at Dublin Airport, and the Authority anticipated that the cost of operating the new terminal, in particular the paybill costs, would be a highly significant factor in awarding the contract to operate T2. The unions were of the view that they had secured a commitment from the government in a medium-term review of the social partnership agreement, Sustaining Progress, in 2004 that there would be a role for unions in the operation of T2—irrespective of the eventual operator. However, this seemed far from being an absolute guarantee, and they could not be secure as to the level of influence they could exercise on a new operator or as to the possible implications for pay and conditions in other DAA locations. Thus, for the unions as for the DAA itself the search for an accommodation that both responded to the effects of the recession and might secure the operation of T2 for the DAA were important background considerations.

7.11   DEVELOPING A RESPONSE STRATEGY

Prior to the onset of the recession in the second half of 2008, the DAA and its unions were occupied with a number of issues. Anticipating the competition for the contract to operate T2, the DAA sought agreement on a series of measures, including the introduction of a defined contribution pension scheme for new entrants, changes to the company's sick-pay scheme, a severance package, revised performance management arrangements and revised work practices, new consultative arrangements and the introduction of a fast-track industrial relations tribunal that might expedite dispute resolution and deliver binding adjudication in disputes over change. This package of measures was rejected by SIPTU, and this union had balloted for industrial action in support of its own claim and that of the other unions for improvements in the company's pension scheme. The dispute and talks on other issues being pursued by the company were referred to the LRC. At the LRC the parties reached agreement on significant changes to the pension scheme for new entrants. The other issues at play between the parties were to carry over into 2009, by which time the effects of the recession were to add both further issues and added pressures to negotiations. December brought another dispute over the payment of an annual bonus, the DAA seeking to pay this on a pro rata basis to part-time staff.

At the end of 2008 the DAA reached a high-level accord with SIPTU, which established agreed parameters for the operation of T2. This deal, unannounced at the time, and presaging less favorable terms and conditions in T2, cleared the way for a bid by the DAA for the operation of Terminal 2. Mandate soon after concluded an interim agreement with the company on terms and conditions in new retail outlets in an extension to Terminal 1, which were less favorable than those in existing airport retail shops. This interim agreement also anticipated that terms and conditions in T2 would diverge from those in existence in T1. Thus, the major DAA unions and the company were already converging on common parameters with regard to the likely character of terms and conditions in T2.

At the end of 2008 the DAA informed the unions that the financial outlook for 2009 and beyond had deteriorated significantly. In early 2009 the company presented the unions with the financial outlook in a large plenary gathering that involved many union representatives as well as full-time officials. The essential message communicated was stark: ongoing cost savings of €25 million would be required through the introduction of a Cost Recovery Program (CRP). This savings target was subsequently to be revised sharply upward several times as business conditions and projections further worsened. The company volunteered independent verification of its financial situation and prospects—grudgingly or unenthusiastically as the unions saw it—and the unions chose a financial expert from Mazar's, who authenticated the financial data presented to the unions by the DAA and who was to play an important continuing role in unfolding developments.

The DAA identified four pillars of a solution to the cost recovery challenge. These involved staff reductions (the largest single components of the cost savings sought), a freeze on pay and bonus payments, the buying out of some existing terms and conditions of employment (principally service-based increment payments) and a series of other changes. From the beginning HR led the strategy of identifying payroll cost-saving areas to be pursued and of determining how these and the financial circumstances of the company would be presented to staff and unions. The stature of HR in the company had been bolstered by the December 2008 agreement with SIPTU on T2 and by the earlier agreement on a new pension scheme for new entrants to the company. HR resolved to engage in intensive, ongoing and direct communications with staff, undeterred by union complaints that this approach might inflame the situation and impair the unions' attempts to gain an understanding among their members of the seriousness of the company's circumstances.

Although the company's chief executive fronted some of the communications activity, HR were the main drivers of the communications program. The governance of HR strategy was conducted through a top-level management group, chaired by the CEO and comprising key senior executives, the HR director and the head of industrial relations.

The company was of the view that negotiations between the sides concerning the CRP itself were from the beginning based on mature and constructive engagement that was 'open and honest,' were built on a platform of common agreement regarding the DAA's financial circumstances and prospects and were affected by few adversarial tactics or ploys. At the same time, management were prepared, as will be seen, to raise the specter of compulsory redundancies and outsourcing and to signal to the unions the company's resolve to stand firm in the event that work stoppages might be mooted. As will be seen, quite conventional forms of industrial relations leverage were also employed by the company to secure eventual agreement with the unions. The unions also portrayed the DAA's approach to achieving payroll cost savings as traditional in character. Rather than seeking to engage with them on a joint basis to examine potential options for cost savings, the company, as the unions saw it, opted to determine cost saving measures unilaterally. The unions felt that the message being conveyed was that if cost savings could not be achieved through a negotiated settlement, they were unavoidable and would in any event be achieved without agreement.

However, before details of the cost-saving measures sought by the DAA were presented to the unions, industrial relations more generally at the DAA became considerably more adversarial and threatened to spill over into industrial conflict. As the company sought to hold the ring on pay costs, pending progress in negotiations on the CRP, the DAA unions, following the lead of the ICTU, balloted for industrial action in protest against the nonpayment of the national pay agreement rises negotiated by the social partners in September 2008. Although developments at national level led to the avoidance of a work stoppage on this issue, SIPTU threatened industrial action over the company's unwillingness to pay annual increments pending CRP talks. Conflict was avoided when the increments dispute was referred to the Labour Court in April. The Court's subsequent recommendation that increments should be paid in return for a commitment by the unions to engage positively with the DAA on the CRP—specifically on alternative cost reductions of similar value to the increment payments—cleared the way for engagement between the parties on concrete CRP proposals and measures.

7.12   IMPLEMENTING THE RESPONSE STRATEGY

Talks between the parties on the CRP began in earnest in May 2009. By this point the anticipated earnings shortfall at the DAA was €60 to €70 million for 2010, and the three airports were expected to record losses in 2009.

This financial projection was conveyed directly to staff in a letter from the CEO. Against this backdrop the company would now seek cost reductions of €55 million, eventually to be scaled back to CRP payroll cost reductions of a minimum of €38 million.

The DAA presented the unions with a diverse range of options for achieving ongoing cost reductions in the paybill of the magnitude now seen to be required. A reduction of 400 jobs was envisaged through a voluntary severance scheme; a pay and bonus freeze was proposed as were changes to overtime and other premium payments, as well as to the sick-pay scheme. There were to be new terms and conditions for new entrants and for staff categories subject to the T2 tendering process. The proposals presented also included career breaks and reduced-working-hours options. The company envisaged gaining agreement through a short intensive period of engagement on the proposals and envisaged that local agreements would be reached on working practices and mobility and other arrangements resulting from staff leaving through the voluntary severance scheme. The company initiated its voluntary severance scheme prior to agreement on a package of measures, and received some 300 expressions of interest with respect to the package on offer.

Negotiations on the CRP continued through June into August. In the talks the unions canvassed what was described as a 'golden share.' This would involve profit sharing or bonus payments on the company's return to profitability. The negotiations reached a turning point in September when the DAA indicated to the unions that the take-up of the voluntary severance scheme had been significantly lower than targeted with the result that higher cost savings would now be required in other payroll areas. An expanded set of cost-saving proposals was now put on the table. These included the outsourcing of various service areas, including cleaning in Dublin, maintenance in Shannon and retail warehousing, management redundancies and possible pay cuts of 10%. SIPTU declared its firm opposition to outsourcing and pay cuts and, in common with the other unions, was staunchly opposed to compulsory redundancies. The company halted the voluntary severance scheme pending agreement on the CRP and declared its intention to refer the program to the LRC.

The negotiations were being conducted in a context in which the parties shared some common principles and interests. The financial disclosure provided to the unions' consultant meant that there was little disagreement with regard to the nature or scale of the company's financial difficulties. Crucially also, both parties were aware that an inability to reach agreement on the CRP could seriously impair their joint objective of the DAA becoming the operator of T2, while any disruption to the airports could prove fatal to this objective. More generally, certainly as perceived by management, the parties had agreed some other objectives early on, particularly the restoration of the DAA to profitability, a commitment to sustainable good employment and an understanding that staff would share in the future success of the company.

Such areas of common interest and understanding aside, the parties were also divided in significant respects. The unions strongly opposed issues such as outsourcing; changes to terms and conditions, such as the payment of increments; and the rescinding of some historic premium payments at the airports. For now they also maintained their opposition to pay cuts. The DAA had a strong awareness that any attempt to force changes in these areas might result in work stoppages that were unlikely to be acceptable to the government. Yet the unions also harbored fears that the management side might still opt to take unilateral action around their preferred agenda for achieving savings. The DAA had gained leverage from initially offering the voluntary severance scheme before an overall agreement was reached with the unions and obtaining, thereby, some 300 expressions of interest—given the level of union organization most of these were from union members. The continuing rollover of about 300 temporary contracts was an additional source of leverage for a successful agreement on the CRP and for progress on T2.

Yet as the parties began to engage in circular arguments and with little further progress in sight, the intervention of the LRC was welcomed by both sides. LRC mediation brokered agreement in areas where the parties had appeared willing to find accommodation—principally voluntary severance and its operational implications, the deferral of the national pay agreement and the nonpayment of discretionary bonuses—and also allowed progress to be made in other areas like reductions in overtime and other premium payments. Critically, the process also created the space for some innovative proposals to emerge in the difficult area of reductions in pay.

Given the limited take up of the voluntary severance scheme and the unions' position on a number of strands of management's proposals, pay reductions appeared to be a necessary component of any agreement. The position of SIPTU's lead negotiator was that standard pay cuts would not work or meet with acceptance at the airports, and particularly at Dublin Airport. The unions also viewed management's proposal to cut pay as a permanent solution for a temporary problem. Once the DAA returned to profitability, lower pay on an ongoing basis would make the company more highly attractive for privatization. As one of the key SIPTU negotiators saw it, it was necessary in the circumstances that prevailed to 'think outside the box' in searching for a solution to the issue of achieving savings in the area of pay. Management also indicated a willingness on their part to adopt an innovative approach to cost saving from the outset of the process.

The SIPTU Aviation Branch official had begun work on a proposal to be known as the Employee Recovery Investment Contribution (ERIC), in which pay cuts would be reversed when the DAA returned to profitability and staff would be accorded a financial dividend in return for their willingness to accept temporary pay cuts. This amounted to a development of the earlier 'golden share' idea, now linked with temporary reductions in pay which would be viewed as an investment by staff in securing the future viability and profitability of the DAA. At LRC conciliation SIPTU undertook to indicate how a proposal of this kind might form part of an overall agreement on cost recovery. The proposal that formed the basis of talks between the parties envisaged pay reductions on a graduated scale, wherein progressively higher earnings attracted larger percentage reductions. These reductions would be temporary and would cease when the company's business and financial circumstances revived. In an early formulation of ERIC the unions envisaged the repayment by the company of pay cuts that had been made. The unions had also favored using passenger numbers as the basis on which the company's revival might be established. In the face of resistance by the management side, these proposals were modified by the dropping of the repayment proposal and by using return-on-equity (ROE) targets or thresholds as the basis on which the company's performance would be assessed and pay cuts rescinded. The employee dividend idea found expression in a commitment by the company to institute a profit sharing scheme. The ERIC proposal was developed and modified with the continued involvement of the unions' financial consultant, who also played a key role in communicating to union members the import of the version ultimately agreed with the company.

The ERIC proposal represented the cornerstone of the agreement on cost recovery brokered by the LRC. The craft unions however refused to continue in the conciliation process, walking out of the talks mainly because of their dissatisfaction with proposals to cut overtime and other premium payments, which they saw as having a disproportionate effect on the members' earnings. They subsequently engaged in a parallel-talks process with the company, finally accepting essentially the same settlement that had been agreed to by the other DAA unions.

The agreement reached at the LRC in December 2009 reflected the parties' common understanding of the financial and business problems and challenges faced by the company. The restoration of the DAA's financial position was seen as the key to sustainable employment. With an eye to Terminal 2, the agreement accepted that new entrants would be appointed on different terms and conditions that would nevertheless be sufficiently attractive to recruit and retain high-caliber staff. One hundred temporary jobs would be lost, and 320 permanent staff would be facilitated in exiting the company. A series of changes to shift rosters and work practices were agreed in different areas to deliver services with fewer people and at higher levels of efficiency. The unions undertook to facilitate staff mobility in that context. The parties agreed €5 to €6 million in headcount reductions in the management grades. For the company this would equate to over 80 management positions. Overtime payments were reduced from double time to time and a half, and the number of permitted uncertified sick days was reduced from four to two. Reflecting a long-established management objective, a new dispute procedure was agreed on, involving the setting up of an internal committee with an agreed independent chair. This committee would adjudicate on any disputes that arose during the implementation phase of the cost-recovery agreement. Adjudication would be nonbinding at the insistence of the unions. However, the stature of the committee was bolstered through the appointment of a former deputy chairman of the Labour Court and former head of conciliation at the LRC, as its chairman.

Pay levels in the DAA were frozen through the nonpayment of the 2008 National Pay Agreement. The agreed form of the ERIC proposal made provision for graduated cuts in earnings, estimated by some observers to amount to average pay cuts of around 5.5%. Pay cuts were graduated from 0% for staff earning up to €30,000 to 8.5% for staff earning between €80,000 and €90,000. The company opted to apply graduated cuts to higher-level management grades not represented by unions, and so those earning more than €90,000 bore pay cuts of between 9% and 12%. During 2010 and 2011, as the company sought to restore its financial position, there would be no restoration of pay levels. In 2012 or beyond there could be a temporary partial (50%) or full restoration of pay levels, by means of lump-sum payments, if a specified level of ROE (or profit target) was achieved. Only if the average ROE reached 4.57% (or after-tax profits reach €60 million) or 6.75% (or after-tax profits reach €80 million) in three consecutive years would pay levels be permanently restored. Pay will be restored by either 50% in the case of the lower of the two return-on-investment (ROI)/profits thresholds or by 100% in the case of the higher thresholds. The agreement also made provision for a €1-million fund to be distributed to employees if budgeted payroll savings for 2010 are achieved. It was further agreed that a profit sharing scheme would be designed and introduced by negotiation.

The management side was surprised at the scale of the pay cuts accepted by the unions. As they saw it, outsourcing, the removal of historical premium payments (for working on bank holidays), the deferment of increments and some other measures resisted by the unions would have made pay cuts unnecessary. The unions were in possession of a radical and technically complex agreement on which their members would be required to ballot. Influenced in part by their experience of the large and unwieldy plenary meeting convened by the company at the outset of the CRP, they opted to communicate the details of the agreement to their members in more than 60 small-group meetings. Not only were union members being asked to accept significant reductions in pay; they also faced radical changes in shift rosters and work practices arising from operating the airports with at least 400 fewer staff. Senior union officials felt that more was required in explaining the agreement to members than could be achieved in large general meetings preceding the conduct of ballots. When the agreement was balloted on the result was decisive. The margin in favor in SIPTU was more than two to one, and the deal also secured a 90% margin in favor from Mandate. The agreement was carried decisively by a majority of members of the DAA unions. A Mandate senior official was quoted as commenting that the "deal has shown how reasonable companies and trade unions can work together for the sustained progress of both the organization and its employees" (Interview). The DAA's Annual Report for 2009 recognized that "voting to accept a reduction in one's pay is a hugely difficult thing to do and the employees that supported the Group's efforts to address its cost base deserve praise and respect in equal measure."

7.13   OUTCOMES OF THE STRATEGY

Soon after the cost recovery agreement was concluded the parties turned their attention to T2, due to open in November 2010. The company's and unions' shared objective of winning the operation of T2 for the DAA had been an important catalyst for the achievement of the CRP agreement. However, as the unions saw it, that deal provided little by way of a 'fair wind' when the parties subsequently sought to reach agreement on terms, conditions and grades for staff categories to be involved in the operation of T2.

The original procurement process for T2 had been terminated by the government on the grounds that none of the candidates met the minimum requirements set for entrance to the competition to operate the new terminal. The DAA was then invited to demonstrate that it could operate the new terminal within stringent cost, including labor cost, parameters set by the aviation regulator. The requirement that T2 be operated at lower cost than T1 came as no surprise to the DAA or the unions. The parties engaged around the issue of new lower-cost grades in T2 within a radically simplified and more flexible grading structure. Agreement was reached on a new grading and pay structure, and management and SIPTU also reached agreement on a deal that would permit people employed in the Airport Search Unit in T1, who would become surplus to requirement when T2 opened, to avail of a severance package and transfer to the new flexible grade and pay structure pertaining to their work in T2.

No major problems have been reported by either side in the implementation of the CRP agreement. More than 400 people applied for voluntary severance, and the company instituted an outplacement program to provide advice for applicants on redundancy pay, tax, social welfare and career and training options. The unions regard the new rosters and work practices instituted by the CRP as highly onerous to many people. The new disputes committee has yet to be convened as of July 2010. The company and unions are on course to achieve budgeted payroll savings for 2010, which, if achieved, will result in payment of the €1-million incentive payments. The most contentious issue surrounds the handling of redundancies for managers. In what the company regarded as an innovative initiative, a Career Development Center (CDC) was established for more than 30 managers seen to occupy redundant positions but not opting for the voluntary severance package. Those managers transferred to the CDC worked with external coaching and facilitation preparing for a new career outside the DAA. This process can involve retraining and reskilling, including attendance at courses outside the company and funded by the DAA. After six months, during which the voluntary package remains open, managers transferred to the CDC appear likely to be made redundant. The CDC has met with opposition from the main union representing managers. IMPACT has sought a collective agreement to regulate the operation of the CDC and has represented members in appeals against their selection for redundancy via the center. In management's eyes, the establishment of the CDC has enabled the company to streamline management structures.

The CRP at the DAA represents an innovative initiative in which management and unions, working mainly through traditional IR postures and processes, succeeded in concluding an agreement that secured the viability of the company and that provided for the restoration of pay levels once the DAA returned to profitability. Financial disclosure to the unions at the outset of the process allowed the parties to focus on measures that might address the commercial problems affecting the company and its staff. Although the company opted for a conventional approach in which management identified a series of measures with which to address commercial problems, they nonetheless responded to the unions' ERIC proposal, paving the way for eventual agreement on a comprehensive set of cost-saving measures. The innovative ERIC proposal developed by SIPTU is worthy of note as a measure to achieve pay cuts of the scale required in the context of a commercial semistate culture, in which the unions had rejected alternative management proposals involving outsourcing and staff would not countenance changes to some historical terms and conditions. The decision to include senior managers in the pay cuts at the highest percentage reduction level provided for was acknowledged by the unions as leadership by example. The eventual agreement was achieved without overt threats of industrial action or work stoppages in a context in which either might have occurred. The unions' involvement of a financial consultant and their use of small-group meetings to explain the agreement to members were also notable features of the case. The parties' shared objective of gaining the operation of T2 for the DAA was a very significant influence on their resolve to reach an agreement on cost reductions.

The HR management team was pivotal to the company's response from the outset and throughout the talks. The function gained in stature on successfully concluding the CRP and reaching agreement on terms and conditions and a new flexible grade structure for T2. HR also managed a program of intensive, direct communications with employees parallel with their ongoing negotiations with the unions.

Ultimately agreement between the parties had been possible in a context in which the unions understood the financial pressures bearing on the company, while resisting outsourcing or changes in some historical terms and conditions; in which management could utilize some traditional forms of IR leverage; that required significant cost reductions but appreciated the risks of pressing for measures staunchly resisted by the unions and were also cognizant of the general significance of good ongoing relations with the unions; and in which both management and unions sought to be involved in the operation of T2. These circumstances were conducive to an agreement with significant innovative features.

7.14   CONCLUSION

A number of conclusions are offered based on the first three case studies. First, all three cases implemented measures aimed at containing job losses and protecting employment, even if all three also found it necessary to introduce voluntary or compulsory redundancy. Thus, IL&P offered staff incentivized career breaks that were availed of by about 6% of employees. A voluntary redundancy program resulted in a further 8% reduction in employment levels. The company also sought to freeze pay, eventually compromising with its unions on modest pay rises in conjunction with a freeze on service-related increments. In both the DAA and Sherry FitzGerald, where the effects of the recession were more acute and severe, career breaks, short-time working and voluntary and compulsory redundancies were also put into operation to reduce headcount, along with curbs on recruitment. In both these companies, significant pay cuts were also introduced as a means of protecting employment. In the DAA, a mechanism was agreed on to restore pay to prerecession levels, contingent on the attainment of agreed business and financial targets. In Sherry FitzGerald, the pay cuts were more open-ended: the company assuring staff that the cuts would be rescinded when more normal business conditions again prevailed.

In both the DAA and Sherry FitzGerald pay cuts were implemented on a tiered basis, with the highest proportionate cuts falling on the most highly paid. This was seen in both companies as an important contributor to the maintenance of a sense of fairness and of organizational cohesion—its value being mainly symbolic in signifying that the highest financial burdens in the adjustment process would be borne by those with the most capacity to concede pay cuts. In the DAA this measure was welcomed by the unions, whereas in Sherry FitzGerald, staff feedback led the company to extend cuts to all staff in a second round of pay reductions—low-paid staff having been exempt in the first round of cuts.

Although these specific measures were influential and well regarded beyond the three companies in which they were devised and introduced, also important in gaining the firms their 'exemplars' accolade was the extent to which employees as stakeholders were involved in the process of adjusting to the cuts, through the aegis of their representative bodies in the case of IL&P and the DAA, and by senior management having significant regard for employees' interests in the case of the nonunion Sherry FitzGerald.

A further feature of all three companies' response to the recession was the extent to which they relied on more intensive communications processes and mechanisms in informing staff of the seriousness of the commercial circumstances that prevailed and the measures being contemplated to respond to these. For the most part, communication was focused directly on employees, sometimes to the irritation of trade unions.

In the case of Sherry FitzGerald senior management initiated and implemented measures for responding to the recession, without structured input from staff—although staff feedback on the acceptability of the measures introduced was monitored and this resulted in a change of emphasis toward across-the-board tiered pay reductions in the second round of cuts implemented by the firm. In the case of IL&P and the DAA, management again opted to formulate response measures unilaterally, although their original proposals were significantly modified based on engagement with the trade unions, resulting in final measures that were more palatable to staff. In terms of both the postures adopted by management in identifying response measures and the processes involved in winning agreement on these (in the case of IL&P and DAA) or bringing about their implementation, strong aspects of continuity with established postures and practices were evident, as well as some departures from established practice. Continuity was apparent in the decision of senior management in Sherry FitzGerald to formulate and implement response measures de haut en bas, and likewise in IL&P and DAA in senior management opting to formulate response measures unilaterally and then to seek accommodation with the trade unions. In the parties' efforts to find accommodation, traditional, arm's-length, 'competitive' negotiation postures and tactics dominated, and there was a considerable degree of reliance, in a traditional manner, on the LRC to broker a final settlement. But in addition to continuity with established postures and practices, some departures beyond what had been familiar territory to the parties should also be noted. First, in IL&P and DAA, both of the parties to industrial relations observed the advent of a more hardheaded, realistic or mature form of engagement, triggered by the seriousness of the challenges they faced. No industrial conflict ensued, although the parties were mindful that industrial action might well have been sparked off, particularly in the case of DAA.

DAA management and unions' shared objective of being involved in the operation of T2 had a major effect on the parties' willingness to reach accommodation on the Cost Recovery Program. Also new to the industrial relations process was the level of financial disclosure sought by the unions and acceded to by management—however reluctant they may have appeared in the eyes of the unions. Thus, the concession bargaining that ensued in IL&P and in DAA involved a combination of competitive and 'cooperative' bargaining, with the balance residing in more traditional and established postures and practices. Unions in DAA and IL&P remained strong, and no decline in their influence was evident in the case research or in commentary by managers or union officials. At the same time, it was clear that they had gained few claw-backs for their members in the form of expanded benefits when recovery was achieved—the DAA unions' achievement of agreement on instituting profit sharing excepted. Nor did they gain any institutional benefits in return for their involvement in concession bargaining.

With respect to union members and employees more generally it was noted that work regimes had become more demanding in DAA and Sherry FitzGerald. New grading systems and more flexible work arrangements added to work intensity in T2 and union officials speculated as to whether these, combined with lower pay rates, would alter the long-prevalent work culture and perception that people working at the airport enjoyed good jobs with matching pay and conditions.

Manifestly the HR function experienced no cataclysm in the three case study firms. Resources remained broadly on a par with the situation prerecession. The HR function was nonetheless stretched in all cases as the volume of strategic and transactional work increased greatly as a result of downsizing and related changes. Also in all cases HR was conscious of the need to demonstrate the value the function added to the business, reinforcing its primary objective of acting as a business partner in support of the business.

In all cases the HR function was pivotal to company responses to the recession, playing a central role in formulating and implementing options and measures supporting revised business strategies and plans. The stature of HR rose from the seriousness of the threats faced by the companies and their resulting level of dependence on HR expertise to achieve the required adjustments in headcount or in the paybill. The pivotal role of HR and industrial relations considerations in the winning of the tender to operate the new T2 facility in Dublin Airport further underscored the stature of HR in that company. In all cases there was respect by top-level management who were willing to take on the challenge of supporting the business as their primary professional responsibility. But some limitations on HR's sometimes newfound strategic prominence and stature should also be recognized. Consistent with the seriousness of the threats and challenges faced by all three companies, the major focus of HR initiatives was on the present and on survival. Less focus on the medium term and on recovery was apparent—HR managers sometimes being very aware that firefighting activity had absorbed all or most of their time and energy, leaving fewer resources to devote to the issue of how the HR strategy might need to be reframed to support business recovery or steady-state development postrecovery. In the case of IL&P, a prerecession initiative to create a unitary HR function, modeled after the template of Ulrich, was placed on the back burner, whereas an ambition to realign industrial relations arrangements through the creation of a unified groupwide bargaining structure was unsuccessful. Thus, initiatives and activities to align the HR function and HR practices in support of the medium-term development of businesses were more a product of prerecession, steady-state commercial conditions than the disjuncture caused by the recession.

Ultimately, therefore, all three cases involve exemplary, widely admired and effective initiatives for responding to the recession: containing job losses; having regard to employees as stakeholders, either through engaging with their unions or by taking their interests into account; being led by influential HR functions and operating through intensive communications and information disclosure; and involving realistic and pragmatic negotiations and conflict resolution. At the same time, no 'meltdown' or radical shift in prevailing HR or employment models was evident, nor seemingly was any contemplated in the context of medium-term recovery or steady-state development beyond this. What the three companies have in common was a concern to work with their stakeholders to remain commercially viable, contain job losses and, at the same time, to stay on course with respect to changes in human resource management and industrial relations practices and systems contemplated prior to the onset of the economic crisis. The recession had not led the companies either to jettison major features of their established HR and employment models, such as job security, career systems, voice systems, performance management systems, HRD and other central policies and practices. Nor, it appears, had anything along these lines been contemplated. In the recession HRD activity was sometimes curtailed but also refocused better to support business strategy. In some cases performance was managed more rigorously, but HR insisted on the continued relevance of performance management processes. In the unionized firms no radical measures aimed at disengaging from collective bargaining or curtailing its scope were undertaken or contemplated. While in some cases, changes to pension schemes were made—in advance of the recession in the case of DAA—or contemplated (IL&P), no major shift in the 'burden of risk' toward employees arose from the recession. No new philosophy of 'fostering self-reliance' on the part of employees was promulgated, and no new employment deal was evident either in practice or in outline. Although in some cases specific employee engagement initiatives were sidelined by the pressures on HR resulting from the recession in IL&P and Sherry FitzGerald, employee engagement remained an objective in all cases. Admittedly, given that these cases were chosen because the companies had sought to accommodate employees' stakeholder interests in responding to the recession, they are unlikely to be in the vanguard of any shift toward an HR or an employment model in which such a principle would be radically recast. At the same time, however, given their HR and industrial relations sophistication and their strong commercial instincts, the three companies selected for in-depth study would be expected to have questioned the continued appeal or viability of their prevailing HR and industrial relations models if any general trend toward the emergence of a new employment deal was underway or imminent.

What emerges from the cases is a pattern in which HR acted decisively to support business survival as an imperative, sought to take account of employee interests in employment security and, to these ends, adopted a series of pragmatic and eclectic measures, guided by largely familiar and well-understood principles of good practice and tempered by the opportunities and constraints that arose.

8 Maintaining Trust and Developing Competencies in Challenging Business Times
Superquinn, Medtronic and Ericsson

Business responses to challenging economic times are difficult to predict in advance. Particularly uncertain is how a business downturn will affect management–employee relations. Sometimes when the abyss appears on the horizon, managers and employees are 'shocked' into leaving behind mutual mistrust and suspicion. New cooperative relations are forged to secure the viability of the organization. On other occasions, the opposite is true, with managers and employees who enjoyed trust relations suddenly at loggerheads, disagreeing over the scale and nature of any consolidation plan to address the decline in sales and profits. And as each side remains emphatic about the strength of their own position, the trust and cooperation that once prevailed evaporates before their eyes. Of course, some organizations might be in the fortunate position of having adopted a challenging business strategy in advance of a turndown which ensures that organizational routines are not disrupted too much even if business conditions easier are tougher. In this chapter, following on from the last, three case studies are presented of how organizations in quite contrasting organizational and business contexts, have rooted their responses to the recession in maintaining and even deepening trust relations inside the organization even if the strategies used to do so are distinctive in each case.

SURVIVING THROUGH PARTNERSHIP AT SUPERQUINN

Context

Superquinn is a privately owned grocery retail chain with 23 stores and approximately 3000 employees. Until 2005 it was a family run business founded by Fergal Quinn in 1960. Fergal Quinn had a 'hands-on,' paternalistic management style. He spent a portion of each week working on the shop floor of his stores, and he was well known by both employees and customers. Under Quinn's leadership Superquinn developed a reputation for quality fresh food, customer care and service excellence, in addition to being recognized as a pioneer in service provision. In its constant search for ways to create and sustain a good relationship with its customers, Superquinn created a significant competitive advantage for the organization. Superquinn was the first Irish retail organization to acquire the Q mark for quality and service excellence. It also pioneered the idea of in-store food preparation (bakeries and delicatessens) and was the first Irish supermarket chain to introduce online shopping.

In terms of its approach to the management of employee relations, Superquinn operates a closed shop and recognizes three trade unions: SIPTU (Services, Industrial, Professional and Technical Union), which represents the butchers employed by Superquinn; the BFAWU (Bakers Food and Allied Workers' Union), which represents the bakers; and Mandate, which represents the majority of employees (2,400) including sales assistants and administrative staff. Traditionally, management and unions enjoyed a good relationship, and Superquinn maintained what could be described as a benign arm's-length relationship with the trade unions. Management operated from what is, in essence, a traditional pluralist perspective in which unions were viewed as adversaries and were kept at a distance but were treated with respect and trust. Management acknowledged that differences of interest would arise between the company and employees, and accepted that unions could play a legitimate role in helping to resolve conflict. However, although the relationship could be categorized as adversarial, neither side adopted a rigid adversarial stance.

The nature of the working relationship between management and unions was very clearly illustrated by the way in which the vexed issue of extended opening hours was handled in the 1990s. Until the summer of 1994, none of the major multiples opened on Sunday with the exception of the Sundays immediately prior to Christmas on which staff were paid triple time. During the summer of 1994, some of Superquinn's competitors began to experiment with Sunday trading and to extend opening hours during the week. This prompted conflict between the unions and management in relation to the appropriate rates of pay for Sunday trading and the ratio of part-time to full-time staff working on the shop floor. One of Superquinn's main competitors, Dunnes Stores, argued that it could not afford to pay premium rates for Sunday working because extended opening hours would not result in an increase in turnover but simply spread existing sales over seven rather than six days. Therefore, in the summer of 1994, Dunnes opened some of its shops on Sundays and paid a flat rate to all staff for hours worked. This initiated a series of disputes that culminated in a long and bitter strike during the summer of 1995. Eventually, with the assistance of the Labour Court, Dunnes Stores and Mandate reached an agreement, and the Labour Court's recommendation became the blueprint for agreements on extended opening hours. Once the Dunnes Stores dispute was settled, other retailers such as Quinnsworth (now Tesco) and Marks & Spencers reached agreement with Mandate, and so all of Superquinn's major competitors operated extended opening hours. However, it was not until five years later that Superquinn extended opening hours during the week, and it did not commence Sunday trading until the spring of 2001. Through this period, Feargal Quinn made it clear that he was opposed to adopting a confrontational approach to the management of employee relations and would only introduce extended opening hours when his employees were readily willing to support such an initiative.

Although there was clearly a sense of trust and mutual respect between management and the trade unions in Superquinn, a partnership-style arrangement did not exist. Management did not routinely share business-related information with unions, and the role of trade unions was limited to handling disciplinary issues and grievances. The good relationship that management traditionally enjoyed with trade unions in Superquinn was to some extent sustained by the national Joint Labour Committee (JLC) structure, which covers the grocery retail trade in Ireland. The JLC consists of an independent chairperson, employer and trade union representatives who agree, through a process of negotiation, the rates of pay and conditions such as hours of work, overtime rates, annual leave and sick pay, for groups of workers in the industry covered by their JLC. The existence of a JLC for the grocery sector meant that bargaining about contentious issues such as pay was done outside the workplace and this factor, combined with management's benign attitude toward trade unions, helps to explain the relatively positive industrial relations climate in Superquinn. Moreover, from the unions' perspective Superquinn was a relatively good employer, and there was therefore no need to adopt an aggressive or rigid adversarial stance. In an industry associated with low-pay and zero-hours contracts, Superquinn had a contributory pension scheme for all employees over the age of 25 and offered opportunities for training, development and promotion.

Although management did not exchange business-related information with shop stewards or union officials, and trade unions did not have any form of joint decision making role in Superquinn, management did routinely share information and consult directly with employees. A key component of Superquinn's voice management system was the Thursday morning meetings, or 'huddles.' Every week, each department in all the stores received a visit from a member of the senior management team. The purpose of these meetings was not only to share information with employees but also to monitor and control commercial performance of every department throughout the organization. The weekly discussions between senior managers and all members of individual departments covered the overall commercial performance of the organization and the results for the individual department. Each week, performance against targets was reviewed using a series of indicators. These meetings served as a very effective mechanism for managing the flow of information around the organization. They provided an opportunity for senior managers to communicate information to employees, and they provided a forum for employees to express their views and communicate with senior managers. Furthermore, the meetings allowed management and employees to engage in problem solving. For example, if sales in a department had declined during the previous week, the group would consider why this had occurred and make suggestions about ways to tackle the problem. From management's perspective, this activity served two purposes. First, staff working in a particular store were best placed to identify local factors that influence local markets, and these meetings gave senior managers access to this information. Second, it gave employees an opportunity to suggest solutions to problems, which made them more comfortable with changes that they would have to implement.

Thus, under Quinn's leadership, Superquinn had a very effective voice management system that placed emphasis on direct employee involvement. Management not only shared information with employees but also actively engaged them in problem solving in relation to the day-to-day operations of the business. The success of Superquinn's voice management strategy was dependent on a human relations–oriented management style and the ability to maintain a relatively benign and arm's-length relationship with trade unions. A series of contingent factors, such as the existence of the JLC structure, limited the sphere of influence of the unions within Superquinn, and as a consequence there was no imperative to involve trade unions in the management of employee voice in any significant sense.

Takeover by Select Retail Holdings

In 2005 the current owners, Select Retail Holdings, a venture capital company, bought the company from its founder, Fergal Quinn. At the time, it was widely believed that they were primarily interested in the property portfolio retained by the business rather than the retail business itself. This speculation appeared to be confirmed when the company entered into a sale and lease back arrangement with Friends First for six of its properties in 2007 (*Irish Times*, August 31, 2008; *Irish Independent*, May 18, 2007). Since the takeover, there has been ongoing speculation that Select Retail Holdings will sell the retail business. For example, in 2008 there was widespread speculation that a number of bidders including BWG (which owns SPAR), Musgraves (which owns SuperValu), Asda (owned by Walmart) and Sainsburys were interested in buying the retail business (*Industrial Relations News*, 2008).

Following the takeover, most of the senior management team were replaced, and Select Retail Holdings introduced a series of cost-reducing initiatives including, for example, the elimination of staff canteen facilities. These factors, combined with a concern for employment prospects in the event of the business being sold, meant that the takeover altered the industrial relations climate within the organization.

8.1   THE IMPACT OF THE RECESSION

Grocery retail outlets in Ireland can be subdivided into three main categories: (1) multiples (supermarkets, e.g., Tesco, Lidl and Superquinn), (2) independents (single proprietors) and (3) symbol groups (collaborative groups of independents, e.g., Supervalu/Centra and SPAR). Six multiples hold 65% of the value of the Irish grocery retail market. Tesco has 27%, Dunnes Stores has 22.6%, Superquinn has 6.5% and the two discount chains Aldi and Lidl have 3.6% and 6% respectively.[1] One symbol group, SPAR also holds a significant share of market value (20%).

The Irish grocery retail sector has always been highly competitive, and the entry of the two German discount chains, Aldi in 1999 and Lidl in 1998, added to the intensity of that competition. Since entering the market over ten years earlier, Aldi and Lidl had acquired almost 10% of the Irish grocery retail market. Because the market was growing year-on-year during the early part of the decade, the impact of the discounters' presence may not have been so keenly felt. Some groups may have lost market share, but most probably experienced either static or small increases in sales. But the arrival of the recession led to a big drop in consumer spending, which has had a dramatic impact on the grocery retail market. In 2008, the value of the grocery market was estimated to be €9.3 billion; in 2010, it had dropped to €8.8 billion (Kantar Worldpanel 2010a). As consumers became more cost-conscious and shifted from premium to budget products, the discount chains, Aldi and Lidl, enjoyed sustained market growth. An analysis of consumer behavior by industry analysts Kantar Worldpanel suggested that consumers were switching from premium brands, shopping around, visiting more stores, shopping more often but spending less per trip (Kantar Worldpanel 2010b). The decline in the market was further compounded by cross-border shopping. A favorable exchange rate with sterling and lower VAT and excise duties enticed significant numbers of shoppers to Northern Ireland. In the weeks leading up to Christmas 2009, two UK-based retailers that do not have outlets in the Republic of Ireland (Asda and Sainsbury) had a 2.9% share of the Irish grocery market (Kantar Worldpanel 2010b). These developments were bad news for Superquinn because it was positioned at the premium segment of the grocery retail market. Unsurprisingly, the shift in consumer behavior away from high-end shopping, led to Superquinn's market share declining from 7.5% in 2008 to 6.4% in 2010 (Kantar Worldpanel 2011). Trading conditions had become particularly difficult for the company.

8.2   DEVELOPING A RESPONSE STRATEGY

Decisive action was required by the company to adjust to these new adverse market conditions. The response strategy had two key components. First, the company negotiated a Survival Plan, the PCC—Programme for Competitiveness and Change 2009–10, which amounted to a substantive collective agreement providing for the introduction of cost-cutting initiatives such as redundancies and a pay freeze. Second, unions and management agreed to the introduction of a new partnership-style procedural agreement called Working Through Partnership.

The Survival Plan, the PCC, was negotiated with Mandate, SIPTU and BAFTW, and agreement was reached in March 2009. The deal was viewed as highly innovative and progressive by both the employer and the trade unions and is credited with securing the survival of the company. The deal provided for almost 400 voluntary redundancies, a 12-month pay pause and the introduction of new profit sharing and gain sharing schemes. Although the primary focus of the deal was to agree the implementation of a range of cost-cutting measures, it also had a number of innovative features. One was the provision relating to 'banded hours' contracts. Prior to the introduction of the survival plan, workers could be scheduled to work anything between 18 to 39 hours per week, and therefore, their earnings could fluctuate quite dramatically from one week to another. The provision relating to banded hours introduced two types of work schedule or 'band of hours.' Employees can now be contracted to work between 18 to 25 hours or 25 to 39 hours per week. The band to which workers are assigned is determined by the average hours worked over a 13-week period. As part of the review on working hours, unions agreed to a two-hour window of flexibility around start and finish times. This means that employees can be scheduled to commence and finish work within two hours of their standard start and finish times. The banded-hours contract offers some stability of earnings for employees and is viewed by trade unions as a major achievement for staff in the Irish retail sector at a time when workers' hours are being cut across the board. A further indication of the willingness of both parties to be flexible and find mutually beneficial working arrangements can be found in the introduction of annualized hours, which allows employees to spread their earnings across periods such as school holidays, whereas in the past they would have taken unpaid leave.

The Procedural Agreement—Working Through Partnership

Consolidating this substantive collective agreement was a new agreement, Working Through Partnership, that established additional procedural arrangements between the unions and management. Triggering this new procedural agreement was the need for the company to comply with the requirements of the Information and Consultation legislation, Employees (Provision of Information and Consultation) Act, 2006. Superquinn had to make arrangements for consulting with employees. However, the arrangements agreed to in Superquinn's Working Through Partnership are more far-reaching and radical than what would have been necessary to meet the requirements of the Information and Consultation legislation.

In essence, the agreement is a partnership-style arrangement in which unions and management have agreed to "nurture and protect a consultative approach" to managing their relationship (Working Through Partnership Agreement: 3). In reaching this agreement, both unions and management were mindful that creating a forum together, that would help them to work effectively, was crucial to the survival of the business. When launching the agreement, Superquinn's chief executive, Simon Burke stated that

> the consultative approach is particularly important during the ongoing challenging trading conditions and Superquinn is committed to maintaining this partnership approach. The principal aim of '*Working Through Partnership*' is to work closely with all of our colleagues and the trade unions to build and grow Superquinn for the future. (*Industrial Relations News*, 2010: 21)

The Working Through Partnership deal was agreed to by the management at Superquinn and the three trade unions, Mandate, BFAWU and SIPTU, that represent the various categories of staff employed by Superquinn. The agreement includes a series of initiatives including

- hosting monthly Store Partnership Forums (SPF) and biannual Company Partnership Forums (CPF),

- enhanced disciplinary and grievance procedures,
- improved communications facilities and training and development opportunities for staff members. (*Industrial Relations News*, 2010)

The structure of the partnership agreement is based on two forums that have differing levels of responsibility and jurisdiction. The Store Partnership Forum (SPF) is a store-based committee with responsibility for addressing a range of store-level issues including routine operational matters such as health and safety and the review of store and company performance. The Company Partnership Forum (CPF) has responsibility for company-level issues and is the ultimate escalation point for all issues from other levels of the Working Through Partnership operation.

Each store has a Store Partnership Forum (SPF) and each SPF is composed of the store manager, the system resource manager, the duty manager and four shop stewards—two from Mandate, one from SIPTU and one from BFAWU. The forum meets in-store once a month, and its purpose and operating procedures are clearly specified in the Working Through Partnership Agreement. As mentioned, the SPF deals with matters relating to local issues. Specifically, it reviews store performance, company performance business plans, local industrial relations issues and can consider some HR matters as well as new initiatives/innovations. The agreement clearly specifies, however, that discussions are confined to topics particular to an individual store. A week prior to the meeting taking place, the union representatives consult with their members and identify agenda items. This list is submitted to the secretary, who then adds management items; an agreed-on final agenda is circulated three days before the meeting. A schedule for the meeting is agreed on, and following the meeting, the secretary circulates the minutes to all members of the group and a copy is posted on the store's Colleague Notice Board. The HR department provides the secretary of each SPF with guidelines on the format for the agenda, and this ensures that the process is consistent across all stores. The SPF does not deal with individual grievances/disciplinary issues. The agreement stipulates that a solution to such issues can be achieved through the application of the grievance/disciplinary procedures and through the involvement of the union official and regional HR manger when appropriate.

In some respects, the form of consultation offered to employees through the SPF is similar to that offered by the informal huddles initiated more than 20 years ago by Fergal Quinn. Both forums provide information to employees about routine operational matters such as store-level sales performance, customer feedback and health, safety and hygiene practices. The huddles were, however, limited to engaging employees to address issues of concern within their own department, and differed from the SPF in two important respects. First, in a SPF trade unions are involved in representing the views and interests of employees whereas huddles were mostly conversations between employees and their immediate line manager. Second, the huddles were informal and the depth and scope of consultation offered to individual employees varied from one store to another, and from one department to another within individual stores. The WTP agreement, on the other hand, specifies the agenda for an SPF and the issues dealt with (and the way in which they are addressed) are consistent across all the stores.

The Company Partnership Forum (CPF) meets twice per year. On the company side, the CPF is comprised of the company CEO, the chief financial officer, the head of HR, the operations director, two store managers, two regional managers, the regional HR manager and the employee relations manager. On the union side the following attend: three Mandate officials, one SIPTU official, one BFAWU official, four Mandate shop stewards, one SIPTU and one BFAWU shop steward. The chair of the forum rotates between a HR management representative and a trade union official. The secretary is the HR manager.

The primary function of this forum is to provide updates on company progress and to address and resolve all relevant issues that may arise nationally or that are referred to it by the SPF. The agreement clearly makes a distinction between local (store-level) issues and national (company-level) issues, and the remit of the CPF is to deal with national issues. The agreement allows for all unresolved issues, which have broader implications, to be referred to an agreed working party or appropriate external third party for consideration. The WTP agreement specifies that the agenda items for the CPF may include a review of store performances, company performance and business plans. In addition, provision is made for the review of industrial relations issues and agreements and for the review and planning of the Working Through Partnership strategy (*Industrial Relations News*, 2010).

In essence, the monthly SPFs and the biannual CPFs, the nub of new partnership framework, give workers and their representatives an opportunity to influence company policy and operational structures. The agreement also provides for the amendment of existing grievance and disciplinary procedures. Specifically, it sets out more detailed procedures for both individual and collective grievances and disputes. For example, it specifies the length of time that a disciplinary warning will be retained on file.

An indication of how committed both management and unions are to developing a consultative approach to the management of employee relations can be seen in the provisions made for training by both unions and management. Management and unions worked together to develop induction and advanced training programs for both union and management representatives. Everyone involved in the partnership forums received at least three days of training. One day of this program was devoted to a joint training session for management and unions, which was delivered in the Mandate Training Offices. The unions also agreed to develop and deliver a shop steward training program specific to Superquinn colleagues. Management agreed to ensure that cover would be provided at departmental level in order that union representatives could fully participate in the process (i.e., attend training sessions and meetings associated with the partnership forum).

In recognition that embedding a culture of consultation and cooperation would require ongoing support, a provision was made for training to take place on an annual basis. The spirit of partnership was further enhanced by an agreement that the SPF union representatives would be given the opportunity to make a presentation at all new-staff induction sessions and that management would be offered the chance to make a presentation at the shop steward training sessions.

8.3   IMPLEMENTING A RESPONSE STRATEGY

Agreement was reached on the Programme for Competitiveness and Change (substantive agreement) and Working Through Partnership (procedural agreement) in the spring of 2009, and the training for the participants in the partnership forums was completed by September 2009. The first monthly SPFs were held in October 2009, and the first CPF took place in the spring of 2010. Since then trading conditions have become even more difficult. There appears, however, to be consensus among management and the trade unions that the forum structures are working well despite increased competitive pressures.

The pay freeze and the redundancies provided significant cost savings for the organization, and obviously the willingness of employees and their union representatives to accept these measures gives an indication of their commitment to support management's attempts to secure the future of the business. These were major concessions, but given the economic climate, they were not unusual. Nevertheless, the willingness of both management and unions to cooperate with each other, to recognize and accommodate each other's needs is a significant development. The new spirit of compromise is reflected in the agreement on banded hours. Unions agreed to a two-hour window of flexibility around start and finish times, and management agreed to limit the control they had over scheduling rosters by agreeing to guarantee employees that they would be employed to work within a fixed range of hours each week.

8.4   OUTCOMES OF THE STRATEGY

In the summer of 2010, unions and management entered into another round of negotiations to review the pay pause agreed in March 2009. Given the ongoing difficult market conditions, management were seeking a pay cut (the need for this had been signaled at the CPF). After detailed discussions, an agreement was reached not to cut pay but instead to freeze contributions to the pension scheme for one year. A provision was, however, made for the full restoration of the pension contributions. Under this arrangement, after one year employees could make a contribution to the pension scheme that would be equivalent to the amount that had been withheld and management would match this contribution.

This arrangement is further illustration of the willingness of both management and unions to address an issue as a mutual problem to be solved. The compromise reached suggests that both sides recognized the difficult circumstances faced by the other and were open to working together to find a creative solution: employees did not have to incur a pay cut while management save, at least in the short-term, on payroll costs. An interesting point to note is that in the course of these negotiations the unions were provided with access to company accounts. The unions' legal experts examined the books and produced a report for the union officials. That the unions were given access to such commercially sensitive information bears testament to the level of trust between management and the trade unions that has developed in recent years.

This relationship was tested when a decision was taken to close a store in Naas in January 2011. The closure occurred because Superquinn's lease had expired and the landlord demanded possession of the premises. Superquinn had been making plans to open a new store on an alternative site. However, due to the downturn in the property market a decision was taken to postpone the development of this site. The unions and employees were aware that the lease was due to expire. They were also aware that management was pursuing alternative options, and so employees were not unduly concerned about the security of their employment. The decision to close the store therefore was unexpected. Within 10 days of this decision being announced, unions and management had concluded an agreement that allowed for the redeployment of 53 of the 104 staff to other Superquinn stores, and provided a redundancy package for the rest of the workforce. The deal also included an innovative arrangement whereby staff who were made redundant would retain the benefit of a staff discount scheme, which had recently been established, and they would also maintain their right to share the €2.5 million 'gain-share pool,' which would arise in the event of the sale of the retail chain. Although the media carried reports of some staff expressing shock and dismay at the sudden and unexpected closure of the Naas store, the assistant general secretary of Mandate, Gerry Light, was reported as commenting on the agreement that

> The process involved in getting the deal over the line was a model of successful industrial relations with both sides dealing honestly and openly with the issues at hand. It shows that constructive outcomes can be achieved when two parties come together with a solution-oriented focus. (*Industrial Relations News*, 2011: 9–10)

The introduction of partnership-style procedural arrangements was a radical change to the way in which unions and management interacted with each other in Superquinn. Clearly the severe economic crisis provided the incentive to embrace such a dramatic change. However, although the crisis may have provided the impetus to be cooperative and engage in joint problem solving, the implementation of such a dramatic change would not have been successful without genuine and ongoing support from both unions and management.

The success of the initiative can be attributed to a number of factors particular to Superquinn. First, there was a strong group of trade unions committed to the introduction of both the substantive and procedural agreements. Superquinn is a closed shop; the unions committed significant resources to training both union officials and management representatives, and they were also proactive in eliciting the support of employees. Second, the HR personnel convinced the senior management team of the merits of engaging in a partnership style arrangement and, in consequence, the company also committed significant resources to support the rollout and implementation of the initiatives. Third, historically in Superquinn unions and management had what could be described as a good working relationship. Although the takeover by Select Retail Holdings altered this relationship, it was not unduly damaged, and there was therefore a basis on which to build a trusting and cooperative relationship.

DEFENDING A SUBSIDIARY MANDATE AT MEDTRONIC

Context

A rich literature has amassed assessing the extent to which multinational subsidiaries have discretion in developing HRM policies that fit with local circumstances or whether their people management policies are passed down from headquarters. The criterion for assessing the character of the HRM function in transnational organizations is not whether it is mainly influenced by its country of origin or adapts to its host country but whether 'best-practice' people-management policies may demand some policies to be operated centrally and others locally. Multinational corporation (MNC) subsidiaries are increasingly likely to have HR systems that are internally more variegated than ever before. The organizational structure of transnational companies is also likely to have an impact on the mentality of HR managers, and even employees and their representatives, in subsidiaries. Within transnational organizations, subsidiaries not only have to produce or deliver high-quality goods and services that are competitive on the external market, but they also have to compete internally with other subsidiaries for what are called mandates: a business or an element of a business in which the subsidiary participates and for which it seeks investment or operating responsibility from the parent MNC. To evolve and develop, subsidiaries must compete in an internal market to either consolidate existing mandates or win new ones. This competitive pressure hangs constantly as a Sword of Damocles over managers and employees in a subsidiary. HR managers, for example, when considering new policies or developments not only have to assess the consequences for people management but also for the subsidiary's mandate. Mandate consolidation or renewal is a decisive factor that separates management–employee interactions in multinational subsidiaries from those in other organizations.

These issues are of major significance in the case of Medtronic, a leading global company in the medical technology industry. It develops and manufactures a wide range of products and therapies and conducts business in more than 120 countries around the world. It regards its business mission as to alleviate pain, restore health and extend life for people with chronic conditions around the world. Medtronic started trading in 1949 in the United States, initially as a product servicing company progressing to developing the world's first battery-powered cardiac pacemaker, a pioneering product at the time. This product proved to be the foundation for dozens more Medtronic therapies that used the company's electrical stimulation expertise to improve the lives of millions of people. Over the years, the company has also adapted additional technologies for the human body, including radio frequency therapies, mechanical devices, diagnostic tools and drug and biologic delivery devices. Today, the technologies developed by Medtronic are used to treat more than 30 chronic diseases affecting many areas of the body.

Headquartered in Minnesota, the company has a number of defining features. One has been its rapid rate of expansion. Since its foundation, the company changed from being a relatively small-scale, although sophisticated, organization to one of the world's most technologically advanced multinationals. Consider the following. In 1992, Medtronic had 8,000 employees; now it has over 43,000; its revenue back then was $1.2 billion, but this has increased to $15.8 billion in 2010. Nowadays, the company spends in excess of $1.5 billion on research and development whereas in 1992 it was a mere $120 million. Currently, the company is valued at near $10 billion. A second defining feature of the organization is the relatively short cycle of many of its products. The continuous advancement in the development of devices to treat a broad range of medical conditions has resulted in a substantial percentage of the organization's annual revenue being generated from products that are less than two years old. Thus, the company experiences constant pressure to innovate, improve existing products, develop new products and move into new, related areas.

Accommodating rapid rates of growth while at the same time maintaining, if not upgrading, its innovative capacity places enormous organizational demands on the company. Over the years, the company has experienced considerable organizational change. For example, in the early 2000s, Medtronic was organized internally into a number of stand-alone businesses. However, this organizational structure has been overhauled in recent years, and a new matrix-type structure has been introduced. To leverage the synergies of these various businesses the company consolidated its business into two operating groups—one focused on its heart rhythm and cardiovascular products and the other on restorative therapies. In addition to this consolidation exercise, several cross-business groups were also created to help leverage best practices, knowledge and technologies across the company.

This organizational matrix structure is designed to meet three challenges: protect and grow core business activities, drive further global expansion and cultivate innovation for new products and markets. The structure is regarded as promoting a global culture supportive of product innovation while simultaneously providing each business unit with the autonomy to nurture organizational collaboration so that high-performance teams could thrive. In a sense, the strategy is to create a transnational organization, with the emphasis on being global and local at the same time. All Medtronic sites, irrespective of location are encouraged to follow HR practices that combine centrally inspired as well as locally designed initiatives. Thus, for example, in recent years the Medtronic site in Galway has recently introduced the Medtronic Corporate talent management program. Similar to many other US multinationals Medtronic's preferred business model is to engage directly with employees rather than via a third party. At Medtronic local business units are given freedom to promote particular bundles of policies that enhances high performances and contributes to the organization's standing as an employer of choice. Thus, Medtronic can be viewed as pursuing a loosely coordinated, decentralized HRM strategy.

Medtronic in Ireland

Medtronic first came to Ireland in 1999 not by establishing a subsidiary in a new greenfield site, but by acquiring a division of another multinational, CR Bard, which had originally established a subsidiary in Galway, Ireland, in 1982. When first started, the focus of CR Bard was very much on low-tech operations and products, but its activities were continuously upgraded to such an extent that by 1998 it had acquired responsibility for global research and development (R&D) as well as for the manufacturing and marketing of two important medical device portfolios, catheters and stents. It is clear that Medtronic was acquiring a strong-performing, highly innovative operation in Galway. This point was not lost on the senior management team at Medtronic as it continued to invest in the Galway site. Under Medtronic ownership, the Galway site has been upgraded even further and is now a state-of-the-art high-performance facility. It is a center of excellence for the development and manufacture of a number of the company's key technologies for the treatment of cardiovascular and cardiac rhythm diseases.

Acquiring an already existing organization poses different HR challenges to those presented when establishing a greenfield site. In particular, the acquiring organization has to decide whether to stay with or change the HR regime in the organization that has been bought. Medtronic was eager to introduce new policies and practices at the Galway plant that encouraged learning and development across the workforce. The company also sought to promote an organizational culture that put a premium on innovative, high-quality work. These new measures were not overly difficult to install as the company had inherited a very-well-qualified workforce and an experienced management team. Thus, the senior management team at Medtronic headquarters was quite prepared to introduce new HRM policies. At the same time, it elected to stay with a trade union recognition agreement that CR Bard had entered into with a trade union, now called SIPTU, even though Medtronic in the main was a nonunion organization.

In total, there are about 2,000 employees at the Galway site, consisting of about 1,300 semiskilled manufacturing team members, referred to as direct labor, and about 700 highly skilled support employees, referred to as support labor. A number of features of the HR system at the site are worthy of note. All of the permanent direct labor resources are unionized due to the recognition agreement at the site whereas most of the support labor are nonunionized. In a global economy Ireland as a location cannot be considered a low-cost operation.

Terms and conditions of employment would be considered as competitive within the local market but above those of employees in some other Medtronic manufacturing sites around the globe. An extensive learning and development program operates on-site. Employees are actively encouraged to upgrade their skills and knowledge through pursuing in-house and external training and educational programs. In support of this expectation of ongoing learning, Medtronic actively develops internal career paths: every year about 50% of vacancies are filled from internal staff pools. A battery of mechanisms exist to facilitate information sharing, including weekly departmental meetings, quarterly general employee updates on the business, newsletters, e-mail and face-to-face meetings in teams. Great efforts are made to ensure that information sharing and consultation are the same for both union and nonunion employees. All in all, a strong commitment exists at the site to involving employees in decisions and to keeping them abreast of how Medtronic is performing.

Employment relations in Medtronic Galway have consistently been good. No time has ever been lost to any form of industrial action and the organization continues to successfully solve problems in the main using in-house dialogue and grievance procedures. Interaction between managers and trade union representatives has been consistently positive. Management and trade union representatives alike feel they can approach each other directly and that their relationship is based on finding solutions to problems. For the most part, the SIPTU branch at Medtronic operates like an enterprise union found in Japan—the emphasis is on insulating internal employment relations from external industrial relations influences and to forge cooperative relations with management. Thus, for example, the Galway site did not directly participate in the national social partnership agreements that prevailed from when Medtronic took over the company until 2009: instead of adhering to the prescribed pay increases established by national agreements, the organization negotiated local wage deals. This practice was to prove be a decisive factor in shaping how the Galway site responded to the recession.

The company can be seen as following a range of soft and hard HR policies. Importantly, within Medtronic, from a financial accounting perspective the Galway site is constituted as a cost center rather than a profit center. Every year the site has to report to headquarters on the extent to which it has met efficiency targets. These annual metrics place responsibilities on all aspects of the Galway operation to leverage opportunities to contain costs. The HR department in conjunction with site leadership team is constantly working to find better ways of securing the full engagement of all employees. Thus, for example, in recent years it has concluded an agreement with the unions on a new absenteeism policy designed to encourage better employee attendance. In addition, it seeks to improve employee productivity on an ongoing basis. This is a standard hard HR orientation. At the same time, the HR department is committed to classic soft HR policies. It actively promotes an inclusive culture within the organization. Senior managers interact informally with all employees on an ongoing, day-to-day basis, whether this is over lunch, in the car park or at workstations. Comprehensive well-being and health-support programs have been developed for the workforce. As already mentioned, an extensive range of information and consultation programs exists at the site to provide employees with a voice on company affairs and to allow them to contribute their views and opinions.

Extensive programs exist to help employees improve their skills and competences. Innovative HRM policies such as financial participation, for example, Annual Incentive Plans and Employee Share Purchase Scheme, are followed to forge positive relationships between the employee and the organization. Thus, although pressures to reduce costs are ever present, equal efforts are made at creating a high-commitment workplace for employees.

8.5 THE IMPACT OF THE RECESSION

To appreciate fully the impact of the recession on employment relations at the Medtronic site in Galway one has to begin in the months prior to the financial crisis in 2007 when the local management and unions were engaged in negotiations about a three-year pay deal. As already stated, trade unions and management at Medtronic Galway had decided to stay outside the pay agreements of the national social partnership arrangement and negotiate their own wage deals. The negotiations of early 2007 were challenging as the company needed to contain costs to advance organizational competitiveness whereas the union sought substantial improvements in pay and conditions of employment as the company was profitable and the Irish economy at that time, continued to be buoyant. Organizations can possess cooperative employment relations and yet experience tough negotiations about pay and working conditions. Finally after protracted negotiations, an agreement was concluded between management and the trade union teams.

However, before the agreement could be implemented it had to be ratified by the employees who were union members. Normally, this process tended to be a formality as employees in almost every case endorse the recommendation of the union representatives. A meeting was called for all unionized employees to vote on whether or not to accept the agreement. The 12-person trade union representative committee had endorsed the agreement, and it anticipated that the agreement would be accepted by the majority of members. At the meeting, the union representatives went through the agreement carefully with members and some skepticism and even hostility was voiced about its contents. Negative comments by an individual trade union representatives on the proposed agreement changed the mood of the meeting entirely, which resulted in the agreement failing to be ratified by the membership. Instead, the union representatives were mandated to go back and renegotiate the agreement with the human resource management team.

But management was of the view that the original agreement that had been concluded could not be improved because it was not in a position to give further concessions. Thus, there was a sizeable gap in the positions of management and the trade unions. In an effort to avoid a stalemate, the conciliation service of the Labour Relations Commission was contacted for support. Officials of the LRC spent a lot of time talking to both sides, particularly trade union representatives. After effectively adjudicating between the positions of both sides, the LRC made a recommendation that the original agreement with relatively minor amendments on clarification of wording be adopted by the workforce. Once again the agreement was voted on by the union membership, only this time the deal was accepted. The conclusion of this pay agreement was unusual: it proved more time consuming than normal, a compromise was more difficult to reach in the negotiations; the refusal to ratify the draft agreement first time round was out of character as was the subsequent involvement of the LRC. All in all, negotiating the pay deal was a challenge for both management and union representatives and the concerns of both sides were allayed when the agreement was finally ratified. Not long after the agreement had been adopted, the financial crisis erupted, throwing the world economy into chaos.

Very few businesses were left untouched by the subsequent downturn in business activity. Many were being brought to the edge of bankruptcy due to the near collapse in consumer confidence. Although the healthcare industry remains generally resilient during economic downturns, the magnitude of what was happening around the world resulted in unprecedented challenges, both competitive and economic, in markets around the world, and Medtronic was not immune to the effects of this downturn. The value of Medtronic stocks fell in 2008. For sure, these developments were not welcomed, but at the same time they were not of a scale to threaten the viability of the organization. Nevertheless, the senior management team in the company was concerned about the challenging external business environment, and the potential impact of the recession on the long-term prospects of the company. Of particular concern was the potential of the recession to influence governments and patients to reduce expenditure on health-related products, with a resulting potential adverse effect on Medtronic's revenues.

8.6   DEVELOPING A RESPONSE STRATEGY

In early 2008 Medtronic launched a restructuring plan, which involved reducing job numbers, to improve performance. This announcement also affected the Galway site, which offered a voluntary severance agreement to employees. However, with the continued deepening worldwide economic crisis and increasing challenging market conditions, it was clear that future action was required. In early 2009 senior leaders at Medtronic headquarters took the decision to revise downward its long-term revenue growth estimates. Remaining committed to delivering profitable growth, Medtronic had to ensure diligent control of operating costs. It was clear that further structural and other changes were required to better align the organization for the challenges ahead. To achieve this required reduction in cost structure Medtronic announced a further reduction in its global workforce. Medtronic also announced a company-wide freeze on promotions and merit-pay increases. All operations across the globe were expected to adhere to this decision. However, the latter part of this decision, that is, the freeze on merit increases, caused specific problems for the Galway site because it meant revisiting the challenging 2007 pay agreement, which had set down that employees would receive a 4.5% pay increase in 2009.

Thus, the pay freeze announcement placed the local management of the Galway site in something of a quandary. If it simply conformed to the call made by headquarters, it would have to renege on the 4.5% pay deal with the local union, a decision that ran the risk of alienating employees, particularly given the agreement's difficult history. Even the cooperative management–union relations that prevailed for years at the site could be jeopardized if this matter was not handled sensitively. Alternatively, local management could have sought an exemption to the company-wide pay freeze and delivered the 4.5% pay increase to employees. For sure, positive relations would have been maintained, if not deepened, with SIPTU and employees generally, but the costs associated with this action would have been significant. To have followed such a strategy could have potentially have had serious negative consequences for the Galway site and future investment decisions. Thus, in reality, the only option open to local managers was to try to comply with headquarters' decision on the pay freeze in a manner that would not jeopardize, at least not to any great extent, the good employment relations climate in the Galway site.

8.7 IMPLEMENTING A RESPONSE STRATEGY

Senior management immediately realized that achieving such an outcome would be difficult because the prospects of having to forgo a 4.5% pay increase would not be greeted well by employees. A concerted communications policy was introduced to counteract this possible reaction. Communications to employees focused on the business rationale for the pay and promotions freeze, that is, to enable the organization get through an uneasy period so that stability and growth could be restored, and the ultimate objective of ensuring Medtronic emerged from the crisis as a stronger and better company. A communication from the chief executive officer was sent to all employees. Managers at all levels were extensively briefed on communications with employees and on the business rationale underpinning the pay and promotions freeze. Thus, intensive communications efforts were made to explain to employees the reasoning behind the company's pay freeze decision.

Actually to implement the pay and promotions freeze meant opening up negotiations with the trade union on the 4.5% pay increase that had already been agreed to. Even though stories were prevalent in Ireland about various companies implementing redundancies and introducing pay freezes, if not pay cuts, the trade union representatives were not going to willingly accept the company's plan. For the union, the case for a pay and promotions freeze was not evident because the company was still making profits and thus on paper had the ability to pay. In addition, the unions were loath to make concessions on an agreement that was difficult to secure in the first place.

Despite an intensive communications strategy by management, these negotiations were made more difficult by various rumors that started to emerge. In consequence, trade union representatives became unsettled and the ensuing environment was not conducive to the conduct cooperative, 'mutual-gains' negotiations. Yet a further complicating factor was that the tight timeline that existed for the conclusion of the negotiations.

The HRM team deliberated long and hard internally about how to approach the negotiations. Extensive discussions were also held with the wider management team at Galway as well as with the vice president of HR based in the corporate headquarters in Minneapolis. Negotiations started, and unsurprisingly there were robust exchanges about the need for a pay and promotions freeze. Management realized that the proposal placed union representatives on the defensive with their members and thus gave the union team as much space and time as possible to have internal discussions. It also realized that when negotiations started that to make the pay freeze more palpable to the unions, management would have to make some type of concession. A persistent demand by trade unions during the negotiations was for contract workers to be made permanent Medtronic employees. Thus, the management team decided to offer to turn 50 contract jobs into permanent positions (which would give the union 50 more members) if the union agreed to a deferral of the pay increase. Finally after intensive discussions, an agreement was concluded, which involved the union accepting the pay and promotions freeze for 2009 and management agreeing to implement the 4.5% pay increase in two tranches in 2010. In addition, management agreed to make 50 contract workers permanent and to a number of other minor concessions.

Again the union membership had to vote to accept/reject these proposals. However, this time round neither management nor unions left anything to chance. Union representatives were true to the assurances they gave to management and actively communicated the relative merits of the agreement to members. Management, in employee communications, also emphasized the importance of union members accepting the agreement. Prior to union members voting on the revised agreement, Galway's general manager at a quarterly employee briefing session communicated openly and directly to employees on the "strategic importance of making the right decision" (Interview). These concerted efforts at promoting the agreement proved effective as the Union membership voted 70:30 to accept the new agreement.

8.8   OUTCOMES OF THE STRATEGY

A number of important points emerge from this case study. First of all, the arrival of hard business times represents a challenge even to organizations with longstanding cooperative relations between managers and employees. Organizational routines and processes that traditionally maintained trust relations tend not to work as smoothly. Rumors begin to circulate about the fate of the organization or about decisions that management is about to make. Trade unions become uncertain about which is the best position to take—whether to maintain close working relationship with management or to try and distance themselves thus reassuring members that they are not in the 'company's pocket.' For their part, management may feel the need to take decisive action to ensure that the organization adjusts effectively to harsher business conditions without winning employee support. Such a course may cause negative rumors, thereby placing established cooperative relations under strain. Thus, in responding to a business downturn, organizations are more fully exposed to the risk of damaging cooperative employment relations.

This scenario did not emerge at Medtronic Ireland. Management and the trade unions were ultimately able to face adverse business relations without jeopardizing trust relations. The senior management team realized that failure to comply with the announced pay and promotions plan could damage the future security of the Galway site. At the same time, no effort was made to impose this freeze on employees without negotiations. An extensive communications strategy was deployed to inform employees why the action was necessary. Although management negotiated hard it also provided space and opportunity for the trade union representatives to discuss the issue and to develop a common position, without recourse to a third party. In adopting this position, management was adopting a central principle of interest-based bargaining, which is to recognize and take on board the constraints of the other negotiating side. Trade unions too acted in an interest-based bargaining manner. One of the mantras of interest-based bargaining is that each side in a negotiation must interact as much with their own constituents as with the other side. Trade unions representatives did this extensively at the Galway site. They worked in a constructive manner to make members aware of the issues at stake and to troubleshoot internal disagreement about which position was the best way forward for the union. Thus, the problem-solving capacities of unions and management ensured that the subsidiary was able to meet the demands of headquarters for a pay and promotions freeze in a manner that maintained good trust relations.

The second important point to emerge from the case study was how the behavior of both the management and the trade unions was heavily influenced by the need not to damage the subsidiary's mandate. The Galway site is unusual within Medtronic in that it recognizes a trade union, but this has not impeded the site from developing its capacity to deliver high-quality products. Over the years, the Galway site has not only been able to meet its designated mandate, but also to win new ones. The autonomy it has enjoyed from headquarters has been used to build a sophisticated internal organizational architecture. Many different elements made up this architecture, but an important component has been cooperative employment relations. Management and the trade unions trusting one another has produced a stable, constructive atmosphere for the conclusion of agreements aimed at creating a high-performance workforce. Rather than being an albatross, trade union–management relations have contributed positively to the comparative advantage enjoyed by Medtronic Galway. To put the matter another way, the pursuit of the site's mandate embedded cooperative relations within the Galway site. Both management and the trade unions realized that to have allowed the pay and promotion freeze announcement to disrupt their previously amicable working relationships would have been short-sighted as it could have jeopardized further investment decisions. Maintaining the site's mandate was the glue binding together management and the unions.

PREEMPTING THE CRISIS AT ERICSSON

Context

Ericsson is a global company that provides telecommunications equipment and related services to mobile and fixed networks around the planet. More than 40% of the world's mobile traffic passes through its 1,000 and more networks. The company was first established in Sweden in 1876 to manufacture telephones, cables and switching equipment. Its headquarters remains in Stockholm. From the very beginning, Ericsson was an international company, a 'born global' firm. Within a decade, the company was exporting to Britain and Russia and soon after to places as far apart as South Africa, the United States and Australia. Its first foreign plant was established in St. Petersburg, Russia, in 1899. The company continued its global expansion in the early part of the 20th century: at the start of the Second World War, the company had established subsidiaries in all of its most important geographical markets. In the second part of the 20th century, further subsidiaries were opened in countries such as Brazil, Argentina, Colombia and Mexico, and more recently it has been expanding in Asia, China and India. Currently more than 88,000 people worldwide, 40,000 of who are service professionals, work for the company.

Ericsson is a highly sophisticated multinational that places great emphasis on innovation, seeking not only to keep pace with, but also to pioneer, technological breakthroughs. In recent years, it has led the technological development of the mobile telephone industry. The company developed one of the first analog mobile systems: it played a leading role in the industry-wide development of the global system of communications, and it pioneered general packet radio systems and third- and fourth-generation mobile technological standards.

The company's present-day corporate strategy has been shaped by events nearly two decades ago. At the end of the nineties, the company rode the crest of a stock market wave due to the dot-com bubble. Technology-based companies were seen as opening the door to the knowledge economy of the future. Ericsson probably allowed itself to be swayed by this market exuberance, which led to the company investing too heavily in R&D. At the end of the nineties, the company employed about 30,000 people in approximately 100 technology centers, with considerable duplication of effort. But when the dot-com bubble burst in 2000, the company was left reeling. To restore profitability, Ericsson was obliged to implement a massive consolidation program, which led to the wholesale closure of technological centers and 60,000 employees being made redundant. This was a salutary episode in the company's history: it allowed itself to be seduced by market sentiment and became oversized. Ever since, the company has been emphatic about the need to be lean as well as innovative. Thus, controlling costs and developing technologies sit cheek by jowl in current corporate strategy.

Until recently, the organizational structure of Ericsson consisted of three business units, Networks, Global Services and Multimedia, with each having responsibility for product management, marketing, development and sourcing of their respective product portfolios. In addition, there were also 24 market units responsible for sales and customer relations in different regions. Finally, there were group-level functions for the development and implementation of strategies and policies in each functional area. The purpose of this organizational structure was to allow Ericsson to meet the transnational challenge of being local and global at the same time. Overall, this structure brought commercial success: for most of the noughties the company experienced market growth and recorded strong profits. Yet the company must have believed further organizational improvements could be wrought as it introduced a new restructuring program in 2010. The main thrust of this program was to create a more pronounced regional organizational structure within the company. In particular, the restructuring initiative condensed the previous 24 market units into 10 regions so that the company could deliver an upgraded, more focused customer care service. In addition, it was anticipated that the new regional structure would promote greater integration and coherence between the various subsidiaries in particular regions.

Human Resource Management at Ericsson

Overall, Ericsson adopts a somewhat differentiated approach to human resource management. Some aspects of the management of the employment relationship are embedded in 'universal' company-wide policies and procedures. For example, each subsidiary is expected to uphold actively, through its human resource management activities, the core company values of professionalism, perseverance and respect. Similarly, all parts of Ericsson are expected to operate the company's Individual Performance Management Program and Leadership Development Program, which are designed to encourage continuous improvement and learning as well as to develop talent inside the organization. But perhaps, the most prominent universal policy followed by Ericsson is competency-based management.

Competency-based management is at the center of how people are managed at Ericsson, and it involves supporting the development of employee competences and learning capacities so that they can operate effectively in a knowledge-based organization: it aims to create the right mix of employee competences to meet ongoing business challenges. The nuts and bolts of such a system include registering the formal education, skills and experience of employees; mapping present and future target competence levels for business units and employees; analyzing competence gaps at various organizational levels; recording and tracking competence development actions; and operating as a repository of employee skills and learning portfolios. Competency management systems help firms identify where knowledge resides in the organization. They also help employees identify colleagues with similar interests and profiles, which facilitates shared learning.

At Ericsson, the competency management process is divided into three stages. The first analysis stage involves identifying the organization's long-term, short-term and obsolete/declining competence requirements by analyzing future market and technological demands facing the company. After establishing the competency gap between present competences and future requirements, the second stage concerns the creation of competence development plans for the organization as well as for individuals. These plans are revised and upgraded regularly. At the third stage, implementation plans are devised, which set out more concretely the theoretical and practical courses that need to be completed. Evaluation is an important element of this stage to ensure that various plans successfully accomplish the tasks they were established to do. Ericsson has developed an extensive set of resources to support competency-based management, and each subsidiary is obliged to do its maximum to implement this system successfully. It is perhaps the number one universal management policy for employees.

But Ericsson does not adopt only universal people management policies. Other parts of the employment relationship are managed through what has been called a 'transversal' approach to human resource management, which seeks to develop policies and practices that are global and local at the same time. Consider the matter of diversity management. Like other state-of-the-art international companies, Ericsson has spent considerable time and resources in developing best practices in this area. In particular, the company has designed a diversity management regime that simultaneously promotes convergence and divergence. After discussions with country-level HR managers, the HR and Organization department based at headquarters develops a global framework for diversity management, which includes a series of global diversity initiatives based not only on best practice at subsidiary level, but also on innovative thinking on the matter from elsewhere. Support is then given to subsidiaries to implement initiatives in a manner that best suits their local circumstances. The strategy has been to adopt coherent, innovative diversity management policies with sufficient inbuilt flexibility to allow subsidiaries navigate country-specific factors.

The company also permits local discretion on some human resource management matters. In most cases, pay rates and negotiations about pay increases are the responsibility of the HR team in subsidiaries. Likewise, grievances and disciplinary matters are usually the preserve of local management. Subsidiary management is also responsible for ensuring compliance with country-specific employment legislation and for interacting with public employment relations bodies such as labor courts and conciliation and arbitration services. To some degree, the recent corporate reorganization that saw the creation of ten regions is likely to constrain the discretion of HR teams in subsidiaries. Part of this restructuring process involved the creation of a HR forum in each of the established regions, consisting of senior HR managers from respective subsidiaries. The task of a regional HR forum is to develop more strategic, regionwide people-management initiatives, which are likely to encroach on the autonomy of subsidiary-level HR management. But to what extent this will occur is still uncertain as the restructuring program has yet to be embedded fully.

Unlike many other multinationals in the telecommunications/technology sector, the company does not have a policy of developing nonunion workplaces. Some subsidiaries are highly unionized while other subsidiaries are nonunion workplaces. But whether or not a subsidiary is heavily unionized, each local HR team has to operate within the confines of a business-relevant human resource management system, which focuses on developing employee competencies.

Ericsson in Ireland

Ericsson has been operating in Ireland since 1957 and has now over 1,400 employees in Clonskeagh, Dublin and Athlone, Co Westmeath. Together the Irish operations are engaged in three main activities, sales and support to local customers, research and development and the operation of a global service delivery center, which has an international focus. Ericsson Ireland, which has its own board of directors, is seen as strategically very important to the overall global company. R&D activity is seen as being particularly important as it plays a critical role for the company in improving the performance and reliability of 3G networks and driving innovative research in network management, wireless sensor networks and M2M (machine-to-machine) communication in the context of mobile networks.

Ericsson Ireland has a relatively small HRM team, employing about 10 people. The HR department has undergone considerable change over the past 13 years. In 1999, Ericsson Ireland was divided into three legal entities, which were serviced by four HR units. This organizational set up was streamlined in 2005 when a single legal entity was created for Ericsson Ireland, with two main operations in Dublin and Athlone. After this legal change, more or less separate HR units looked after personnel matters at the two sites. There was no rivalry between the two sites on HR matters, but each tended to focus on their own bailiwick. After the 2010 global restructuring program that led to the creation of 10 new regions, a single, more integrated HR team emerged in Ericsson Ireland. A new head of HR was appointed. The Head of HR divides her time between Athlone and Dublin and is responsible for developing a more common approach to managing people in Ericsson Ireland. She also participates in a regional-level HR forum that is charged with developing strategic HR polices for subsidiaries in the Central and Western European region. In addition, she reports into the head of HR at headquarters. Since the restructuring, HR, at least in the region in which Ericsson Ireland is involved, is trying to develop what might be termed a coordinated decentralized approach to managing people: some people management policies will be regionally inspired while others will be driven more by local considerations. The new HR team recognizes that they have to be active and display considerable capabilities to influence regional HR deliberations in their favor.

Only about 20% of the workforce in Ericson Ireland is unionized, with the remainder being nonunion. To some extent this is an historical legacy of Ericsson being involved in rigging operations at Dublin Port, which required them to recognize a union. SIPTU, the biggest union in the country, negotiates terms and conditions for the unionized employees while the company determines these for nonunion employees. This situation creates a number of organizational anomalies and inconveniences, which although important should not be overstated. Thus, for example, the company operates performance pay for virtually all nonunion employees whereas until recently it operated the national pay agreements for unionized employees. With the breakup of the national social partnership it will have to start negotiating locally with the union on pay and other matters.

Different terms and conditions for employees make it much more difficult for the subsidiary to operate an integrated human resource management system. Operating information and consultation procedures, for example, are made more complicated, particularly in terms of timing the release of information and consultation. Union representatives believe that they should be able to receive information well in advance of any decision so that representations or even negotiations can take place on the matter. But to provide the union with information in advance of nonunion employees would create problems in terms of horizontal procedural fairness: nonunion employees may consider their unionized colleagues to be receiving more privileged treatment. To avoid this situation, the company releases information and news to all employees—whether unionized or not—at the same time. This of course makes the union disgruntled.

Generally, relations between the union and the company can be considered workmanlike: management recognizes that it is the function of the union to represent its members and the union understands that management is in the business of obtaining agreements with employees that improve the competitiveness of the company. Thus, relations are neither excessively adversarial nor overly consensual. Because both sides engage with each other in a workmanlike fashion, negotiations can be tough and protracted. Sometimes an agreement can prove elusive. On occasions, the services of the LRC have been used to assist discussions that had reached an impasse. On several occasions, some industrial relations disputes in the company, mostly relating to pay grades, have reached the Labour Court. For the most part, however, agreements are reached internally. In terms of managing nonunion employees, a range of information and consultation arrangements, including a staff forum have been put in place. Performance management processes are used to assess and monitor employee progress. Overall, Ericsson Ireland follows a comprehensive range of people management policies for nonunion employees.

The HR team is very much committed to developing a suite of business-relevant people-management policies. However, it has not followed the path of many other organizations in diffusing an Ulrich-style business partner model for HR, which involves dividing the HR function into transactional services, centers of excellence for particular functional issues and participation in strategy development. For one thing, the HR team is too small to warrant reorganization on such lines. Instead, the HR team considers that the best way it can be business relevant is to help implement the business strategy for Ericsson Ireland. The senior HR manager participates in the business strategy–making process, but the focus of the team is on implementation.

Controlling costs and developing employee competencies have been core aspects of Ericsson Ireland's business strategies for the past decade. Pursuing these twin objectives in tandem is considered the best way of advancing the subsidiary's mandate and of consolidating the reputation of the two sites in Ireland for employing talented people who deliver high-quality products and services. The senior management team at Ericsson Ireland has kept relentless pressure on operational costs. An interview by John Hennessy, chief executive of Ericsson Ireland since 2003, is revealing on this score as he said, "Over the past seven years, we at Ericsson Ireland have benchmarked our centres of excellence on a monthly basis against our competition right across Europe. That's because we firmly believe that in order to give ourselves that element of sustainability or competitiveness that we all talk so much about in Ireland, we must be able to compete with those countries" (Interview). Thus, controlling costs to ensure that Ericsson Ireland is not out of line with competitors is considered a central plank in protecting and advancing the subsidiary's mandate.

At the same time, Hennessy recognized that corporate strategy for the subsidiary cannot be solely about controlling costs: as he suggested that "it's not necessary for companies based in Ireland to compete with China or India, or even, to a lesser extent with countries such as Poland or Hungary, but we have to be able to benchmark ourselves against, and compete with, other economically developed countries like ourselves, countries which are world leaders" (Interview). In other words, as well as competing on costs, Ericsson—and other Irish companies—also have to compete on productivity and quality. At the subsidiary, this is achieved through rigorously implementing the company-wide commitment to competency management.

Considerable effort goes into developing competencies at Ericsson Ireland. Ericsson has developed an extensive set of resources to support its competency management system in line with the template established by headquarters. Thus, employees must engage with the performance management process, and the vast majority will be actively involved in a competency development program. In addition, an academy has been established in Ireland to provide training and learning programs for both the company's employees and customers. Programs for employees are sometimes delivered in-house, but at other times are delivered by specialist outside people and institutions. Thus, for example, the academy has worked with the ICT Learning Network at an Institute of Technology in Dublin to provide customized training programs. One such program involved developing a tailor-made program for 100 Ericsson employees, in particular covering IP and other networking technologies. Continuously upgrading the skill base at both Dublin and Athlone is seen by the senior management team as key to maintaining Ericsson Ireland's reputation as a hotspot for talent. More generally, competency development is considered a route to developing a modern, sustainable psychological contract at the workplace between employees and the organization. By increasing their portfolio of skills and competences, employees are enriching their individual integrity and self-esteem and the organizations benefits too as internal human capital deepens: it is a win–win relationship that fosters a symbiosis between employees and the organization.

8.9 THE IMPACT OF THE RECESSION

Ericsson's global performance, overall, since the onset of the recession has been flat. In 2007, company performance was rather sluggish, which resulted in the company announcing that it would have to make 4,000 redundancies worldwide. A year later, the CEO considered the company to have turned in a 'flattish' performance. Yet this was above market expectation to the extent that it led to a 20% hike in its share price. But in 2009 performance once again was lackluster, with profits falling 31%, which resulted in the company announcing that it would need to shed 5,000 jobs. The indications were that the company had been performing reasonably well in 2010. Overall, although not insulated from the recession, the markets in which Ericsson operates have not been severely hit by the recession. For the most part, heavy investment by some emerging markets, most notably China and India, in telecommunication infrastructures has ensured relatively stable business conditions for the company. At the same time, the senior management team is very aware that the telecommunications sector is highly competitive to the extent that any hint of the company not being able to control costs could potentially send the company's reputation into a tailspin. This is why the team responded to unimpressive profit results by announcing cost cutting, which invariably took the form of job cuts.

8.10   DEVELOPING A RESPONSE STRATEGY

To understand fully how Ericsson Ireland responded to the recession, it is necessary to start in 2005 and not 2007/2008. In what has turned out to be a very prescient move, the senior management team in 2005, after assessing benchmarking reports, concluded that operating costs both internally, and in Ireland more generally, were becoming increasingly out of line with competitor companies. Decisive corrective measures were considered necessary to halt the slide into poor performance. As a result, Ericsson Ireland adopted a far-reaching competitiveness program designed to drive down costs and increase productivity without making employees redundant. Ever since, the subsidiary has been aggressively pursuing policies aimed at improving competitiveness. In a sense, the recession of 2007 arrived two years early at Ericsson Ireland. The great merit of launching a cost reduction plan in 2005 was that the recession, when it did arrive, was not a major market shock to the subsidiary. It did not have to uproot established organizational routines, but simply continue with existing policies and practices.

The HR team has made a major contribution to the implementation of this competiveness program, which unsurprisingly took on added import with the arrival of the economic crisis. It has overseen changes to the subsidiaries pension scheme that resulted in new recruits being obliged to join a defined contribution scheme rather than the defined benefits scheme that exists for established employees. In 2009, the team managed to secure agreement for an increase in the working week from 37.5 hours to 40 hours. Incrementally, it has led changes to work practices and arrangements designed to create a highly flexible workplace. Additionally, the team has also been able successfully to operate a pay freeze since 2009. Thus, a battery of HR-related measures has been introduced to restore productivity. These various cost-controlling measures have been introduced at a breakneck pace. Although employees have been kept abreast of these measures, the HR team considered it was not necessary to intensify communication efforts with them. Established arrangements were seen as sufficient to secure employee buy-in.

Of course the HR team has been pursuing more than cost-reducing policies. The commitment to developing people's skills and competencies has remained undiminished during the recession. It is seen as equally important to the success of the business as controlling costs. The HR team has been doing a lot to support competency development. Thus, for example, the HR team has been loath to go beyond pay freezes and introduce pay cuts in an effort to improve Ericsson Ireland's competitiveness. Reducing pay is seen as potentially making employees less willing to engage in competency development on an ongoing basis. The HR team also oversees the performance management system that monitors and guides the formation of competencies inside the organization. In addition, the recruitment and selection process is molded in such as a way to not only choose bright, well-qualified people, but also those who are well motivated and appear to have the disposition for continuous learning and development. All in all, the HR team is open and eager to provide policies and programs that will advance skill and competency acquisition in the organization.

8.11   OUTCOMES OF THE STRATEGY

Ericsson Ireland has been doing everything within its control to make the business successful. But sometimes a subsidiary in a multinational has to enact policies that emanate from headquarters and over which they have little control. This has been the case with Ericsson Ireland as it has been obliged since the onset of the recession to introduce several different redundancy programs. These job cuts have had more to do with organizational-specific factors than with the business downturn. Perhaps the most high profile redundancy program involved the loss of 300 jobs from the research and development section of the Dublin site in early 2009. These job cuts were part of a worldwide restructuring program announced by Ericsson headquarters—most of the jobs were not lost due to the recession, but were transferred to China, Poland and Sweden for cost reasons. SIPTU was unhappy with the way the job losses were announced. The company had e-mailed the news to affected workers before bringing them to a large auditorium in Dublin for a meeting to explain more fully the reasons for the decisions. News reports suggest that the employees were almost disbelieving and listened to senior management in 'stunned silence.' The union complained that they were provided with no opportunity to make any meaningful presentations about the redundancies. Once the job losses were announced, the HR team introduced a thoroughgoing support program to provide those employees losing their jobs with comprehensive guidance and advice.

The other redundancy program introduced was the result of the 2010 regional restructuring exercise. The result of this organizational change was closer integration and in some cases full merger of managerial activity across the Dublin and Athlone sites, which led to a surplus of management positions. A number of voluntary and mandatory redundancies were required to address this situation. In addition, the new regional management team introduced a voluntary redundancy scheme that all subsidiaries were to introduce in an effort to reduce costs. The management team was given the responsibility of determining the conditions of the redundancy package in Ireland and the criteria that would be used to choose volunteers. So far about 75 employees have availed of the opportunity to leave the organization. So Ericsson Ireland has been obliged to let people go during the recession, but the job losses have not been the result of locally made decisions.

Despite the redundancies that have occurred in recent years, Ericsson Ireland remains a lynchpin of global Ericsson. Within the multinational, Ireland is still seen as possessing highly skilled and motivated people in both Dublin and Athlone who contribute considerable value to the company. Ericsson Ireland is also considered to have a highly dynamic managerial team that consistently delivers on the company's objectives. But being a valuable strategic asset does not exclude the sites in Ireland from the ebb and flow of international business strategy making. Being a subsidiary of a multinational company can bring many benefits, most notably access to the latest technology and management thinking. But on occasions it has a downside, particularly when the subsidiary is adversely affected by a global restructuring plan. Unfortunately, Ericsson Ireland has faced this predicament recently. In this situation, all the subsidiary can do is to accept that such decisions are beyond its control and continue with efforts to realize fully its mandate. The managing director of Ericsson Ireland captured this sentiment when he stated, "The world of multi-nationals is a very dynamic and constantly changing place. The day you're at the top of the curve is the day to be most concerned. That's why, to be successful, you have to have a constant lust for action and that action must be executed with consistent excellence" (Interview).

To stay leading edge, multinationals have continuously to upgrade business strategies. Sometimes this process results in subsidiaries gaining new investment and mandates. At other times it leads to subsidiaries losing business and jobs. Unfortunately, Ericsson Ireland has experienced the job-loss scenario recently, although this was only tangentially related to the recession. In reality, the subsidiary had to do little that was new to face off the business recession as it was already aggressively pursuing a competitiveness program, based on controlling costs and building competencies. In rolling out this program, the HR team felt it did not need to develop any additional 'relational'-type policies such as an intensified employee communications or involvement schemes to secure employee buy-in. This would have been the strategy of many organizations embarking upon a competitiveness drive: the calculus being that deeper forms of consultation, participation and negotiations can create a form of *relational* trust between employees and managers, thereby providing social foundations for the competitiveness policies.

For sure, Ericsson Ireland uses extensive voice mechanisms to foster engagement between employees and managers, but it appears to assign less weight to these arrangements than to competency development to establish trust in the organization. The subsidiary has created a competency regime in which both employees and managers unambiguously commit to continuous training and learning. For their part, managers commit to providing a regime of training, learning and competency development that operates as a form of organizational public good. Competency development does not create rivalry: the provision of training for one employee does not exclude another employee from training; all employees have the ability to 'consume' some form of training. Providing competency development as an organizational public good has the effect of creating shared understandings between employees and managers about the professional conduct and behavorial standards that are expected of both. Employees get an assurance that the organization will provide the necessary support to allow them continuously to upgrade their skills and that managerial behavior will be consistent with fostering a high-skills workplace. Managers get an assurance that employees will commit to continuous improvement and learning so that they have the capabilities to do what is required to deliver high-quality products and services. Thus, it is through the competency regime that employees and managers develop a commitment to each other, a form of competence trust rather than relational trust is created in the organization.

8.12 CONCLUSION

Firms operate in different business environments, pursue contrasting business strategies and possess distinctive organizational characteristics. Thus, while recessions have an economy-wide depressing effect on the demand for products and services, they tend also to impact on firms in idiosyncratic ways. As a result, the strategies used by firms to respond to a business downturn will always be customized, at least to some extent, to deal with organizational-specific challenges. The organizations that were the subject of these case studies had to deal with quite different problems brought on by the recession. One firm, Superquinn, found itself very quickly in a battle for survival as the economic crisis triggered a large-scale shift in demand from the premium end of the retail grocery market to the more price sensitive end: the recession had delivered a massive blow to the business strategy that had brought commercial success to the organization for so many years. In these circumstances, the company had no option but to take decisive action, which included making voluntary redundancies and pay cuts, to secure the viability of the organization. The Medtronic subsidiary in Galway faced an entirely different situation. The challenge it encountered was to introduce a pay freeze not only to help the multinational restore cost competitiveness globally, but also to signal to the organization's headquarters that the Galway plant could deliver on commitments and on company strategy. The subsidiary was actively engaged in defending its mandate within the multinational. A different scenario yet again emerged in Ericsson Ireland. For organizational-specific reasons, it had to commit to a radical competitiveness plan that led to the implementation of hefty cost-cutting measures as well as a competency development program several years before the arrival of the recession. This meant that when the business downturn did arrive the organization did not have to depart from established organizational policies and routines. Nevertheless, during this period the subsidiary did experience a business shock in the form of a decision by headquarters to relocate 300 jobs based in Dublin to other parts of the global company. This is a salutary lesson of business life in the new global economy: even subsidiaries that are performing very well can have business decisions, which are effectively outside their control, go against them.

Although different problems were encountered and contrasting bundles of policies implemented, the responses of the three case study companies to the recession shared some common features. In particular, even though hard HRM policies had to be pursued, each company made sustained efforts to maintain, if not deepen cooperation and trust inside the organizations, sometimes by management and unions engaging intensely with each other and sometimes by the organization remaining committed to competency and talent management. But why did the organizations act in such a manner? The most straightforward answer is that a calculation was made in each case that committing to trust relations would enable more effective buy-in for retrenchment policies. For management, when deciding to introduce hard HRM policies to cope with challenging economic times, it is not sufficient to declare that such measures are required to safeguard the business, but also to ensure that such declarations are believed. Without trust, management retrenchment strategies may be hard to sell and even more difficult to implement. Employees may prevaricate and not fully support the strategies, which may create suspicion and bad feeling in the organization.

When trust relations between management and unions are strong, employees, along with their trade unions in some cases, are likely to give their imprimatur to retrenchment policies, which increases the credibility of management statements: employees are more likely to accept that their interests are being incorporated into adjustment plans. Why would employees/trade unions be willing to be parties to such a scenario? The obvious answer is that there is unlikely to be any other credible alternative for them to follow. In such circumstances, employees or a trade union may provide their imprimatur in the hope, at least, that their posture will be reciprocated by management in the future. At the same time, this is not specified in the accommodation reached and is effectively left to the discretion of management. If management does reciprocate then trust deepens further in the organization. Credible commitments have been forged between management and unions as each are assured about the other's willingness to work together to advance the interests of the organization.

But the case studies also highlight that trust relations are not self-organizing or self-sustaining, but instead require deliberate and ongoing actions and interventions by both management, particularly HR managers, employees and trade unions. Sometimes, for example, HR managers have to act as advocates for the need for cooperation and reciprocity between management, employees and unions. For example, HR managers may have to persuade other skeptical managers of the benefits that can accrue from developing trust relations with employees and trade union representatives. This is what happened in Superquinn, as HR managers played a decisive role in influencing other managers to accept the creation of a partnership arrangement. Similarly, trade union officials may have to win over reluctant employees to the idea of greater cooperation with management. There may even be times when each side has to give the other space to sort out problems that could jeopardize trust and cooperation. In Medtronic, for example, the HR department did everything to facilitate internal discussions within the union to signal that it was eager to maintain trust relations and to provide the means for the union to sort out its internal difficulties. At Ericsson, the HR team went to great lengths to ensure that the competency development of employees was not compromised by the need to introduce cost-cutting measures. Thus, ongoing efforts are required to sustain trust relations among management, employees and their trade union representatives, but the prize is significant as noncooperative behavior is pushed to the margins inside organizations.

9 Human Resources in the Recession
Summary and Conclusions

The individual chapters of the book contain summaries of the detailed findings in each of the areas examined, and these are not repeated here. This chapter discusses the conclusions that can be drawn from the study's empirical findings and their implications for the perspectives considered in Chapter 2 on the effects of the recession on HRM and work and employment arrangements more generally. The chapter also addresses the more general import of the Irish case for understanding the effects of the recession.

9.1 HR RETRENCHMENT PROGRAMS

Managers responsible for HRM in the survey and focus groups indicated that a wide range of practices had been adopted to respond to the severe pressures presented by the recession. These practices range from changes to pay and pensions, HR systems and staffing to changes in working time arrangements. Although pay freezes for some or all employees were common, pay cuts too operated in a substantial number of firms. Other pay-related measures adopted include lower pay or salary scales for new entrants, bonus cuts and changes in pension arrangements. In terms of headcount and staffing arrangements, changes were also pronounced in that most firms in the survey experienced redundancy (compulsory and voluntary) for some employees. Freezes on recruitment were also commonly instituted. Firms with more than half the employees in the survey were also engaged in redeploying staff to new positions or product lines within the business. Changes in working-time arrangements, involving inter alia reductions in overtime working, increased short-time working and the increased use of contingent working arrangements (part-time and contract workers) were also common. Training budgets were commonly cut, and substantial proportions of firms also reported managing staff performance more rigorously and otherwise tightening up on work regimes through a more exacting approach to discipline, timekeeping and attendance.

By and large, while most of the measures adopted were aimed at reducing pay costs in one way or another, the survey results also showed that HR mangers have been steadfast with regard to implementing the softer side of HR practices. The importance of intensive communication emerged as a key issue for firms to help manage the effects of the recession. So also sometimes had been attempts to hold onto staff through redeployment. Many firms had retained HRD initiatives (around half of the survey respondents did not say that they had cut their training and development budgets), and a significant proportion of firms had sought to retain high-potential or high-performance staff. Other measures that could have helped to promote organizational cohesion, such as higher proportionate cuts in pay and bonuses for senior managers, however, have not been implemented on a widespread basis.

The research revealed two broad patterns of response in terms of the manner in which firms combined hard HR responses concerned with controlling or reducing payroll costs. Around half implemented what were described as general HR retrenchment programs focusing primarily on pay freezes, curbs on overtime, short-time working, redundancies and more rigorous work regimes. The other half of firms implemented fewer measures overall and were mainly concerned with freezing pay and curbing overtime working. Both types of retrenchment programs combined measured focused on making payroll savings with measures concerned to maintain motivation and commitment. In the case of most unionized firms these HR retrenchment programs were aligned with voice-related practices that pointed to the limited engagement of unions in measures for responding to the recession.

The features of the bundles of HR practices making up the alternative HR retrenchment programs identified sit uneasily with perspectives that claim either that the recession heralds a new deal in employment or alternatively establishes a platform for the transformation of high-commitment HRM. Rather than pointing toward a primary reliance on market forces and mechanisms in managing people or an accelerated adoption of the high-commitment HR model, the survey results point rather toward attempts to balance market-attuned measures, focused on immediate savings in costs, with measures designed to maintain motivation and commitment—the particular combinations of measures of both types adopted being contingent on a number of features of firms' circumstances that include scale, ownership type, the structural severity of the recession (in terms of the occurrence or otherwise of business restructuring), sector-specific experiences and employment relations legacies. A similar picture of improvisation under often extreme pressure and a concern to balance cost savings with maintaining goodwill on the part of employees (and sometimes trade unions) emerges in the HR focus groups and case studies where it is the absence of any new guiding template for change or innovation and the continuing influence of a largely traditional model of 'good HR practice' that stand out.

9.2 THE HR FUNCTION: BUSINESS PARTNERS AND 'WORKING THE PUMPS'

The international literature shows no consensus regarding the experience of HR managers and departments during the recession, nor regarding their prospects beyond it. Some have predicted cataclysm, large job losses and extensive outsourcing; others, modest changes in staffing downwards or even upward; and others still have portrayed the recession as an opportunity for HR to gain lasting influence as a key business partner and strategic player.

The research conducted in this study reveals the advent in the Irish recession of HR functions that have commonly avoided radical reconfiguration or depletion of resources and that have gained new influence as 'business partners,' mainly on foot of a hard HR agenda dictated by short-term responses to commercial challenges. Relative to the extent and scale of downsizing identified in this study and in other reviews of the Irish labor market, people working in HR have fared lightly, although they have not been entirely spared. HR functions have been restructured infrequently, especially when compared with the incidence of corporate restructuring reported. While the focus groups identified a number of incidences and models of restructuring, for example based on the creation of centers of excellence and on the general centralization of HR in multinational companies, these seem very much the minority. Transactional HR processes and services also appear in the main to have escaped strong pressure to reduce costs. Only in the area of using HR consultants have a significant minority experienced cutbacks.

The new centrality of HR as a business partner in firms in Ireland has emerged from the survey, focus groups and case studies. Most HR managers report that their business role has strengthened, though they are divided as to whether that role has been mainly restricted to implementing measures decided upon by other managers (the business), or have played the major role in decisions as to the choice of measures adopted by firms. The new influence of HR managers as business partners and contributors to decisions on company's responses to the recession emerged clearly from the HR focus groups and was illustrated in the case studies where senior HR executives had a major influence on the development and/or implementation of response measures. It was clear from the focus groups, in particular, that many HR managers now define their professional identities squarely in terms of adding value to the business and in supporting the business. The old image of the personnel manager as the mediator or buffer between employees, their unions and the employer has little resonance with the experience and self-understanding of focus group participants. Participants in the union focus groups commented on this also, pointing out, sometimes in an almost elegiac manner, how different people now occupying this role were to their 'personnel' predecessors and how commonly they nowadays expected to move onward and upward in the HR career system. They saw this development as something that predated the recession but which had formed professional priorities that had been starkly in evidence in recent years.

The basis of HR's newfound centrality to business is manifestly the increased dependency of firms on HR expertise and knowledge in successfully introducing controls or reductions in areas like pay and headcount and related changes in working-time regimes and work practices. In some instances, as illustrated by the case studies, HR had won respect from senior management before the recession and this provided a platform on which they could extend their influence and contribution to firms grappling with acute commercial challenges. The dependence of line managers on HR expertise has also grown as redundancy programs, and other retrenchment measures have become common.

Few instances were reported in the focus groups or case studies in which HR managers were active in positioning HR practices, systems or processes to support business revival postrecession. Sometimes such activities had been displaced or at least eclipsed by the acute pressures of the recession. When they were reported, they tended to be found in firms where HR strategy focused on the medium-term development of the business had been in play prior to the recession and remained in place as a guiding vision, or in firms relatively little affected by recessionary setbacks. In Ericsson the HR competency framework that allows HR to support efforts to position the firm for the medium and long term in global markets preceded the current recession. It has been continued in the firm's Irish subsidiary despite significant job losses rooted in global restructuring. The image suggested by the study overall is one of HR managers frequently 'working the pumps' but only infrequently 'navigating from the bridge.'

If this picture is at variance with the more pessimistic prognostications regarding HR in the recession, it is also significantly at variance with the projections of HR gurus like Ulrich or Cooper or theorists like Mohrman and Worley. For sure HR in Ireland has come to the fore during the recession and has gained a new centrality by adding value to firms as a business partner. But this new centrality does not appear to have commonly translated into leadership with respect to HR strategy over the medium to long term, nor into strong advocacy regarding the pivotal role of many soft HR practices in harnessing commitment and engagement for sustainable business success. As for the idea of specialist HR managers as a professional services group, or as a kind of business within a business, HR managers have clearly mastered the lexicon of adding value and serving the business and its various stakeholders. However, as discussed, the dominant image is one of HR managers busy working the pumps, mainly by implementing hard, short-term HR measures that form but part of the wider repertoire of professional HR knowledge and skills. Mohrman and Worley's appealing image of organizations reconfiguring themselves and deploying human capital to 'thrive and survive in rough times' also seems at variance with the picture emerging from the study. In essence the Mohrman–Worley thesis is that organizational structures and systems have become more fluid and dynamic in recessionary conditions to facilitate the intensive bottom-up involvement of employees in firms' operational and strategic activities. The balance of effort and activity in many firms in Ireland seems to be less with these softer sides of organizations and their functioning than with the hard slog of survival through cost cutting and short-term measures, while, at the same time, preserving motivation and commitment, and keeping HR and industrial relations practices and systems that were contemplated or developed prior to the recession on course in the face of acute recessionary pressures.

In conclusion the study indicates that the HR functions of many organizations have changed significantly during the recession, but not in the kinds of radical or even revolutionary ways portrayed by either the heralds of cataclysm or the gurus and theorists proclaiming transformation. Because the newfound leverage of the function is rooted primarily in firms' high level of dependence on HR knowledge and expertise in recessionary conditions, it cannot be predicated with any confidence that HR managers will remain influential when more normal business conditions return. Whether they succeed in doing so will depend in part on the extent to which they are capable of using their newfound influence among senior management to institutionalize their role by proving their worth. It will also depend on the success with which they can convince senior colleagues of the continuing centrality of HR when business conditions revive.

9.3   UNION REPRESENTATION IN THE RECESSION: SILENT DISPLACEMENT?

No evidence emerges from the survey, focus groups or case studies that employers in Ireland had launched any onslaught against unions, whether coordinated or mimetic in character. Yet unions were often under extreme pressure to defend their members' terms and conditions and employment security. Collective bargaining usually took the form of concession bargaining, with unions trading changes in pay and conditions for enhances job security or fewer job losses and otherwise gaining little in terms of organization, representation for themselves or claw-back mechanisms for their members.

From the focus groups conducted with trade unions, it is evident that they have a fairly clear idea of their preferred good practice framework that companies should follow when making adjustments to cope with the recession. A key aspect of this framework is management recognizing that trade unions are a key stakeholder in the company and thus should be closely involved in any discussions about how to secure the future viability of a business in the face of the economic downturn. Unions believe that the interests of employees will only be fully accommodated if collective bargaining is used to negotiate a restructuring plan. In addition, unions believe that negotiated solutions to the recession are more likely in firms with robust HR structures and policies and when senior management commits to working with trade unions. Gaining and maintaining trust between the two sides are considered critical by the unions to securing employee buy-in for restructuring plans. This is why unions put so much emphasis on gaining access to the financial books of companies.

Unions believed that a good practice framework not only involves the procedures used to reach a restructuring agreement, but also the nature of the substantive policies that are subsequently implemented—good practice covers both processes and outcomes. The trade union priority is for restructuring plans to save as many jobs in companies as possible and to provide employees with the strongest possible job security guarantee. In addition, when employees are obliged to accept a pay freeze or even a pay cut to help a company stave off the recession, unions believe that some claw-back provision should exist to allow them recoup forgone earnings when prosperous business times return. A further principle which unions deem important is that higher earning employees should bear a disproportionate amount of any restructuring burden. Providing greater protection to more vulnerable or less-paid employees is seen as building fairness into a restructuring plan. A commitment to provide unions and employees with full information about the financial state of the company on an ongoing basis is considered another key element of a restructuring plan as it allows trust to be maintained between management and unions.

A restructuring plan that contains these various elements would be considered by trade unions to be a 'high-road' (progressive or good practice) strategy.

But the evidence presented in this study suggests that the incidence of such high-road restructuring plans is low. The survey evidence presented in Chapter 3 suggests that although management in many firms actively engaged with unions when developing HR policies to respond to the recession, only a handful of firms said that union engagement led management to change its original plans. In most cases, the discussions held between unions and employees were not preference changing; management stayed with their initial proposals. The survey also found that unions were able to secure an agreement on some type of financial claw-back mechanism in very few companies. Unions were also able to gain greater access to financial information in only a small number of companies. Thus, few firms appeared to be travelling along the high road to restructuring or at least the one mapped out by the trade unions. Certainly there appear to be relatively few firms following the Superquinn example and using economic adversity to attempt to forge a new consensus between management and unions to improve the productivity of the organization in a manner that advances the interests of employees. This finding correspond with the findings of the focus groups and the case studies, which suggest that the recession has placed trade unions on the defensive, unable to exert decisive influence on the direction companies elect to follow in response to the recession.

At the same time, it is wrong to paint an apocalyptic picture of the fate of trade unions during the recession. There appears to be little evidence of employers 'not wasting a good recession' by either launching a concerted offensive to bypass unions when developing a response to the crisis or even to marginalize union representation. Nearly half of unionized firms thought that the unions were realistic and constructive in negotiations compared to about a third saying that unions were not particularly cooperative. Thus, the picture that emerges is of collective bargaining and other engagement processes being used mainly in an attempt to gain consensus on management plans and not to negotiate solutions about how to restructure the enterprise in response to the business downturn. A kind of equilibrium appears to have emerged which involves management agreeing often to work within established collective bargaining procedures and unions accepting that management will be the decisive drivers behind company policies for the recession. To some degree, this balance benefitted both sides. Whereas management avoided relations with unions turning sour—which could have had the effect of damaging any restructuring plans—unions kept representational channels intact in the hope that these could be used to reassert influence when more buoyant economic times return. At the same time, the impatience of many employers with the pace of established bargaining practices needs to be recognized, as does the newly reported tendency in some cases to seek to short-circuit these by working toward quick and definitive outcomes—often putting unions 'on the back foot' in the process. Union officials also reported significant numbers of instances in which firms sought to proceed as if past agreements no longer had any status. So firms' postures toward unions in implementing measures to respond the recession seem to vary significantly between involving and seeking to find accommodation with unions, often in short bargaining cycles, seeking only to accommodate unions when resistance has arisen.

A number of factors account for the inability of unions to act more assertively to secure for themselves an active role in the creation of restructuring plans. First of all, the sheer scale of the recession has resulted in trade unions being caught in situations where they could do no more than acquiesce to managerial priorities. Second, the collapse of the national social partnership framework has weakened extra-firm industrial relations institutional structures that could have strengthened the bargaining hand of unions inside organizations. Third, the weak position of trade unions may to some extent reflect the outlook of their members. Although there is a seething public anger about the scale and nature of the recession, employees at the workplace are subdued and compliant, fearful for their jobs, pensions and livelihoods. Thus, trade unions are engaging with muted workplaces, which have weakened their bargaining positions in individual companies. Compounding this problem for unions is the willingness of a sizeable number of employees in firms proposing job cuts to take voluntary redundancy packages. In this situation, it is difficult for the union to muster support for any alternative plan that involves saving jobs. Union representatives are instead encouraged to get the best possible redundancy deal for their members. In other words, the willingness of many employees to exit the workplace through the redundancy door has the effect of weakening union voice on job retention inside organizations.

Thus, the recession has debilitated trade unions even though they may have experienced increased membership here and there because some employees join in an effort to secure greater protection at work. In particular, unions have found that the slump has weakened their capacity to mobilize their members at the workplace, which inevitably has made it more difficult for them to advance their goals. The current bleak situation for trade unions is unlikely to improve in the near future as economic conditions are destined to remain depressed for some time to come. While unions may have suffered no frontal onslaught by employers, the question remains as to whether they may nevertheless have been largely displaced in an undramatic and silent manner. The big concern for unions is that the current situation will have permanent negative consequences and that they might be unable to recoup lost members and bargaining power when economic conditions improve (Hyman 2010).

9.4 RECESSION AND WORK AND EMPLOYMENT ARRANGEMENTS

The last recession during the 1980s sparked considerable international commentary and analysis regarding its likely effects on the future conduct of HR and the character of employment arrangements more generally. Commentary has proceeded along similar lines during the current recession. Some projections, whether or academic or professional provenance, claim that the recession is driving disjuncture in work and employment. The nature of this disjuncture is disputed: some have pointed toward developments akin to the emergence of a more market-driven model; others have pointed toward the growing prevalence of a commitment-based model. Alongside these projections are found more empirically based commentaries that emphasize the pragmatic, eclectic and contradictory nature of many of the measures adopted by firms in recent years.

In considering what the study can add to this important strand of commentary and debate the first thing that should be admitted is the difficulty of making sound projections about trends and disjunctures based on developments during a few years when the onset and the impact of the recession have been both rapid and very severe. Salutary lessons can be learned from previous prognostications about the peril of mistaking cyclical changes for secular trends or disjunctures. This caveat aside, the study's findings are relevant in a number of ways to thinking about the effects of the recession on work and employment arrangements.

To begin with, a striking feature of the research is the degree to which principles of good HR and industrial relations in the recession identified by focus group participants reveal continuities with long-abiding ideas about the features of exemplary people management and relations with trade unions. In general and nearly unanimously when asked to identify principles of good HRM and industrial relations in recessionary conditions focus group participants have pointed to well-established and well-understood precepts and practices. Managers have stressed the role of intensive communications, advocacy of values that include integrity, forthrightness and fairness and of acting in accordance with established company policies and procedures. The importance of engaging or reengaging staff has been underscored, albeit less unanimously or more problematically. They have continued to espouse the principle—if not so often, it seems, embraced the practice—of engaging constructively with trade unions and of information disclosure.

Although espousing the need to engage constructively with unions, HR managers have also identified the need to expedite negotiating cycles and to leave behind the prolonged and detailed negotiating activities seen to be commonplace in the past. Overall, few new principles or practices have been espoused or practiced with respect to how work and employment arrangements should be (re)configured in response to the recession. Nor are there any significant signs from the focus groups or case studies of the advent of appealing new HR fashions or fads borne out of the challenges of the recession. The case studies reveal firms in different sectors and circumstances acting in accordance with established—though sometimes reprioritized—principles and practices in their dealings with employees and trade unions.

Union focus group participants largely underscored many of the principles and practices of good HR in the recession identified by HR managers—while often being critical of the degree and extent to which firms had acted in accordance with espoused principles. So union officials defined good HR and industrial relations in terms of honoring existing agreements and procedures, having meaningful consultation and a willingness to consider alternative proposals, communications and the disclosure of financial information. These are familiar and long-established principles of good industrial relations. Less familiar and more specific to recessionary conditions is the emphasis on firms producing viable business plans when seeking concessions from union members, or on review mechanisms and claw-back arrangements in agreements arising from concession bargaining.

Overall, therefore, whether we consider managers' or unions' understandings of good HR in the recession we find little evidence of any really significant change in the ideas guiding practice, and no real sense that the ground has been shifting and that new principles and practices are coming to the fore or fundamentally altering long-established precepts and ways of working. It is also significant in this regard that the case study firms, chosen for study because they are widely viewed as having managed HR effectively in recessionary conditions, have largely acted in accordance with these principles. The innovative practices adopted in HR response programs in these firms (e.g., the ERIC mechanism in the DAA or tiered pay cuts in the DAA and Sherry FitzGerald) mainly reflect established principles such as fairness and transparency. Ericsson has continued to operate its pivotal competency program, rooted in a prerecession concern to manage costs and productivity rigorously. If the ground had been shifting with respect to good HR principles and practices this would have been expected to be evident in sophisticated, leading-edge firms of this kind, admired in the HR and industrial relations professions for their success in managing the effects of the recession.

The critical thing in assessing competing strands of commentary on the long-run effects of the recession is whether the changes that have been made to work and employment arrangements during the recession are congealing—or seem likely to congeal—into new patterns or models of work and employment that will abide when the recession passes. Throughout this study skepticism has been expressed about apocalyptic prophesies pointing to the imminence of a market-driven new employment deal or alternatively prophesying what might be referred to as the 'second coming' of high-commitment HRM.[1] This skepticism is underscored here by drawing together the pattern of findings of particular relevance to this issue.

The preceding conclusions regarding principles of good HR in recessionary conditions is significant also for debates about the effects of the recession on work and employment. In the cauldron of the recession to date, no significant changes in guiding ideas of effective people management have emerged that might reflect profound change or disjuncture in underlying employment arrangements or ways of organizing work and careers. No such changes are evident either in the case study firms, where considerable improvisation and some innovations have been apparent. But firms' and unions activities have been largely in line with established principles and ways of working. For the most part, changes and response programs in the case study firms have been 'path dependent': in the sense that they reflect long-established relationships between the parties and the parties' concern to sustain these through the recession. Thus, the ERIC proposal in DAA reflects a heritage of stable industrial relations and significant past innovation. The agreement in Metronic reflects good industrial relations and a shared awareness of the need to cooperate to protect and extend the subsidiary's mandate from the parent company. Tiered salary reductions in Sherry FitzGerald reflect an organization that has traditionally valued staff cohesion and commitment as key brand attributes. The survival and partnership agreements in Superquinn reflect a tradition of good if paternalistic industrial relations extending back to the company's previous owner. The continuing centrality of the competency framework in Ericsson has not been disturbed by significant job losses caused by global restructuring. The point is that the cases overall highlight continuities with preexisting practices, traditions and actions concerned mainly with sustaining HRM and industrial relations through the recession. None of the case studies involved path innovation, where firms have sought to transform established patterns of work and employment and point them in a new direction.

It is perhaps the union officials in the focus groups whose comments and experiences point toward some of the most significant changes in prevailing work and employment arrangements and models. The union officials gave the strong impression of being people on the defensive, at best holding on to what they had with great difficulty in organizations under severe pressure. This picture fits uneasily with the prescribed principle in the high-commitment model that unions should be involved more deeply in company decision making. Perhaps it fits better with the concept of a market-driven workforce, managed in accordance with a new deal. But caution is warranted in inferring the advent of such a new deal based on evidence of the recent experience of trade unions. Unionization has been in decline in Ireland for three decades, and unions generally have been unsuccessful in extending their influence in Irish firms and workplaces commensurate with their influence at national level. The recession has certainly contributed to this decline and may have accelerated it. Some union officials in the focus groups were emphatic that there had been much opportunism and short-termism in employers' postures. Yet, as discussed, the evidence of the union focus groups overall seems discordant with any notion of a widespread onslaught by employers bent on exploiting the recession to reinstitute market mechanisms for the hiring, deployment and firing of labor and to deliver a terminal blow to unions and their influence within firms. Consistent with this view are survey results that present a picture of employers continuing pragmatically to engage with unions and being divided in their assessments of whether union influence had declined.

The evidence in support of any shift in the direction of a new-deal, market-driven employment model is not impressive. Although significant numbers of firms reveal evidence of possibly shifting the burden of uncertainty toward employees by changing pension arrangements, the incidence of forms of employment flexibility such as outsourcing remains very low. The net rise in the incidence of firms employing contract workers remains very modest, whereas the net level of use of agency workers has declined. Some proponents of the new deal model lay emphasis on employees no longer expecting a secure career or career progression within firms. However, more than 6 out of 10 employees work in firms indicating in the survey that formal career progression was an objective for all of their employees. This represents a rise in the level of workforce penetration of internal labor markets or career systems as reported in a 2008 survey conducted by some of the authors.[2] A comparison with the same survey also shows a rise in contingent reward systems like individual performance-related pay and profit sharing/share ownership. These reward systems are not, however, specific to a market-driven employment model but are consistent with a range of different models. The agreement in a new grading system and work practices in T2 at Dublin Airport, and related developments in parts of T1, are the closest developments in the case studies to a shift in the direction of a more market-driven model of employment. However, these developments arose less out of the pressures unleashed by the recession than out of the functioning and priorities of the aviation regulatory system. The DAA unions have continued to exercise influence on terms and conditions at T2, not least with a view to precluding the spread of the T2 model to other parts of the company.

All in all, the survey evidence and other strands of research reported in the study provide little support for the emergence of a new social contract at work based on growing employee self-reliance and related HR practices. The survey, focus group and case study evidence revealing that firms have commonly sought to balance hard and soft HR practices in managing the recession might be taken as evidence in favor of high-commitment HRM. However, what matters in assessing the view of heralds of the high-commitment model is whether the circumstances of the recession have acted as a catalyst by accelerating the incidence and workforce penetration of this HR and employment model. This seems doubtful. The survey results provide some relevant data and the focus groups and case studies are also highly pertinent to assessing this line of commentary.

The standard prescription of the high-commitment model involves responding to declining output by activating 'employment stabilization measures' (insourcing, short-time working, reductions in contract work, curbs on overtime, higher performance standards, the redeployment of staff and pay cuts) as ways of buffering firms' employees and avoiding compulsory layoffs. Hardly surprising, given the severity of the Irish recession, these measures have often been adopted in programs (described in Chapter 3 as general HR retrenchment programs) that have commonly included compulsory job losses.

Turning to softer HR practices, the survey suggests that communications, engagement and employee involvement measures have commonly been allied to harder measures focused on pay and headcount. Other measures such as the promotion of organizational cohesion through higher pay or bonus reductions for senior staff have been a good deal less in evidence. When turning to relations with trade unions, it appears from the survey that the recession has not commonly prompted firms to deepen unions' involvement in response and recovery measures. Union representatives—commonly portrayed as realistic, constructive and pragmatic—have only uncommonly been allowed more access to business and financial data or succeeded in modifying employers' initial proposals for responding to the recession. Nor have unions gained institutional supports in areas such as organizing or representation in compensation for agreeing response measures. Finally, union members have only very exceptionally gained financial claw-backs aimed at recovering pay and conditions or financial participation when business recovery sets in. All in all, the survey evidence hardly points to any blossoming of high-commitment practices and postures during the descent into recession.

Survey data, while useful, only allows for a snapshot of HR practices. The focus group and case study data are useful in allowing for a more dynamic appraisal of firms' HR postures during the recession. The HR focus groups appear consistent with the survey data in revealing the degree to which firms have sought to balance hard and soft HR measures and to sustain or preserve their existing approaches during the recession and have tended to proceed in a cautious and incremental manner. Thus, it had sometimes been necessary to 'park' employee engagement initiatives, with a commensurate decline in morale and commitment, in order to attend to pay and headcount priorities. HR managers commonly battled to sustain HRD budgets and often lost this battle. The big HR advance reported in the focus groups and illustrated also in the case studies involved the area of communications. More intensive communications have been allied pragmatically and nearly exclusively to the handling of retrenchment programs rather than allied to wider programs aimed at transformation or changing the 'rules of the game.' The new centrality of top-level managers in the formulation and communication of HR policies was focused on the same concern.

The case studies fill out this picture. What they show are efforts to manage severe setbacks or significant commercial challenges, while in the main seeking to sustain existing HR and industrial relations postures and practices. Thus, the DAA and IL&P both sought to control payroll costs by engaging unions on a largely traditional basis. In each case significant innovations occurred in the areas of union access to financial information and the use or creation of new dispute resolution mechanisms. But in neither instance did the parties seek to break the mold of established HR or industrial relations practices. In the case of IL&P, a medium-term project of unifying the HR function, guided by Ulrich's framework for HR, was put on the back burner as management sought to address the immediate challenges of the recession. In both cases management adopted an eclectic approach: opting to remain with tried-and-trusted postures, while also being prepared to modify these in response to union demands for access to financial information. In Sherry FitzGerald tiered pay cuts were instituted to minimize involuntary redundancies and sustain organizational cohesion and esprit de corps. But here too the recession had forced management to set aside a medium-term strategic review of HRM, geared to the firm's future position in the sector. In Medtronic, the parties were able to harness their preexisting positive industrial relations heritage to ensure that the subsidiary's mandate was sustained within the parent multinational. In Superquinn the recession had been a catalyst for moving ahead with a partnership approach—an approach which built on the firm's established industrial relations tradition and that seemed not to be intended as any radical departure beyond this. Ericsson's Irish subsidiary had continued to operate a pivotal HR practice, the competency management program, notwithstanding significant job losses caused by corporate restructuring.

The picture of HR in the recession that emerges from the survey, focus groups and case studies, therefore, seems to be marked by the following major features. Firms, their employees and unions have experienced considerable tumult and have responded by controlling or reducing pay and headcount, while seeking to balance these with soft HR policies concerned to preserve motivation and commitment and seeking also, for the most part, to sustain prevailing approaches to human resource management and industrial relations. In this process there has been much cautious and incremental improvisation and some innovation. There have been few attempts to break the mold and either reverse or significantly deepen existing models of HR and employment arrangements. The recession per se seems unlikely to cause any disjuncture or transformation in work and employment arrangements.

9.5 THE EFFECTS OF THE RECESSION: THE IMPORT OF THE IRISH CASE

Few countries have experienced the scale and intensity of the economic crisis that descended on Ireland in 2007. As a result, we need to be careful not to overplay the wider significance of how firms in Ireland responded to the economic downturn. Nevertheless, the Irish case throws up a number of features that impinges on our understanding of how the employment relationship is managed in adverse economic times. First of all, the Irish case stands apart from a strong theme in the relevant literature that suggests employers take the opportunity offered by business slumps radically to restructure established employment relations. Thus, for example, Cappelli (1999a) argues that firms in the United States introduced a series of far reaching reforms to the management of employment relationship during the economic recession of the early nineties. In particular, firms sought to reduce career jobs while at the same time increase the numbers on part-time and temporary employment contracts. The overall thrust was to the intensify firm-level employment flexibility. The Irish case, however, does not conform to this pattern of change. There is little evidence of firms seeking to use the recession to introduce radical change and move decisively toward some type of marketized or new deal employment model. In Ireland, at least, the economic downturn, dramatic and abiding though it has been, did not trigger any kind of radical disjuncture. Thus, the recession has not transformed established work and employment practices. For the most part, employers have sought pragmatically to deploy sets of practices, often involving internal tensions and contradictions (for example, between cost-cutting and engagement), frequently directly geared to handling the immediate effects of the recession and commonly characterized by strong elements of continuity with past practice. Thus, the Irish case emphasizes the plausibility of firms adapting to recessionary times without recasting rules and procedures that govern the employment relationship.

A second key insight from the study, which more or less corresponds with the experience of other countries, is that the economic crisis has put trade unions in Ireland very much on the defensive. Trade unions have found it well-nigh impossible to persuade firms to follow restructuring strategies that fully incorporate the interests of employees. Ideally, trade unions want firms to give them full access to all relevant financial information, commit to making people redundant only as a very last resort, enact a comprehensive retaining strategy so that employees can be up-skilled to exploit new market opportunities rather than be laid off, and agree to financial payback arrangements whereby any reductions in pay employees accept to help stave off the recession are recouped when buoyant business times return. These high-road restructuring plans have not been comprehensively enacted by any firms in Ireland, which more or less accords with the experience of other countries. In their review of collective bargaining outcomes during the economic crisis across most OECD countries, Haipeter and Lehndorff (2009: 41) laconically conclude that "the 'high road' is not too busy." The most positive things that can be said about the fate of trade unions during the recession is that firms in Ireland have not sought to marginalize or derecognize them during the recession: although they have not been influential, trade unions continue to maintain an organizational presence in many firms in Ireland. But overall the Irish case suggests that the argument mooting that recessions are good for organized labor by encouraging employees to join trade unions is way of the mark.

A third point worthy of comment is that the study provides further support for the growing trend in the literature to suggest that the presence or absence of labor market institutions can strongly influence the character of adjustment strategies pursued by firms. In particular, collective bargaining agreements and employment legislation are seen as having obliged firms in many countries in northern Europe such as Germany, Austria and the Netherlands to use working time flexibility (shorter working hours and work-time accounts) and functional flexibility (job rotation and retraining) in response to the economic crisis . These strategies encourage firms to 'labor hoard' in harsh economic times. In contrast, Anglo-Saxon countries, where there is a relative absence of labor-market institutions that constrain the behavior of firms, the tendency is for organizations to pursue numerical and wage flexibility strategies that place emphasis on job and pay reductions in response to the business downturn. Firms in Ireland, long a member of the Anglo-Saxon industrial relations family, have by and large followed this pattern of restructuring. Although many adjustment strategies have been tempered with increased communication and engagement efforts, firms have either responded to the recession by either reducing jobs (quantities) or wages (prices) and when things getting really tough by introducing both. There is relatively little evidence of firms seeking to labor hoard by pursuing some form of internal employment flexibility. All this suggests that the presence or absence of labor market institutions matters not only in terms of the behavior of firms but also to employment outcomes.

This study of the Irish case also speaks to the ongoing international debate about the nature of the HR function in organizations. Two sharply contrasting views dominate the international literature on the state of the HR profession. One view, probably most commonly referred to as the Ulrich et al (2008) model, is that the future integrity of HR is tied to the profession getting closer to corporate strategy making. In other words, if HR managers do not discard their traditional identity of being the organizational nanny and become business partners, they will remain the poor relation of the management family. The alternative message is that the HR profession is in crisis precisely because it has been too eager to embrace a business partner role only to have its efforts shunned. This account suggests that top management treat HR as something akin to an ugly bride with a large dowry (Wright 2008). As a result, HR finds itself in no-man's land in many organizations, having repudiated its past role without fully acquiring the status of business partner. Thus, the international literature on HR is facing in two opposite ways simultaneously: one way pointing to a bright future for the profession if it becomes fully integrated into senior management teams in organizations and the other envisaging a legitimacy crisis as HR managers without the confidence and trust of employees struggle to carry out core activities effectively.

A rather more nuanced view of the contemporary role of HR emerges from this study. Human resource managers are found to have gained influence in decision making in many firms, particularly in terms of identifying and implementing short-term measures designed to keep businesses. Thus, the dependency of firms on HR knowledge and expertise with respect to retrenchment programs has led to HR managers acquiring the role of businesses partners. At the same time, HR managers have been preoccupied with implementing multiple retrenchment policies. They have 'worked the pumps' by hand-holding, counseling and problem solving with line managers to secure the survival of their organizations. In other words, the study found that many HR managers were blending a business partner role with a more traditional role of implementing employment practices. In performing this hybrid role, HR managers did not operate in the highly integrated, strategic manner as envisaged by Ulrich and others. Equally, HR managers did not regard themselves as being in the midst of a legitimacy crisis, caught in a vortex of professional ambiguity and uncertainty. Above all, this study found HR managers confident and assured as they went about smoothing out the constraints, tensions and ambiguities that emerged in the wake of introducing pragmatic adaptations to the recession. Thus, in contrast to the international literature, we found a HR profession neither moving decisively toward a business partner role inside organizations nor in the midst of a legitimacy crisis that threatens their professional viability. Instead, we found HR managers that first and foremost proclaimed their problem-solving capabilities, which enabled them to adapt to contrasting different business circumstances.

Notes

NOTES TO CHAPTER 2

1. The Hackett Group restricts the circulation of its research to clients and does not make it available for review by third parties. As such, the provenance of these research findings is unclear.
2. The provenance of terms such as *eclectic* and *pragmatic* with respect to portrayals of HR changes can be traced back to the work of Marino Regini (1995) on the very different circumstances of prerecession European companies.

NOTES TO CHAPTER 3

1. Respondents were also asked if these categories of employees had been increased. Levels of part-time working had increased in 32% of firms, of contract working in 21% of firms and of agency work in 5% of firms.
2. Details of the software program used for the latent class analysis can be found at http://statisticalinnovations.com/products/latentgold.html.
3. Cross-tabulations of the incidence of HR response measures compared firms recognizing unions and nonunion firms to determine whether any systematic differences were evident. Second, in estimating exploratory latent class models, union recognition was included as a covariate to determine whether this feature of firms was helpful in distinguishing between clusters of firms with different HR response programs. Third, union recognition was included as an explanatory variable in logistic regressions exploring influences on the adoption of different response programs identified in the latent class modeling. None of these tests suggested that a basis existed for partitioning the sample into union and nonunion firms when identifying HR retrenchment programs.
4. Wald statistics and their significance levels perform this function in latent-class modeling. When HR response measures were of no statistical significance in distinguishing between the HR response programs of firms, these were often dropped from subsequent analysis in a manner analogous to the backward elimination procedure in regression analysis.
5. An examination of the bivariate residuals for the two-cluster model revealed several large values, especially for the association between more importance being assigned to communicating the demands of the business and specific employee engagement measures and/or employees being actively engaged in developing options for responding to the recession. This suggests a pattern of association between these variables for which the latent model fails adequately to account statistically. Of the remedies for local dependence of this kind

between variables, which include dropping and combining affected variables and including direct effects between variables likely to be highly correlated, the option of fitting additional latent classes was investigated (see Magidson and Vermunt 2003). The effect of this was to distribute cases in the 'pay-freeze focused' latent class across more classes, without, at the same time, altering much the substantive character of the classes thus identified. As a result, we remain satisfied with the portrayal of latent classes in Table 3.7.

6. The HR practices included in the index were (1) a formal performance management system; (2) performance-related pay; (3) profit sharing/share ownership; (4) regular employee surveys; (5) formal assessment of employees at the time of hiring for values, attitudes or personality; (6) formally designated team working; (7) common terms and conditions of employment; (8) a system of regular team briefing that provides employees with business information; and (9) internal career progression as a formal objective for all employees. Latent-class factor analysis revealed that the scale was unidimensional.

NOTE TO CHAPTER 8

1. Data based on Kantar Worldpanel briefing, October 2010. Data relates to value for year ending October 3, 2010. See www.kantarworldpanel.com.

NOTES TO CHAPTER 9

1. To continue the metaphor, the 'first coming' of high-commitment HRM as a widely prevailing model was prophesied by many HR commentators during the 1990s.
2. For details of the survey see Hahn et al. 2009. In that survey firms accounting for 56 per cent of the workforce (in firms with 50 of more employees) claimed that internal career progression was a formal objective for all employees.

References

Advisory Conciliation and Arbitration Service (ACAS), (2008), *Layoffs and Short Time Working*, London: ACAS.
—— (2009), 'The Recession: What the Future Holds for Employment Relations', London: ACAS Policy Discussion Papers, June.
—— (2010), 'Riding Out the Storm: Managing Conflict in the Recession and Beyond', London: ACAS Policy Discussion Papers, March.
Akerlof, G. and Shiller, R., (2009), *Animal Spirits: How Human Psychology Drives the Economy, and Why It Matters for Global Capitalism*, Princeton, NJ: Princeton University Press.
Armstrong, S. J. and Overton, T. S. (1977). 'Estimating Nonresponse Bias in Surveys', *Journal of Marketing Research*, 14: 396–402.
Arpaia, A., Curcui, C., Meyermans, E., Peschner, J. and Pierini, F., (2010),' Short-time working arrangements as a response to cyclical fluctuations', Brussels: European Economy Occasional Papers No 64, June.
Balakrishnan, R. and Berger, H., (2009), 'Comparing Recessions in Germany, Spain, and United Kingdom', *IMF Survey Magazine* (December) 6–14.
Bank of Ireland, (2010), *The Irish Property Market June 2010*, Dublin: Bank of Ireland.
Baron, J.N. and Kreps, D.M., (1999), *Strategic Human Resources: Frameworks for General Managers*, New York: John Wiley & Sons.
Becker, B., (1988), 'Concession Bargaining: The Meaning of Union Gains', *Academy of Management Journal*, 31(2): 377–87.
Berg, P., (2008), 'Working Time Flexibility in the German Employment Relations System: Implications for Germany and Lessons for the United States', *Industrielle Beziehungen*, 15(2): 133–50.
Bergin, A., Conefrey, T., FitzGerald, J. and Kearney, I., (2010) 'Recovery Scenarios for Ireland: An Update', ESRI *Quarterly Economic Commentary* (Summer), 56–101.
Bosch G., (2009), 'Working Time and Working Time Policy in Germany', paper prepared for the 2009 Conference JILPT International Workshop, Tokyo, January 21–23.
Bowers, J. and Davis, C., (2010), *Termination of Employment*. London: Wildy, Simmonds and Hill Publishing.
Briner, R. (2010), 'Deal Breakers', *People Management*, July 29, pp. 22–25.
Brockett, J., (2010), 'See HR as a Professional Services Firm, Says Ulrich', *People Management*, March 25, pp. 11–13.
Brown, D. and Reilly, P., (2009), 'HR in Recession: What Are the Prospects and Priorities for HR Management in 2009', London: Institute for Employment Studies, March.
Bureau of National Affairs, (1982), *Labor Relations in an Economic Recession: Job Losses and Concession Bargaining*, Washington, DC: Bureau of National Affairs.

Cappelli, P., (1999a), *The New Deal at Work: Managing the Market-Driven Work-force*, Boston, MA: Harvard Business School Press.

――― (1999b), 'Career Jobs Are Dead' *California Management Review*, 42: 146–66.

Cappelli, P., Bossi, L., Katz, H., Knocke, P., Osterman, P. and Useem, M., (1997), *Change at Work*, New York: Oxford University Press.

Cascio W., (2002), *Responsible Restructuring: Creative and Profitable Alternatives to Layoffs*, San Francisco: Berrett-Koehler

Cazes, S., Verick, S., and Heuer, C., (2009), 'Labour Market Policies in Times of Crisis,' Employment Working Paper No. 35, Gevena: ILO, August.

Cedefop, (2010), *Socially Responsible Restructuring: Effective Strategies for Support-ing Redundant workers*, Luxembourg: Publications Office of the European Union.

Charlton, J., (2008), 'Training Budget Cuts Predicted by Learning and Development Managers', *Personnel Today*, July: 7–9.

CIPD, (2008), 'How to Manage Your Workforce in a Recession', A Joint ACAS and CIPD Guidance Note, London: CIPD, February.

――― (2009), *A False Economy? The Cost to Employers of Redundancy*, London: CIPD.

Cooper, C., (2009), 'The Recession Could be the Making of HR', *HRM Magazine*, February 3, pp. 17–18.

Craft, J., Labovitz T. and Abboushi, S., (1985), 'Concession Bargaining and Unions: Impacts and Implications', *Journal of Labor Research*, 6(2): 167–180.

Daft, (2010), *The Daft.ie House Price report: An Analysis of Recent Trends in the Irish Residential Sales Market*, Dublin: Daft.ie, available at http://www.daft.ie/report/Daft-House-Price-Report-Q1-2012.pdf.

Doherty, N., (2009), 'How to Manage Through Recession and Redundancy: Build-ing on Past Lessons Knowledge', Bedford, UK: Cranfield School of Management, Cranfield Knowledge Interchange Online, September.

Dribbusch, H., (2009), 'Working-Time Accounts and Short-Time Work Used to Maintain Employment', Eironline, available at http://www.eurofound.europa.eu/eiro/2009/12/articles/de0912059i.htm.

Dyer, L., Milkovicz, G. And Foltman, F., (1985), 'Contemporary Employment Sta-bilization Practices', in Kochan, T.A. and Barocci, T. (eds.), *Human Resource Management and Industrial Relations*, Boston: Little Brown.

ESRI, (2010), *Quarterly Economic Commentary, Summer 2010*, Dublin: ESRI.

Estlund, C., (2009), 'Just the Facts: The Case for Workplace Transparency', New York: New York University School of Law, Public Law Research Paper No. 09–55, October.

European Commission, (2009), *Employment in Europe*, Brussels: European Com-mission.

――― (2010), 'Labour Market and Wage Developments in 2009', Brussels: Euro-pean Economy No. 5, July.

European Foundation for Living and Working Conditions, (2009a), *Europe in Recession: Employment Initiatives at Company and Member State Level*, Dublin: European Foundation for the Improvement of Living and Working Conditions.

――― (2009b), *Tackling the Recession: Employment-Related Public Initiatives in the EU Member States and Norway*, Dublin, European Foundation for the Improvement of Living and Working Conditions.

Farndale, E., Paauwe, J. and Hoeksma, L., (2009), In-sourcing HR: Shared Service Centres in the Netherlands', *International Journal of Human Resource Manage-ment*, 20(3): 544–61.

Felstead, A., Green, F. and Jewson N., (2010), The Impact of the 2008–9 Reces-sion on the Extent, Form and Patterns of Training at Work, LLAKES Research Paper 22.

Freyssinet, J., (2010), 'Tripartite Responses to the Economic Crisis in Essential West-ern European Countries', Geneva: ILO: Industrial and Employment Relations Department, Working Paper 12, October.

Gallie, D., Marsh, C., and Vogler, C. ed., (1994), *Social Change and the Experience of Unemployment*, Oxford: Oxford University Press.

Gallie, D., Penn, M. and Rose, M, (1996), *Trade Unionism in Recession*, Oxford: Oxford University Press.

Glassner, V. and Keune, M., (2010), 'Negotiating the Crisis? Collective Bargaining in Europe during the Economic Downturn', Geneva: ILO Industrial and Employment Relations Department, Working Paper No 10, March.

Gospel, H. and Sako M., (2010), 'The Unbundling of Corporate Functions: The Evolution of Shared Services and Outsourcing in Human Resource Management', *Industrial and Corporate Change*, 19(5): 1367–96.

Green, F., (2006), *Demanding Work*, Princeton: Princeton University Press.

Griffin, E. and Smith, G., (2010), 'Recession: A Shot in the Arm for HR', *Strategic HR Review*, 9(1): 17–22.

Gunnigle, P., (2002), 'Organized Labour in the New Economy: Trade Unions and Public Policy in the Republic of Ireland', in D. D'Art and T. Turner (eds.), *Irish Employment Relations in the New Economy*, 44–61, Dublin: Blackhall Publishing.

Hackett Group, The, (2009a), 'Offshoring of back office Jobs is Accelerating. Global 1000 to Move More than 350,000 Jobs Over the Next two Years', Atlanta and London: The Hackett Group, January 6.

——— (2009b), 'Extended Jobless Recovery Likely for Back Office. 1.4 Million Jobs in IT, Finance and Other Areas Face Elimination by 2010', Atlanta and London: The Hackett Group, December 3.

Hahn, D., Roche, W. K. and Teague, P., (2009), *Managing Workplace Conflict in Ireland*, Dublin: Government Publications.

Haipeter, T. and Lehndorff, S., (2009), "Collective Bargaining on Employment", Geneva: ILO, Industrial and Employment Relations Working Paper 3, May.

Hallock, K., (2009), 'Job Loss and the Fraying of the Implicit Contract', *Journal of Economic Perspectives*, 23(2): 69–93.

Hardiman, N., (1987), *Pay Politics and Economic Performance in Ireland, 1970–1987*, Oxford: Oxford University Press.

Honahan, P., (2006), 'To What Extent Has Finance Been a Driver of Ireland's Economic Success?' *Quarterly Economic Commentary* (Winter), 59–72.

Houseman, S. and Abraham, K, (1995), 'Labor Adjustment under Different Institutional Structures: A Case Study of Germany and the United States', in F. Buttler, W. Franz, R. Schettkat, and D. Soskice (eds.), *Institutional Frameworks and Labour Market Performance: Comparative Views on the German and USA Economies*, 285–315, New York: Routledge.

Hyman, R., (2010), 'Social Dialogue and Industrial Relations during the Economic Crisis: Innovative Practices or Business as Usual?', Geneva: ILO, Industrial and Employment Relations Dept, Working Paper 11, March.

Incomes Data Services, (2009), *Managing Redundancy*. London: IDS, HR Studies.

Industrial Relations News, (2008), 'Uncertainty Mounts over Speculation about Superquinn Sale', *Industrial Relations News*, 33: 11–12.

——— (2010), 'Superquinn—"Working through Partnership" Agreement, *Industrial Relations News*, 12: 21–23.

——— (2011), 'Superquinn—Deal on Redundancy and Redeployment', *Industrial Relations News*, 3: 9–10.

International Monetary Fund (IMF), (2009), *Regional Economic Outlook: Europe*, Washington, DC: IMF.

Jacoby, S., (1997), *Modern Manors: Welfare Capitalism since the New Deal*, Princeton, NJ: Princeton University Press.

——— (1999a), 'Are Career Jobs headed for Extinction?', *California Management Review*, 42: 123–45.

——— (1999b), 'Reply: Premature Reports of Demise', *California Management Review*, 42: 168–79.

Jørgensen, C., (2009), 'Economic Crisis Leads to Extensive Use of Work-Sharing', Dublin: European Foundation for the Improvement of Living and Working Conditions. Eironline, available at www.eurofound.europa.eu/eiro/2009/03/articles/dk0903021i.htm. Accessed on 23 November, 2010

Kantar Worldpanel, (2010a), *A Summary Update of The Irish Grocery Market To 21st March 2010, A presentation to the National Consumer Agency, May 2010*, Dublin: NCA.ie, available at: http://corporate.nca.ie/eng/Research_Zone/kantar-research/March_2010_research_on_shopping_trends.html. Accessed on 23 November, 2010

—————— (2010b), *A Summary Update of Grocery and Shopper Trends up to and including Christmas 2009, A presentation to the National Consumer Agency, 2010*, Dublin: NCA.ie, available at: http://corporate.nca.ie/eng/Research_Zone/kantar-research/Research_by_Kantar_Worldpanel_on_shopper_trends.html. Accessed on 23 November, 2010

—————— (2010c), *A Summary Update of The Irish Grocery Market To 21st March 2010, A presentation to the National Consumer Agency, May 2010*, Dublin: NCA.ie, available at: http://corporate.nca.ie/eng/Research_Zone/kantar-research/March_2010_research_on_shopping_trends.html. Accessed on 23 November, 2010

—————— (2011), *Promotions Push—Retailers Help Shoppers to Save*, Dublin, *Quarterly Up Date*, Retail Excellence.ie, available at: http://www.retailexcellence.ie/images/uploads/downloads/members_resources/14_11_11_-_Kantar_Worldpanel_Supermarket_Share_Data.pdf. Accessed on 4 December 2011

Kochan, T., Katz, H. and McKersie, R., (1986), *The Transformation of American Industrial Relations*, New York: Basic Books.

Legge, K., (1988), 'Personnel Management in Recession and Recovery: A Comparative Analysis of What the Surveys Say', *Personnel Review*, 17(2): 2–72.

MacLeod Review, (2009), *Engaging for Success,* London: HMSO.

Maertz, C. P., Wiley, J. W., LeRouge, L. and Campion, M. A., (2010), 'Downsizing Effects on Survivors: Layoffs, Offshoring and Outsourcing', *Industrial Relations*, 49(2): 275–85.

Magidson, J. and Vermunt, J. K. (2003), 'Latent Class Models', Belmont, MA: Statistical Innovations Inc.

McGovern, P., (1989), 'Union Recognition and Union Avoidance in the 1980s', in e T. Murphy, B. Hillery and A. Kelly (eds.), *Industrial Relations in Ireland: Contemporary Issues and Developments*, 61–72, Dublin: Department of Industrial Relations, University College Dublin.

McGovern, P., Hill, S., Mills, C. and White, M., (2007), *Market, Class and Employment*, Oxford: Oxford University Press.

McKersie R. and Cappelli P., (1981) 'The Concession Bargaining Experience', in L. Cohen (ed.), *Avoiding Confrontation in Labour Relations*, 15–32, Montreal: McGill University Press.

McLoughlin, I. and Gourlay, S., (1992), 'Enterprise without Unions: The Management of Employee Relations in Non-Union Firms', *Journal of Management Studies*, 29(5): 669–91.

Mellahi, K. and Wilkinson, A., (2010), 'Slash and Burn or Nip and Tuck? Downsizing, Innovation and Human Resources', *International Journal of Human Resource Management,* 21(13): 2291–2305.

Mohrman, S. and Worley, C. G., (2009), 'Dealing with Rough Times: A Capabilities Development Approach to Surviving and Thriving', *Human Resource Management*, 48(3): 433–45.

O'Connell, P. and Russell, H., (2007), 'Employment and the Quality of Work', in T. Fahy, H. Russell, and C. T. Whelan (eds.), *Best of Times? The Social Impact of the Celtic Tiger*, 79–94, Dublin: Institute of Public Administration.

O'Hearn, D., (1998), *Inside the Celtic Tiger: The Irish Economy and the Asian Model*, London: Pluto Press.

Peacock, L. ,(2008), 'Dave Ulrich Calls on HR to Exploit the Downturn to Get Rid of Duds', *Personnel Today*, 5 December: 27–29.

Phelps, E., (1994), *Structural Slumps: The Modern Equilibrium Theory of Unemployment, Interest, and Assets*, Cambridge, MA: Harvard University Press.

Phillips, L., (2008), 'Firms Plan to Hire More HR Staff Despite UK Job Cuts, *People Management*, January 21, p. 5.

—— (2009), 'Firms Get Savvy with Training in Downturn', *People Management*, March 23, p. 9.

Pickard, J., (2010), 'A Cut Above', *People Management*, May 6, pp. 27–20.

Pitcher, G., (2008), 'The Global Economic Crisis Will Decimate HR Departments in 2009', December 8, *People Management* pp. 10–11.

Regini, M., (1995), *Uncertain Boundaries: The Social and Political Construction of European Economies*. Cambridge: Cambridge University Press.

Robinson-Smith, G. and Markwick, C., (2009), *Employee Engagement: A Review of Current Thinking*, Brighton, UK: Institute of Employment Studies.

Roche, W. K., (2001), 'Accounting for the Trend in Trade Union Recognition in Ireland', *Industrial Relations Journal*, 21(1): 37–54.

—— (2006), 'The Changing Industrial Relations Landscape in the Republic of Ireland', *Administration,* 54(2): 86–96.

—— (1997a), 'The State, Pay Determination and the Politics of Industrial Relations', in T. Murphy and W. K. Roche, (eds.), *Irish Industrial Relations in Practice*, 41–74, Dublin: Oak Tree Press.

—— (1997b), 'The Trend of Unionization', in T. Murphy and W. K. Roche, (eds.), *Irish Industrial Relations in Practice*, 145–226, Dublin: Oak Tree Press.

—— (2007a), 'Social Partnership and Workplace Regimes in Ireland', *Industrial Relations Journal*, 38: 188–209.

—— (2007b), 'Developments in Industrial Relations and Human Resource Management in Ireland', *Quarterly Economic Commentary* (Spring), 62–77.

—— (2009), 'Social Partnership: From Lemass to Cowen', *The Economic and Social Review,* 40(2): 183–205.

—— (1998), 'Public Service Reform and Human Resource Management', *Administration,* 46(2): 3–24.

Roche, W. K. and Geary, J., (2000), 'Collaborative Production and the Irish Boom: Work Organization, Partnership and Direct Involvement in Irish Workplaces', *The Economic and Social Review*, 31(1): 1–36.

Schumann, P., (2001), 'A Moral Principles Framework for Human Resource Management Ethics', *Human Resource Management Review*, 11(1–2): 93–11.

Slichter, S., Healy, J. and Livernash, R., (1960), *The Impact of Collective Bargaining on Management*, Washington, DC: The Brookings Institution.

Towers Watson, (2010), *The New Employment Deal: How Far, How Fast and How Enduring?*, New York: Towers Watson.

Ulrich, D., (1997), *Human Resource Champions: The Next Agenda for Adding Value to HR Practices*, Boston: Harvard Business School Press.

Ulrich, D., Younger, J. and Brockbank, W., (2008), 'The Twenty-First Century HR Organization', *Human Resource Management*, 47(4): 829–50.

Van Gyes, G., (2009), 'Reducing Working Time as Anti-Crisis Measure', Dublin: European Foundation for the Improvement of Living and Working Conditions, Eironline, available at www.eurofound.europa.eu/eiro/2009/06/articles/be0906029i.htm.

Vance, R, (2006), *Employee Engagement and Commitment: A Guide to Understanding, Measuring and Increasing Commitment in Your Organization*, New York: SHRM Foundation.

Walker, T., (2007), 'Why Economists Dislike a Lump of Labor', *Review of Social Economy,* 65(3): 279–91.

Wall, T., (2004), *Understanding Irish Social Partnership: An Assessment of Competitive Corporatist and Post-Corporatist Perspectives*, University College Dublin: unpublished Master of Commerce Dissertation.

Webb, T., (2009), 'Grass of Home Grows Greener as UK Firms Discover In-Sourcing', *The Observer*, March 8, p. 48.

Whelan, K., (2009), 'Deadweight Loss and "Job Creation" Plans', available at http://www.irisheconomy.ie/index.php/2009/06/02/deadweight-loss-and-%E2%80%9Cjob-creation%E2%80%9D-plans/. Accessed on 10 November 2011

——— (2010), 'Policy Lessons from Ireland's Latest Depression', *Economic and Social Review*, 41(2): 225–54.

Wright, C., (2008), 'Reinventing human resource management: business partners, internal consultants and professionalization', *Human Relations* 61(8): 1063–86.

Index